FROM PRAIRIE TO PRISON

Missouri Biography Series

William E. Foley, Editor

FROM PRAIRIE
TO PRISON

The Life of Social Activist
Kate Richards O'Hare

Sally M. Miller

University of Missouri Press
Columbia and London

Library of Congress Cataloging-in-Publication Data

Miller, Sally M., 1937–
    From prairie to prison : the life of social activist Kate Richards
O'Hare / Sally M. Miller.
      p.   cm. — (Missouri biography series)
    Includes bibliographical references (p.   ) and index.
    ISBN 0-8262-0898-3 (alk. paper)
    1. O'Hare, Kate Richards, 1877–1948. 2. Women social reformers—
United States—Biography. 3. Women political prisoners—United
States—Biography. I. Title. II. Series.
HQ1413.O53M55   1993
303.48′4′092—dc20
[B]   93–12223
                                                      CIP

Designer: Rhonda Miller
Typesetter: Connell-Zeko Type & Graphics
Printer and Binder: Thomson-Shore, Inc.
Typefaces: Musketeer, Berkeley Oldstyle, and Times.

To Peg, long-term critic *par excellence*

CONTENTS

ꙮ ACKNOWLEDGMENTS

I had been interested in the career of Kate Richards O'Hare for over a dozen years before I undertook work on her biography. In 1977, I was invited by Philip S. Foner, professor emeritus at Lincoln University and one of the most prolific authors in the field of American history, to join him in a project. He proposed that I edit the published works and extant letters of O'Hare, most of which he had already collected, and that the book be published under both our names.

That collection was published as *Kate Richards O'Hare: Selected Writings and Speeches* by Louisiana State University Press in 1982. At LSU, it was my good fortune to work with Beverly Jarrett, an editor and a very fine collaborator. Some years later, she moved to the University of Missouri Press to become its director and editor-in-chief. She then invited me to write the long-overdue biography of O'Hare. Accordingly, I want to thank Phil Foner and Beverly Jarrett for leading me to the writing of this book.

Of course, a historian cannot write her books without the resources and helpfulness of repositories and librarians; it is my pleasure to acknowledge the many institutions and individuals that provided assistance to me during my work on this book. I am pleased to thank Martha Clevenger, associate archivist of the Missouri Historical Society in St. Louis; Kenn Thomas, manuscripts librarian of the Western Historical Manuscript Collection of the University of Missouri–St. Louis; Randy Roberts, manuscript specialist of the Western Historical Manuscript Collection of the University of Missouri–Columbia; the staff of the Newspaper Division of the State Historical Society of Missouri, Columbia; and also the staff of the Kansas State Historical Society, Topeka. I enjoyed visiting these repositories located in O'Hare country.

For their assistance in obtaining primary sources I also acknowledge Raymond Roryczka, research archivist of the Walter P. Reuther Archives of Wayne State University, and Sandra Kimberley, also at Wayne State, who acted briefly as a research assistant for me; the State Historical Society of Wisconsin; the Newspaper Division of the Oklahoma Historical Society; Saundra Taylor, curator of manuscripts, the Lily Library of Indiana University; Robert L. Carter, Rare Books and Special Collections librarian at Indiana State University; and the International Institute of Social History in Amsterdam.

For helpful information and leads to material in archives, I am pleased to thank Michael J. Dabrishus, Head of Special Collections, the University of Arkansas Library; Suzanne Maberry, Assistant Editor, *Arkansas Historical Quarterly,* the Special Collections Division of the University of North Dakota Library; and the University of Washington at Seattle Libraries.

I owe a great debt to colleagues, both friends and writers whom I know only through their work. The following individuals helped me to find my way to resources: Robert W. Cherny of San Francisco State University; Robert H. Zieger of the University of Florida; William C. Pratt of the University of Nebraska at Lincoln; David Roediger of the University of Missouri–Columbia; Homer Socolofsky, the dean of Kansas history studies, of Kansas State University; Gene DeGruson, curator of Special Collections at Pittsburg State University; Lawrence O. Christensen of the University of Missouri–Rolla: Stuart B. Kaufman, editor of *Labor's Heritage,* of the University of Maryland; David Thelen, editor of the *Journal of American History,* of Indiana University; Nancy Hewitt of the University of South Florida; Dana Frank of the University of California at Santa Cruz, formerly of the University of Missouri–St. Louis; James N. Gregory of the University of California at Berkeley; James M. Lorence of the University of Wisconsin Center at Wausau; Gary R. Kremer, former Missouri state archivist; and Kenneth H. Winn, former editor of *Gateway Heritage* and current Missouri State Archivist.

Very special thanks go to the following individuals without whom this work could not have come to fruition: Mary Beth Corrigan, who undertook research for me in O'Hare files at the National Archives; Coralee Paul, who checked collections in St. Louis that I did not have time to research during my visit there: Mary Beth Figgins of Kansas, a descendant of the Richards's and a family genealogist; and William Foley of Central Missouri State University, who is the congenial and most helpful general editor of the Missouri Biography Series, of which this work is a volume. I wish also to acknowledge the warm support and cheerful assistance extended to me by the entire staff of the University of Missouri Press, especially Sara Fefer and Jane Lago.

Saving some of the greatest debts for last, I am happy to acknowledge the help of two Kate O'Hare scholars who shared both materials and insights with me: Erling N. Sannes of Bismarck, North Dakota, and Neil K. Basen of the University of Iowa. I also thank Peter Buckingham of Linfield College, Oregon, for discussing with me his research into the life of Frank P. O'Hare. In addition, I appreciate the generosity of Meredith Tax, who lent me tapes of her interviews with Kate O'Hare's late daughter, Kathleen, recorded in the 1970s. I am very grateful to the colleagues who kindly took time from their busy schedules to review one or more chapters of the manuscript: Gary M. Fink of Georgia State University; Candace Falk, editor of the Emma Goldman Papers at the University of California at Berkeley; and Robert Reinders, professor emeritus at the University of Nottingham; and Estelle B. Freedman of Stanford University. I wish to thank colleagues at the University of the Pacific who read early drafts: Erling A. Erickson of the Department of History and the late Marjorie Bruce of the Department of English; and

Patricia Youmans, professor emeritus of the Department of Sociology for the use of her dissertation on the social service milieu of Kansas City, Missouri. The University of the Pacific was enormously helpful to me in several ways. It awarded me an Eberhardt grant, which allowed me to travel to the necessary archives in the Midwest during one summer, and I received a semester-long faculty development leave, which enabled me to concentrate on the writing of the manuscript. I am in debt for this indispensable assistance to Vice-President Joseph L. Subbiondo, Dean Robert Benedetti, and the members of the Faculty Research Committee. I am also most appreciative to staff people who went beyond the call of duty in assisting me. They include Judith Andrews and other reference librarians of the University of the Pacific, who, for twenty-five years, have enabled me to complete research projects that would have been impossible without their cheerful assistance. The interlibrary-loan office was also indispensable, and I wish to thank Marina Tarala especially. I am delighted to acknowledge in a heartfelt way the assistance of my secretary, Pamela Altree, who was interested in the material, was helpful in substantive ways through her questions about issues, and who was always there for the additional assistance that I—the antithesis of a mechanical genius—needed with word processing and copying machines. I also express deep thanks for cheerful computer assistance from a local expert and friend, Lynn Welch of Fairfield, California.

I am grateful for a second time in this second book about O'Hare to her longest-lived offspring, Eugene R. O'Hare, who died in 1982, and who, just before his death, granted me permission to use and to reprint written materials of his late mother's. I also wish to thank two publishers for granting me permission to reprint here materials from my earlier publications: the Louisiana State University Press, for the book cited above, and *Kansas History,* in which "Kate Richards O'Hare: Progression Toward Feminism" appeared.

My special thanks to family, friends, and, yes, even pets, for their encouragement of and interest in this project (not *much* interest in the case of the pets but they are always there for authors all the time, day in and day out and at all hours) over the past few years, and for their under-standing of my preoccupation while daily life continued around me.

As authors always write, and I am no exception, while I appreciate all the help people provided, the responsibility for interpretation and for any errors in fact rest with me alone.

This work has been a pleasure.

FROM PRAIRIE TO PRISON

1

BEGINNINGS

As an adult, Kate Richards O'Hare often recalled her idyllic childhood on the Great Plains in the boom years of the 1880s. Her family homesteaded in central Kansas, and she thrived in the open spaces, seemingly endless time, and environment of security and warmth. To the hundreds of thousands of homesteaders in post–Civil War Kansas, a prosperous future seemed inevitable, but the boom led to bust. Kate was forced from the rural environment of her youth, exiled to the unfamiliar urban world, and set on a far different path from that which she could have imagined. After that she would live much of her life in metropolitan areas—Kansas City, Kansas and Missouri, St. Louis, and the urbanized enclaves of California. But she never lost the perspective of her early years; she always retained a feel for the land and its people and their concerns. Kate Richards maintained her tie to farmers, and as far as she was able, she struggled to promote understanding of agrarian Americans and to seek solutions to their problems.

Life in Kansas had given O'Hare a well-developed understanding of the agricultural environment. Nature's unpredictability was an ever-present factor in the lives of the homesteaders. While good weather promised a bountiful harvest, recurrent natural disasters could wreak havoc. In spring, floods might engulf the landscape or, perhaps

worse, tornadoes might appear. In summer, droughts and high winds
were not uncommon. Autumn often brought the danger of prairie fires,
and winter meant devastating blizzards and subzero temperatures. Occasional grasshopper infestations, such as the infamous one in 1874,
added to the pattern of calamities. The eastern part of the state was
normally rather well watered, and the High Plains, in western Kansas,
was semiarid; central Kansas, located in what is considered the Great
Plains proper, was subject to extremes of temperature and an erratic
rainfall pattern. Sandstone outcroppings and buffalo grass were prevalent, but few trees grew. The granular soil was ideal for agriculture, but
settlers required the tenacity to withstand natural disasters and the strength
to carve out homes on what had recently been the frontier.

By the end of the 1870s, strife between the whites and the native Osage
Indians was virtually concluded, and the land belonged to the newcomers.
In just a few decades, the Native-American culture had been replaced
by a Caucasian one. Most of Kansas's settlers came from Iowa and Missouri, respectively; others hailed from states farther to the east, such as
Kentucky and Virginia. Immigrants made up 13 percent of the Kansas
population in 1870. They settled especially in north central Kansas, drawn
by the location of the railroads and land grants. Some counties held at
least twice the state average of foreign-born residents. Among the various ethnic groups living in the center of the state were Norwegians,
Swedes, Danes, Scots, Irish, Bohemians, French, and, most notably,
German Mennonites.

In that decade, Kansas was in its first generation of European settlement. The Civil War, which had delayed economic and political development, was over, and migrants, including many veterans and widows,
rushed in. Whole counties were established overnight or, as historian
Everett Dick remarked, appeared as if by a magic wand. The state's
population increased from 528,437, in 1875, to 996,096, in 1880, with
the biggest influx occurring in central Kansas. Some potential homesteaders were lured by the "Ho for Kansas!" posters sprinkled everywhere, or by railroad advertisements that called Kansas "the Garden of

the Grasslands." A great real estate boom occurred: land values inflated, and over 50 percent of the homesteaders carried mortgages; the percentage was even higher in central Kansas. Despite a general trend of declining agricultural prices and increasing importation of cereal foodstuffs, homesteaders were optimistic about the future. Both corn- and wheat-growing areas produced especially high yields in the years 1883 and 1884.

One of the homesteaders in central Kansas was Andrew Richards. He and his family settled in Ottawa County, in north-central Kansas. Ottawa (a name meaning "trading post") was one of several counties organized in the 1860s. Since the county was located west of Kansas's tree-growing area, its only source of timber came from the relatively few trees along creeks and rivers. The land was some of the richest in the state, but to turn over the hard soil, farmers had to use sodbusters or breaker plows, first available in the 1870s. The sod strips cut from the earth became home-building material. Fenceposts were often made of limestone, while hedges were used as fences. The county attracted a scattering of Irish settlers and an especially large number of German Mennonites. The Richards's land was located near the town of Ada. Four blocks long and one block wide, Ada was slightly north of Salina, in Saline County, which was the marketing center for the area and the location of the Kansas Pacific Railroad's land office. Concordia, just to the north of Ada, in Cloud County, also boasted a rail connection and, for a few years in the 1870s, it had a state normal school. Perhaps the only noteworthy aspect of early development in the area was a communal farming project, a cooperative colony of New Yorkers known as the Thompson Colony, about fifty miles from Salina.

Andrew Richards and Lucy Sullivan were both descended from colonial Americans. Andrew's grandfather, James Robert Richards, was born in Virginia in 1777. A century before, three Richards brothers had immigrated from Wales, and Andrew's branch had settled in Virginia. Immediately following the war for independence, the family began to migrate to Kentucky. There, they lived in log cabins and farmed and hunted Andrew's father, Jesse, was born in Kentucky about 1810, and he married Amanda Zornes in Scioto County, Ohio, in 1835. Like earlier generations of Richardses, the couple moved west—from Ohio to Illinois to Iowa. Members of the Richards clan fought in the Civil War; some joined the Union army, and some crossed the Ohio River and fought for the Confederacy. Andrew's family and at least two of his uncles and their families moved to Kansas on the eve of the Civil War, traveling in prairie schooners.

Andrew, the second of eleven children, was born in Ohio in 1844. He grew to be a serious, taciturn young man who joined the Universalist church and took an interest in politics. A staunch abolitionist, Andrew volunteered at Leavenworth, fought for the Union at Gettysburg, and led a division up Lookout Mountain. He met Lucy Sullivan, whose birthplace has been variously reported as Illinois, Tennessee, Kentucky, or Kansas, but she was probably born in Illinois. They married in 1866 in Miami County, Kansas, and then settled in Ottawa County. With Andrew's parents as well as uncles, aunts, and cousins from both their families nearby, Andrew and Lucy Richards, like many Americans, homesteaded within a kinship network. They reared five children of their own—Clarence, John, Kate, Cora, and Jessie—and when one uncle died six years later, they made room now and then for some of his children.

Carrie Kathleen Richards, to be known as Kate, was born on March 26, 1876. She was the Richards's fourth child and their eldest daughter; a boy named James had been born in 1874 but had died in infancy. Kate Richards was born in, as she later described it, a sod-walled, dirt-roofed structure, but it had an upstairs, unlike many nearby houses. Sod provided a dark, dank, close environment into which it sometimes rained or snowed. The sod walls were about two and a half inches thick and were laid in furrow slices twelve inches wide and eighteen inches in length, with water used to cement the sod together. The walls were plastered with a mixture of sand and native clay to keep cold air from entering through the crevices. The Richardses might have whitewashed the plaster to lighten the interior or, perhaps, have papered the walls with newspapers. Whatever they tried, the wind inevitably shook the sod house fiercely at times. When the cold was too extreme, the family would pile on quilts and, possibly, as others reported, have the children sleep spoon-fashion in their featherbeds. During particularly inclement weather, the poultry was probably brought into the house.

The diet of the Richards family was simple. As late as 1867, federal government agents in the area issued rations of beans and flour to ensure a balanced diet for the homesteaders. Big game, such as bear, for the most part had been all "shot out," as it was expressed in the vernacular of the time, and the dangers Indians represented were gone. Hunters might find an occasional antelope, deer, or elk. Andrew Richards and his children brought home small game—geese, coons, prairie chickens, wild grouse, and quail—and whatever fish the streams could provide. They fished with pinhooks, and Kate enjoyed fishing in the creek as an escape from chores. For the most part the Richardses and their neighbors depended on what the land produced for the bulk of their diets. They planted wheat and corn and collected wild fruits, such as chokeberries, gooseberries, crabapples, and grapes for jams and pies, and nuts, such as hazel and hickory. Plants were dried for both cooking and medicinal purposes.

Corn formed the bulk of the average homesteader's diet. In season it was the staple at each meal: families ate it as grits, mush, pudding, bread, pancakes; and in good years, it was used in pies, fried doughnuts, and heavy cakes. Kate Richards particularly enjoyed johnny cakes and buttermilk. The Richards children, no doubt, took sandwiches of cornbread and molasses to school. Homegrown produce and poultry rounded out the typical diet. Excess foods might be traded to neighbors, who would have tended to have only the same staples. Coffee was a luxury, and substitutes were commonplace. Proper nutrition was lacking and scurvy in children was not unknown.

All the children helped with farm chores. The boys worked outdoors more, the girls indoors, but they all participated, especially at harvest time. Kate O'Hare remembered churning butter "for many a weary hour" on her aunt's prized churn, all the while longing to be outside playing or hunting. Kate enjoyed riding horses, and the outdoors attracted her, as she later recalled, from the time she was able to walk. She and her brother John often got into mischief. Once they planned to run away with one of the horses and the buckboard and seek buried treasure. The children managed to squirrel away some eggs from the henhouse, bacon, and applebutter—but Andrew discovered the cache and canceled their plans.

This fiasco apparently did not undermine Kate's adventurousness and curiosity; she was just as apt to get into difficulties at home as outdoors. She developed a reputation as an errant "Miss Fixit" of whatever items she could find, showing at an early age an interest in mechanics. Of all her nearby relatives, young Kate especially admired her mother's sister, Katy, a young widow with three small children who had held down a claim of her own and turned it into a thriving farm. Kate wanted to emulate her favored aunt.

Young children usually attended school for a few months out of the year. Most children attended for no more than six years, and few proceeded to high school since that required leaving home and boarding with strangers near a regional secondary school. At that time, Kansas was moving away from "subscription schools," for which parents hired, boarded, and employed semitrained teachers, toward systematized school districts with state-certified teachers. Young Kate attended the local one-room Glendale School. In the Richards's area a square dance had been held to celebrate the opening of the limestone school. A large crowd attended, musicians were hired from east of the county seat, Minneapolis, a distance of fifteen miles, and a tub of oysters was procured from Kansas City for the supper.

Besides such community social events, the Richards family also participated in church activities. Unlike the many Methodist or Lutheran settlers, Andrew Richards, as a member of the Universalist fellowship, did not believe in ritual to any great extent. He taught his children, in the words of his eldest daughter, that "the only religion acceptable to God was to serve the people with all our hearts and souls." The family avoided the revival and camp meetings held by visiting, circuit-riding ministers, but they did join in the social activities of the local church. Events sponsored by neighboring churches were occasions in homesteaders' lives, and everyone turned out for the picnics, bazaars, and ice cream socials.

Holidays were of special significance to the family. In Andrew's opinion, the Fourth of July, with its waving flags and fireworks, had been taken over by flaunting hypocrites; he viewed Memorial Day as the key summer holiday. Each year the Richards family attended a solemn religious service and then paraded with relatives and friends. Andrew and the other Civil War veterans wore their faded blue uniforms; the children dressed in their finest, and each of the girls wore a red sash labeled with the name of a state. Kate later recalled often being assigned Texas because of her long legs and her perpetually sunburned face. The formal opening events led to an all-day picnic for which families brought wagonloads of food. For the Richards family, a washtub packed with food and carried by John and Clarence provided them with a feast. Even decades later, the adult Kate felt strong emotions for this annual event of her childhood.

Christmas, too, seemed overly commercialized to Andrew, but it was, nevertheless, an important holiday for the family. The Richardses exchanged few gifts, but there was always a gathering of the extended family, for which the women prepared an elaborate meal with, however, limited dietary choices. Everyone stayed over, sleeping in what Kate called the barracks system, rather than make the cold, dark ride home on Christmas night. There was also a festive get-together on New Year's Day. January 1, 1886, was their most memorable holiday; the worst snowstorm in recorded Kansas history struck. Referred to for years thereafter as "the big die-up," the sudden, enormous snowstorm paralyzed the state: businesses closed, and the railroads could not run. Unusually severe cold spells continued for months; as many as one hundred people and one million cattle froze to death. The blizzard can be seen as a sign of a change for the worse in the lives of the homesteaders. The bust of 1887 was coming.

Until the age of at least eleven, Kate Richards was enveloped in an emotionally secure and loving environment. She idolized her father, but she apparently did not have such a close relationship with her mother, Lucy. While she lauded her mother in later years for her undying support of Andrew, Kate Richards seemed not to view Lucy as an individual in her own right. She saw her as wife, mother, and later, as grandmother. Lucy was not to be a role model for her ever-active and intellectually curious daughter.

Kate Richards was gradually maturing in a world in which primary, face-to-face relationships were the cornerstone of life. Neighbors knew and depended upon one another. Writers have described the world of the plains families as a *folk society,* a term coined by the anthropologist Robert Redfield. In only one generation, a distinct culture had evolved in which strong individualists learned to cooperate with and help each other. In the isolation of their microcosm, tested by their chosen tasks and by nature, they developed a strong sense of identity and of community. Even as a child, Kate knew her family could depend on friends and neighbors to help raise a barn or to share their hay if a crop failed.

The state of Kansas in the 1870s and 1880s was known for its free thought and politically open environment, despite an electorate overwhelmingly loyal to the Republican party. Farmers who visited the Richards's home would have discussed popular economic tracts, like *Progress and Poverty* by Henry George, and analyzed the increasingly downward economic trend for American farmers. As early as her preadolescent years, Kate seemed to adopt Andrew Richards's interest in political and economic matters. She listened to the discussions among the farmers who visited and read the books about which the men debated. In her preoccupation with politics, she was a true Kansan. In 1887 the *New York Times* called Kansas "the great experimental ground of the nation." In 1867, Kansas was the first state to allow the electorate to vote on female suffrage. Despite campaigning for its passage by Lucy Stone, Henry Blackwell, Susan B. Anthony, and Elizabeth Cady Stanton, suffrage was denied, but twenty years later Kansas became the first state to grant women the right to vote in municipal and school elections. A woman mayor immediately won office in Argonia and an all-woman administration was elected in Cottonwood Falls. Meanwhile, numbers of utopian or socialist colonies were established, however briefly. For example, Louis Pio and Paul Geloff, founders of the Danish Social-Democratic party, established a socialist commune near Hayes in 1887. While there was little labor organizational activity in Kansas cities in the 1870s and 1880s, Topeka had a workingmen's movement briefly, and Fort Scott was home to a chapter of the Knights of Labor.

Even the smallest towns had their own newspapers. In 1889, the number of newspapers in Kansas peaked at an astounding 733. Competition was intense for the highly literate reading public, and editorial policies of great diversity were promoted. In Enterprise, located in the county adjacent to Ottawa, a paper called the *Anti-Monopolist* was published. Winfield, in south central Kansas, had the skeptical *American Non-Conformist.* The most iconoclastic and notorious of all Kansas sheets was *Lucifer, the Light-Bearer,* which promoted anarchy and free love. Associated with a free-thought society—with some initial support from Robert Ingersoll, Charles Robinson, the state's first governor, and Annie L. Diggs, later a Populist leader—*Lucifer* promoted free speech, women's emancipation, sex education and sexual reforms, the rights of the poor and workers, and anticlericalism. An associated paper, the *Cloud County Blade,* was published briefly in central Kansas. It was undoubtedly known to and perhaps read by Andrew Richards in the next county. No matter which papers the Richards family read, young Kate would have been influenced by the remarkable freedom of expression represented by the papers.

Kansas also had a colorful history of third-party activity beginning in 1872. The constant effort made during the 1870s and 1880s to represent those whose interests might not be voiced by either the Republican or the Democratic party was evident in the appearance of the Independent Reform party, the Greenback party, the Greenback-Labor, the Union Labor, and the Prohibition parties. These various parties embodied virtually every reform for which the Populist party in the 1890s would attract greater attention. Alternative parties attracted 10 to 11 percent of the vote and could, by joining together, win state and national offices. In Kansas, young Kate Richards absorbed lessons about people left out of the political mainstream and about the potential role of third parties.

In 1887 the economic boom collapsed, and a decade of drought began. The impact of the double blow on homesteaders like the Richards family was staggering. It was the end of the cycle of large crops, decent prices, and rapid appreciation of land values. As a result of profligate public bond issues and extensive private debt, Kansas was second in the country in the ratio of real estate mortgage debt to the true value of all taxed real estate, according to John D. Hicks, an early historian of the region. In western Kansas, many of the residents pulled up stakes and retreated east, leaving behind ghost towns and abandoned claims, and sporting signs that became famous: "In God we trusted, in Kansas we busted." In some counties, banks foreclosed on up to 90 percent of the homesteads. The state's population dropped by 200,000 over the next few years, and in Ottawa County, the population dwindled from 12,740 in 1885, its highest ever, to 10,861 by 1900.

Andrew Richards was among those who decided that they could not continue to homestead. Apparently fearing he would be forced into tenant farming (35 percent of all Kansas farmers in the 1880s were tenants), Richards left central Kansas. Richards and his neighbors had tried other solutions. In 1887 farmers in Washington County, slightly northeast of Ottawa County, organized a chapter of the Farmers' Alliance, a self-help group. In 1888 the Kansas State Alliance was organized, and it soon joined the national Southern Alliance. Perhaps reflective of the desperate situation of the farmers of Kansas, the Kansas Alliance seemed to enter politics at once. Within two years the state organization had enrolled 130,000 members, uniting those who had previously supported different political groups.

From 1887 to 1890 thousands of Kansas farmers participated in the largest political wave ever to sweep over agrarian America. The rapid politicalization of the alliance led to the formation in 1890 of a state farmers' ticket. The ticket's success in the state election was largely due to its victories in the central counties where mortgage pressures and, thus, alliance activities were strongest. By 1892 it would be part of a new national party, the Populist, or People's, party, whose greatest showings at the polls would occur in the rural precincts of central Kansas.

Andrew Richards certainly fit the profile of the Kansas homesteader who turned to the alliance and then to the Populist party. He was a struggling farmer, dependent on what he made from each year's corn and wheat crops to support his family. He was also by instinct politically aware, an embryonic organizer who held meetings in his home to discuss current issues and ideas. He had responded to the Union Labor party's appeals, just as other residents of his heavily mortgaged region, ripe for politicalization, supported the various new organizational impulses. However, Andrew and Lucy Richards did not seek political solutions to their problems; it would be left to their daughter Kate, a decade later, to respond to the economic problems of her time by becoming radicalized and a political activist.

As the economic picture worsened, Andrew and Lucy Richards had tried to conceal from their children the scope of the dismal situation, but they recognized the charged atmosphere, as the adult Kate's letters later showed. In the winter of 1887–1888, apparently without any family discussion, Richards sold the stock and traveled east to Kansas City, Missouri, to find work. He got a job paying nine dollars per week, hardly enough for a family of seven. Now a member of the poorly paid, wage-earning class, he could only afford housing in the West Bottoms, an industrial area with squalid hovels. The Richardses had always been independent, self-sufficient, and proud, and living in the city's worst slum was a searing experience. It was also awesome for eleven-year-old Kate. She later wrote, "Of that long, wretched winter . . . the memory can never be erased, never grow less bitter." She witnessed others even worse off than her own family—hungry children and tramps—walking the streets. After a year, Andrew's fortunes revived, and he managed to open a machine shop, but Kate dwelled on the poverty and suffering of the new world into which she had been thrust. She was morally outraged over the helplessness of families like hers. Already victims of economic and natural disasters beyond their control, they were sentenced to, at best, menial, subservient work or, at worst, joblessness and utter hopelessness. Her anger over the unattainability of the Jeffersonian dream by those around her was to set her on an unexpected path. The child was very much being shaped into the adult she would become.

When the Richards family arrived, Kansas City, Missouri, was evolving from a frontier town into an urban community. It was no longer merely the jumping-off point for the great migration west but the largest city between St. Louis and San Francisco. Between 1890 and 1900, its population grew from 132,000 to 165,000. Many new residents were immigrants. Also, Kansas City was on a direct route from the South, so by 1880, 14.5 percent of the city's population was black. Since blacks were limited to housing in the West Bottoms, Kate Richards became acquainted with blacks for the first time. All of the area's residents were increasingly cramped for living space as shops and factories expanded, and black residents experienced the beginnings of firm segregation.

Throughout the city, Kate and her family would have seen vacant business properties and "to let" signs, symbols of the "bust" of 1887. Nevertheless, the city must have been impressive to these farming folk. It had one ten-story building, a public library, a telephone system, and cable-car lines. The legendary journalist William Allen White arrived in Kansas City, Missouri, about the same time as Richards. White, who also came from rural Kansas, found the city to be "a gilded metropolis" but "consciously citified, like a country jake in his first store clothes" and "drab" rather than "regal" since the good times of the 1880s were over.

Kansas City was not heavily industrialized. Most of the factories were across the Missouri River in the smaller city of Kansas City, Kansas. It had several packing plants, the stockyards in the West Bottoms (which, according to White, "smelled to high heaven"), and milling plants. Kansas City's workers were not strongly organized; the unstable and fluctuating character of the population interfered with worker solidarity. Unions existed, but they lacked sufficient leverage to strike effectively and could not win favorable terms, such as an eight-hour day. A local assembly of the Knights of Labor existed for a time, and some Germans sponsored socialist meetings in the 1880s. A talk by Henry George attracted an audience of two thousand, but the Union Labor party was unable to develop a following. The public was more indifferent than hostile to labor's situation.

In this new setting, Kate Richards continued her education; her family somehow managed to do without her financial contribution. Kate enrolled in Central High School in Kansas City, where she studied Latin and Greek. She graduated in 1892 and spent the next year earning a teaching certificate at nearby Pawnee City Academy in southeast Nebraska. (It is not known why she chose Pawnee City over a school in Missouri or Kansas. The faculty was not particularly illustrious, although one newspaper biographical account did report, erroneously, that William Jennings Bryan had been one of her teachers there.) Richards became a teacher, as did perhaps one-fourth of all nineteenth-century women. She taught in a typical ungraded elementary school, earning thirty dollars per month, about one-half the salary of a male teacher. Although Catherine Beecher instructed young women that teaching was "the road to honorable independence," it was poorly paid, hard work. Richards was responsible for her one-room schoolhouse; heating the schoolhouse was up to her, as was sweeping and washing the floor. She was expected to teach various grades using whatever assortment of books, if any, families might provide and to provide any rudimentary equipment needed herself. Somehow she found the time and had the inclination to start writing for the protest press, publishing in a Nebraska populist newspaper. But eventually the load became too much for the tall, gangling nineteen-year-old. In 1895, suffering from exhaustion, she resigned her position and returned to her family in Kansas City.

Kate Richards was at one of several crossroads of her life. She apparently was not interested in marrying at that time, but she lacked a clear sense of direction. She needed to support herself, but teaching had lost its appeal and, furthermore, was clearly an underpaid profession. She worked as a seamstress and then as a stenographer, but neither paid well, nor did she really enjoy the work. She ended up investing her time and idealism, as well as satisfying her psychological needs, in various religious and reform efforts through the women's voluntarist network of Kansas City. From the 1870s through the 1890s, thousands of urban and rural women's clubs and associations were organized across the United States to respond to social problems and to meet women's needs. Ultimately, many volunteers were led into suffrage work, and a smaller percentage into more radical challenges to society. Reflective of this enormous activity, the General Federation of Women's Clubs was organized nationally in 1890.

As a sensitive young woman who had been reared in a religious household, Kate felt a need to make a personal religious commitment. Andrew Richards's coolly intellectual Universalist faith had minimized certain, especially revivalist, religious impulses, but others in her family, including her Uncle Jim, of whom she was fond, belonged to the Campbellite Disciples of Christ. The Christian, or Disciples of Christ, movement had been founded in the Ohio Valley by two Scottish immigrants. It dismissed church dogma in favor of the New Testament as the sole source of faith and knowledge. This emphasis on Scripture addressed her needs, and the stress on grace and a religion of the heart was more appealing to Kate at that time than the heady components of faith that satisfied Andrew Richards. Kate had taken courses in college to prepare herself for a life as a missionary or possibly a minister (although the latter path was virtually closed to her as a woman).

Kate Richards was also involved in the temperance movement in the inner city. She had been shocked by Kansas City's wide-openness and by the numbers of people with broken lives. When she saw the effects of the depression of the 1890s, she experienced a crisis of conscience. Like the legendary Jane Addams of Hull House, Richards's initial encounter with the problems of the urban-industrial milieu led her into a socially responsive career. Kate Richards focused on the liquor traffic (and resultant drunkenness) around her, which she believed to be the basic cause of endemic poverty. Her belief in temperance and even prohibition might have been formed in childhood. Kansas was the first state to impose prohibition, with some of its enthusiasm spilling over the border into Missouri. Because of a local option law enacted in the mid–1850s, the Kansas in which Kate grew up consisted of mainly dry counties. Then, in 1880, Kansas voters endorsed the prohibition amendment and proceeded to squabble over its enforcement, with the "extreme drys" led by a Disciples of Christ minister. Temperance societies flourished, and a state branch of the Woman's Christian Temperance Union (WCTU) was formed in 1878, only a few years after the national organization was established. The religious cast to WCTU meetings no doubt provided an example to young Kate of the link between religious work and prohibition. Later, as an impressionable young person, she prayed long and earnestly for the salvation of those around her in Kansas City—the men lost to drink and the women to prostitution. With what she later described as religious fanaticism, she worked to reclaim the erring.

The WCTU also pursued many problems it considered drink related. For example, it founded an industrial school for young girls where they were trained to be independent and able to withstand the entrapments of modern life. In Kansas City in the 1890s, the first organized charities based on private donations emerged and they, too, actively confronted social problems. As a railroad terminus, Kansas City had a large transient population. Abandoned women with children were everywhere, as well as thousands of young, single women, who were attracted to the city as a source of jobs or husbands. While some women saw such hopes realized, many more suffered destitution and out-of-wedlock births and turned to prostitution or other socially condemned options to survive. Among the relatively new institutions battling these social ills, besides the WCTU, were the local Women's Christian Association, the Provident Association, and the Young Women's Christian Association (YWCA).

Among other efforts, they sponsored a children's home, several employment agencies for women, the Industrial Home for Friendless Women and Children, the Protestant Door of Hope for homeless and wayward young women, the Industrial School for Girls, and several other women's refuges. As elsewhere in the west, it was through such rescue work that young women created charitable networks in cities where only male-dominated social institutions, such as saloons and houses of prostitution, had been common.

Kate Richards worked for the Florence Crittenton Mission and Home, the Kansas City branch of a national string of missions, which tried to "rescue" prostitutes by uplifting them morally and teaching them job skills. The young women who worked at the Crittenton Mission matched the profile of so many such volunteers of the time: they tended to be fairly well educated, not-yet-married, evangelical daughters of middle-class families. These pious young women were not trained in the embryonic social work skills of the day but rather brought their empathy, earnestness, and piety to the mission. They drew on their religious and nurturing qualities to try to reach across class lines to redeem and rehabilitate fallen sisters. Based on the nineteenth-century belief in female moral superiority, such benevolent work imposed Victorian standards on charges who were shaped, at best, to adapt middle-class lifestyles or, failing that, at least to become domestic servants.

The Kansas City Crittenton Mission opened in 1896 in the red-light area, just north of the central business district. The main task of Kate and the other volunteers was to round up people to attend the mission's programs. Kate walked through the neighborhood around the mission, visiting the local saloons and dance halls to try to convince the errant to participate in the nightly prayer meetings. Their success, in building an audience at least, was noticeable. Sixty thousand people attended such services during the mission's first year of operation. The mission also provided a temporary shelter, with programmed religious, educational, and social activities, for up to one dozen women at a time. It also provided maternity care and job referrals for its inmates. Despite all her efforts, the thrust of these programs came to seem hollow to Kate Richards. She began to question her own judgment, and she later wrote, "The corner saloon still flourished . . . and new inmates came to fill the brothel as fast as the old ones were carried out to the Potter's Field, and the grim grist of human misery and suffering still ground on in defiance to [*sic*] church and temperance society and rescue mission." Perhaps poverty, not sin, was the cause of all the misery around her. A crisis of conscience had led her to Christian charity work, but now she experienced a crisis of faith.

Kate Richards went to work for her father's machine shop in Kansas City, Kansas. At first she handled the correspondence, filing and bookkeeping, but soon, because she "hated ledgers and daybooks and loved mechanics" and because clerical work paid no better than teaching, she maneuvered her way into the shop. She convinced both her father and the foreman to let her apprentice as a machinist only to face teasing or outright hostility from her coworkers. Despite their resentment, she built on her youthful aptitude for mechanics and she worked in the shop for a couple of years, experiencing deep job satisfaction. Drawn to broad labor issues, she joined the International Association of Machinists as one of its first women members and was always proud of that distinction. Gradually, Kate Richards began to read popular critiques of the social and economic system in those depression-torn years of the 1890s. She read *Caesar's Column* by Ignatius Donnelly, *Wealth vs. Commonwealth* by Henry Demarest Lloyd, and reread *Progress and Poverty* by Henry George, to which her father had already introduced her. Increasingly engaged by economic and political issues, she joined in debate at the union meetings, which she faithfully attended. Although taunted by her shop mates for "daring to talk politics," she continued to grapple with current questions. One day, she heard a street corner speaker demanding that workers organize a political party of their own, and his words struck a sympathetic chord in her. Then she encountered one of the legendary labor orators of the era. Kate attended a dance given by the cigar maker's union, and the speaker was Mary Harris "Mother" Jones who, at nearly seventy, still had thirty years of labor organizing ahead of her. Her espousal of socialism as the solution to the problems confronting working people captured Kate's attention. She managed to speak briefly to Mother Jones, who referred her to the few Socialists in the hall. They provided her with a reading list of socialist classics. One worker she met talked her into joining the Socialist Labor party, but the Kansas City branch was then about to collapse, and she was not yet prepared to play a role in it anyway. She had already met Eugene V. Debs. Andrew Richards had brought him home to supper after Debs's release from Woodstock jail, but, as a young person, she had ignored his formal talk. Now, however, Kate Richards was becoming enthralled by this strange new world.

From the moment that young Kate Richards abandoned the field of teaching and returned to her family in Kansas City, she had wandered in what is known in the psychological literature as a *moratorium period*. According to this concept, identified by the psychiatrist Erik H. Erikson, some young persons experience an interim period in which they flail about, the dimensions of the struggle varying with the individual. Such a crisis in development is not universal, but it is common. Those suffering it do not know their path; they doubt which way to proceed, and they may not be able to pursue anything concrete during this interim. They are not wasting time; they are nourishing their latent needs and preparing for their later tasks, possibly gathering experience essential to their life's work while waiting for a path to open to them. During a crisis, such a person, as Erikson observed, may be recruited by an ideological movement.

Great figures like Martin Luther and George Bernard Shaw floundered during their respective moratoriums before destiny revealed itself. However, the moratorium has rarely been treated as a possible stage of female human development, except implicitly in recent writings by Carolyn G. Heilbrun. But clearly Kate Richards was developing skills during her interim that would be useful to her in her work as a radical agitator. As did the thousands of young women active in the late nineteenth-century female networks, most of whom would not ultimately choose a lifework, she learned how to work with others, to organize events, to structure meetings, and to speak in group situations. All these skills and methods would prove important to the work she eventually chose.

Another common thread in the moratorium saga is that individuals often fail in their early work. This was not quite true of Kate Richards: she had not failed, but she lost her respect for the Crittenton movement. Of course, as a young woman, Kate Richards was not required by society to find a path or to have a voice of her own, unlike her male peers. Historian Jill Conway has observed that young women, lacking models for finding a public or political path, tend to believe that politics finds them rather than that they seek it. Indeed, Kate Richards O'Hare always insisted, in contrast to many comparable men, that she stumbled into her life's work by chance. Yet circumstantial evidence does indicate that she had been seeking it all along. The fact that she did not marry until the age of almost twenty-six, an age at which most American women then were already married, does imply, at least, that she was holding herself ready for other possibilities. Richards married, and pursued a personal life, only after she had embarked on a public career.

Her father clearly influenced her choices. He, rather than her mother, was her role model. The young woman followed the path to which her father had pointed, throwing her lot in with a "club of men," as Carolyn Heilbrun has written about accomplished women in male-dominated lines of work. Several factors in Kate Richards's childhood seem to have come into play in her choice. As is already clear, her father's public concerns and activities suggested to the young woman the possibility of making some kind of commitment to the larger world. Neither the eldest child nor the only child, she was most clearly the child of her father. In fact, she somehow accepted a son's mantle. Conversely, her mother represented a destiny that she was not interest in emulating. Throughout her childhood, she had ignored her mother's interests and pursuits in favor of her father's. This is not atypical in the intellectual and emotional development of achieving daughters, for mothers have not tended to be the overriding influences in those instances.

Kate Richards chose to leave the path that she had followed for the previous few years—teaching, machine shop and rescue work—and threw away social restraints and made a radical shift in her life. But she did not abandon norms entirely. She married and reared a family. In fact, she represents a minority within a minority. She became a woman activist but one whose private life mirrored the norm. Unlike Eleanor Roosevelt, who came to her work after her several children began to mature or, more typical of a woman activist, Emma Goldman, who, after a failed marriage, eschewed home life and motherhood, Kate Richards O'Hare brought the two ends of the spectrum together.

Kate Richards O'Hare lived by two sets of values: those learned during her childhood in rural Kansas and those acquired after her traumatic move to Kansas City. Economic adversity and forced relocation taught her that life was unpredictable and unjust, with rewards not necessarily related to effort. She was exposed to exploitation and insecurity, and she would remember those facts throughout her adult life. Her new awareness, allied with the political and social values she had inherited from her father and intensified by her employment alongside fellow unionists in the labor movement, turned her toward the work she would assume at the opening of the twentieth century.

2

NOVICE ACTIVIST

Kate Richards began meeting with a handful of Socialists, some of whom she had first encountered at the dance. She struggled with the difficult readings they lent to her, and she bombarded the group with questions. One day, a stranger who had joined the group criticized the others for failing to provide her with appropriate introductory readings, and he thrust into her hands several booklets of socialist classics. The newcomer proved to be Julius A. Wayland, publisher of the *Appeal to Reason*. Wayland, described by Elliott Shore as a quintessential American, was an entrepreneur who lent his energies to an anticapitalist cause. He would become one of the most influential journalists in American history; his paper, the largest mass-circulation socialist periodical in the United States. With the *Appeal to Reason,* Wayland helped create a socialist milieu in the heart of America. Kate Richards soon became one of his most significant converts.

In October 1901, Kate Richards enrolled in the initial class of the International School of Socialist Economy, a school for socialist organizers. Located over a furniture store in Girard, Kansas, it was partially funded by Wayland, who had moved his newspaper to Girard from Kansas City. The school was run by the colorful Walter Thomas Mills, a former Bryanite, minister, and prohibitionist.

Mills was the author of a minor socialist classic, *The Struggle for Existence,* and was a successful speaker before audiences of farmers. Called the "little professor," he was regarded as somewhat eccentric but influential in socialist circles. To attract local attention to the school on the eve of its opening, Mills gave a talk in Girard in early October on "What is Socialism?" The school was an expanded version of a small night school that Mills had recently operated in Chicago. Besides the on-site course, there was also an extensive correspondence program, which attracted students from every state and from other countries as well and spawned dozens of similar programs.

Kate Richards was one of twenty-four full-time students in the school's first class. In a twelve-week course, students studied socialist classics and learned a variety of the practical skills needed to make them effective community organizers, such as elocution, grammar, forensics, and parliamentary procedures. Among the few other women students, there was a teacher of physical culture and a spiritualist. Among the men, there was an attorney, a salesman, and several farmers. The students hailed not only from Kansas and Missouri, but also from Iowa, Illinois, Ohio, Texas, Louisiana, Oklahoma, and Arizona. Richards found the focused work gratifying, and she studied Mills's book and worked conscientiously to become a knowledgeable, skillful agitator. She and her classmates spent Saturdays "soapboxing" on street corners in Girard and nearby towns to improve their speaking skills. Sometimes Mills joined them. On one Saturday, just before Thanksgiving, a scuffle developed during his remarks. At the request of the police the nascent Socialists postponed speaking publicly until the mood had calmed, but they continued to keep busy in their hours outside of class; for example, they drove to Parsons, Kansas, to attend the socialist state convention. They also formed a glee club and wrote a school yell: "I.S.S.E.! / Bis! boom! bah!/ Socialism! Socialism! / Rah! Rah! Rah!"

Richards was fully committed to the cause. In a school examination she wrote, "The trade union provided for the wage workers, the grange and alliance for the farmer, but Socialism embraces them all." This became her first article to appear in the socialist press when the *Appeal* printed a sampling from the exams. A class photograph in a socialist newspaper depicts Richards as a very earnest-looking young woman. She later recalled feeling enthusiastic but uncertain, idealistic but ignorant. Her classmates must have felt much the same way; it is not surprising that she remained in contact with some of them for the next twenty years. Kate Richards discovered in Girard the sense of community for which she had been searching almost fifteen years. Since childhood, when her family was uprooted from its homestead, she had looked for some semblance of caring in a world that seemed to her so indifferent to human need. The folk society of her rural childhood, in which everyone depended on one another, was echoed in socialist society, in which comrades of similar ideals and commitments interacted. It was no wonder that she was so comfortable in the socialist milieu of Girard.

Girard, in southeastern Kansas, had a population of twenty-five hundred. It had wide streets lined with catalpa trees. Small stores surrounded the town square, facing the courthouse situated in its center. The advantage of a railroad—the Missouri River, Ft. Scott, and Gulf—and the low cost of living had attracted Julius A. Wayland. His printing plant was the major employer, and Wayland used the railroad line to send his newspapers nationwide. Also, Girard was not far from a socialist colony in adjacent Bourbon County, which had thrived in the previous decade, perhaps a good sign. Girard itself had a socialist club, founded in 1897. The town was the county seat and was located within several miles of the county's largest city, Pittsburg. Girard was an agricultural, mining, and manufacturing center whose residents processed, sold, and transported the products of the hinterland. The population included a small number of blacks, and the nearby mines had drawn so many southern European immigrants that the region was known as the "Little Balkans." In the early twentieth century, essentially because of the presence of Julius A. Wayland, Girard became an unlikely mecca for American Socialists.

By establishing the *Appeal to Reason* and its subsidiary enterprises in

Girard, Wayland was able to create a mini-fiefdom over which he presided. In Kansas City, his interests could not have dominated the local economy and culture as they did in the small town of Girard. Despite initial misgivings and some antagonism from townspeople, Wayland became one of the most significant figures in the local community. Julius Augustus Wayland was a forty-seven-year-old editor and publisher of weekly newspapers at the time Kate Richards moved to Girard. He had begun his career as a self-educated printer. He had traveled around the country, editing newspapers and establishing a number of his own in Indiana, Colorado, and Missouri. He had moved ideologically as well. An ardent Republican initially, he became first a Populist, then a Socialist. Reading Edward Bellamy's *Looking Backward* and Laurence Gronlund's *The Cooperative Commonwealth,* as well as talking with a Fabian socialist worker, turned Wayland in a new political direction: he started his first socialist newspaper, the *Coming Nation.* Wayland prided himself on his ability to reach people. His Marxism was a folksy concoction of socialist teachings and midwestern American values; the combination won readers and earned utter disdain from Daniel De Leon of the Socialist Labor party, perhaps the leading Marxist ideologue of the time. Wayland also dabbled in utopian socialism, virtually a fad among social democrats in the 1890s, and he established the short-lived Ruskin Colony in rural Tennessee in 1894.

From its debut on August 31, 1895, until World War I, the *Appeal to Reason* was a media phenomenon. In addition to Wayland's pithy paragraphs of "one-hoss philosophy," it ran serialized classics, by writers such as Marx and Engels, William Morris, Edward Bellamy, and Tom Paine, and contemporary works, by Jack London and Upton Sinclair, including the initial printing of *The Jungle.* Eugene V. Debs was on the staff for five years. The paper published four to eighteen regional editions of each issue, and its success led to a lending library and a traveling lecture series, among other activities. Wayland's *Appeal* accepted advertisements, including those for patent medicines and unscrupulous real estate rip-offs, for which the publisher always vouched. He sold subscriptions using an expansive network of volunteer salesmen, the "*Appeal* army." Circulation reached a peak of five hundred thousand during World War I, and single issue printings ran as high as four million copies. An able editor, Fred D. Warren, gradually took over direction of the paper from Wayland, but its editorial mission remained the conversion, through education, of its readers to socialism. In 1901 the paper was a firm supporter of the newly organized Socialist Party of America.

The citizens of Girard came to accept their most famous resident. The paper, the school it helped establish, and its other subsidiaries proved to be major economic assets. Wayland attracted Socialists from across the country. Girard became a waystop for those en route to socialist events or conventions. An informal network of boarding houses arose for the visitors, where local Socialists lodged and fed them. Some of the visitors stayed to be near "The Temple of the Revolution," which was the name of the fourth in the ever-larger series of buildings needed to house the *Appeal*. The socialist circle in Girard had blossomed.

One young man who was drawn to Girard was Francis Patrick O'Hare from St. Louis. He was born in 1876 in Iowa to Elizabeth and Peter Paul O'Hare. Frank's father was an immigrant from Belfast and an unsuccessful entrepreneur, who often left his family while he pursued various money-making schemes and even participated in the Boer War. Frank's mother was of Dutch background; she died when he was fourteen, and his half-sister, Gertrude Petzold, twelve years his senior, became his surrogate parent in the absence of Peter Paul O'Hare. Frank earned money by delivering papers while he attended elementary school and one year of high school in St. Louis, and then he worked for several hardware wholesalers. He was introduced to socialist literature by one of his workmates. He joined both the Public Fund and Welfare Association and the Rochdale Co-operative Association. By 1901 he was reading the *Appeal to Reason*, which circulated widely in Missouri, had organized a socialist study club called the Clarion Club, and had started to write for the local labor press. The lanky Irish-American took his place in the first class of the International School of Social Economy, where Mills immediately pegged him as a natural organizer.

He met Kate Richards on October 9, 1901, in a classroom. Frank later said that four days after meeting they decided to marry. The young couple seemed very much alike. They were the same age and even about the same height. They had similar ideas and backgrounds, although Frank was more the urbanite, and he was taciturn while Kate was talkative. There were hints of difficult traits that would later intensify, for example, Kate's opinionatedness and Frank's volatile temper. Kate had a "great mass" of reddish hair and was described as thin as a beanpole with an irresistible "Irish" smile. In no time, Frank and Kate were keeping company. In the course of their twelve-week program at the school, their romance did not remain a secret. They could be observed "spooning" at the front gate of Kate's lodgings, the home of Lillian and M. V. Tubbs, whom the O'Hares would ever after refer to as Mother and Daddy Tubbs. The Tubbses often hosted socialist visitors to Girard and were party activists at the local level. Despite the frigid and windy December weather in southeastern Kansas, the young couple's evening walks became a daily event. Recalling those evenings together three years later, Kate Richards O'Hare wrote a flowery, generalized piece entitled "Happiness." In it she rhapsodized, "Do you remember that moonlight [*sic*] night when the snow creaked beneath your feet and all the world was radiant with its frost jewels on, do you remember that someone held your hand to keep it warm, how heartbeats smothered voices but without the spoken word you knew for the first time love's young dream?"

Kate Richards's conversion to socialism was complete at this point. She later wrote, "[I] awoke in a new world, with new viewpoints, new aspirations and the dazzling view of the new and wonderful work to do. All the universe pulsated with new life that swept away the last vestige of the mists of creed and dogma and the old ideas and beliefs." Her romance with Frank O'Hare only enhanced her ideological commitment. They spent their first Christmas together with seventy-five friends at a community dinner for local Socialists hosted by Mills. Kate Richards was assigned to prepare the dinner and was more than grateful when some "good Girard matrons" contributed their culinary expertise.

The school term ended on December 30, 1901, and Kate and Frank were married on New Year's Day, 1902, at Wayland's home. The house was an imposing Victorian on the outskirts of town, one of the show-places of Girard. It was situated on a half-block of land that Wayland operated as a miniature farm. It boasted a pasture, rows of fruit trees, a large barn, and a yard full of chickens and berry bushes. The structure itself was of three stories with several verandas, and it contained a library and all of the comforts that turn-of-the-century American civilization could provide. The wedding was certainly the social occasion of the year for the socialist comrades of Girard. Among the thirty guests were the recently widowed and remarried Wayland, his second wife, a former employee of the *Appeal,* and some of Wayland's children. Mills officiated at the ceremony, and his wife and daughter attended. Many of the classmates of the bridal couple attended as did Mother and Daddy Tubbs. Standing up were Wilbur Clark Benton, a classmate, Mrs. Fred Warren, and Kate's sister, Jessie. Other Richards relatives came for the wedding but, surprisingly, not her parents. Mother Jones was not present, but she sent a silver soap dish, which became one of the O'Hares' most treasured possessions.

Following the wedding, the young couple left on a working honeymoon. They stopped for a visit with Kate's parents in Kansas City, and then they implemented their training by touring the region as socialist agitators and organizers. The uniqueness of such a honeymoon brought them media attention: feature stories appeared in the *Kansas City Times,* the *St. Louis Post-Dispatch,* and other area newspapers. From then on, they shared lives within the framework of the Socialist party. Kate earnestly assured Frank's disapproving sister, who evidently was concerned about their future, that they were "uplifting humanity" but that she would, nevertheless, find time to take care of Frank. The couple established a home in Kansas City, Kansas, and Frank lectured at the training school and worked as a socialist organizer, while Kate became a journalist and promoted the cause.

The cause for which Kate and Frank O'Hare worked already had a history, but the Socialist party, organized in Indianapolis at a convention in July 1901, was relatively new. The coalition that emerged was made up of socialist groups that had spent the 1890s fighting with each other rather than the capitalist system. The oldest contingent was the Socialist Labor party, founded in 1876, which chose to remain separate under the leadership of the inflexible, contentious Daniel De Leon. Eugene V. Debs, originally of the American Railway Union, had converted to socialism following the famous Pullman strike and a jail term. He and a number of colleagues organized a series of new parties, including the Social Democratic party. It nominated Debs for president in 1900, and the party garnered one hundred thousand votes in the general election. By 1901 these Socialists were able to bring together all American Socialists, except for the coterie that remained in the S.L.P.. The Socialist party became the largest and most electorally successful radical party in the history of the United States.

Between 1901 and 1912 the party drew members and increased electoral support. In 1903 national membership stood at 15,000, and in 1912 there were almost 120,000 members. In the meantime, itinerant organizers, lecturers, and journalists spread through all regions of the country, converting people to their cause. A strong network of local and state party activists developed, and Socialists were elected to public office across the nation. The party enjoyed support in the plains states and the Southwest among native-born American farmers, as well as among followers in ethnic enclaves in the Midwest and the East. An entire culture emerged; people spent their lives within the socialist community, participating in local events, fundraisers, and a variety of party-organized activities.

Until recently, historians characterized party members as essentially professional, middle-class, native-born Americans. Writings by James R. Green and others have demonstrated, in fact, that the Socialist party had a strong base among workers. Although the majority of American work-ers did not align with the party, its core of active members tended to be skilled and unskilled workers. They were the volunteers who walked the precincts and sold subscriptions to the *Appeal to Reason*. Women were a visible presence in the party. When Kate Richards O'Hare became a card-carrying member, perhaps 5 percent of the membership was female. Exact gender-identified membership figures do not exist, but fragmen-tary evidence suggests that by 1912, 10 percent of the members were women, and the percentage grew in the next few years to perhaps 17. The majority of women who joined the Socialist party were American-born with college educations. They were middle-class women who had very frequently been active in earlier social purity movements, such as temperance, evangelical work, or suffrage campaigns. A minority of the female members were working-class immigrants. They tended to be either Jewish or Finnish, reflective of the strong involvement of these two ethnic groups in the Socialist party. Rank-and-file women members distributed propaganda, served as poll watchers, and observed gender-suggested roles by organizing cake-bakes, bazaars, and picnics and by generally supporting the cause in auxiliary functions. However, women also worked for the party in many nontraditional ways as lecturers and organizers, which was a marked difference between the Socialist party and other political parties in the early twentieth century.

Revisionist Marxism dominated the Socialist party. It held that so-cialism would inevitably triumph over capitalism without any need for violence: The continued concentration of American industry and finance was transforming the economic system. Through party propaganda and political action, the American public would become convinced to sup-port socialism. Thus, the party conducted campaigns and elected its members to public office as a means of educating the public about socio-economic issues and of achieving reforms to improve the lives of the workers under capitalism, while simultaneously promoting its full trans-formation. This strategy, promoted by the majority of officeholders in the party, was challenged by those who considered themselves scientific, or orthodox, Marxists. This vocal minority believed that increasing tensions between capital and labor would soon lead to a revolution. They argued that the party's role was to remain prepared to lead the workers at the moment of revolution rather than to elect members to public office during the capitalist phase or to ameliorate tensions in any way. These two factions were often in conflict, but the revisionists dominated party policy-making, and most members accepted their views.

Kate Richards O'Hare accepted and endorsed the views of the leadership of the Socialist party. She, like Frank, was a revisionist, or reformist, Socialist who believed that the increasing exploitation of the proletariat would help undermine the existing capitalist structure and that socialism could be built into the system through reforms. Though she would later be known in the national media as "Red Kate," an epithet that seemed to identify her with the revolutionary socialists, that nickname misrepresented her.

From January 1902 onward the O'Hares were, as she described them, "traveling speakers and organizers" who "followd the stony, rough hewn path. . . . From the coal fields of Pennsylvania and West Virginia and Indian Territory, to the farms of Kansas and Iowa and Missouri, through the plains of Texas and into the cotton fields of Oklahoma and Arkansas and Tennessee, from the Ghetto of New York to the Rocky Maintains." They spent their first long trip organizing among Pennsylvania anthracite miners. The lengthy strike that year, the longest up to then in the mining industry, led President Theodore Roosevelt to assume a precedent-setting role of arbitrator between labor and management. It was Kate O'Hare's first extended experience working among the various immigrant miners since her acquaintance with the miners of the "Little Balkans." Some of the Pennsylvania miners, trying to figure out why this young, educated American woman was spending time among them, and perhaps noting characteristics left over from her rescue-work past, assumed that she was a social worker.

From Pennsylvania, Frank and Kate went to New York City, where they spent months working among the "huddled masses" of the East Coast. The penniless young couple was boarded by party comrades in their tenement flat until they could find a furnished room. As Frank later wrote, he and Kate never worried about money in those days. He became a tutor to a boys' socialist study group, and then a lecturer for the I.A.M., speaking before members of their New York lodges. Both he and Kate wrote for the popular socialist press, and Kate earned more money than Frank by selling articles to Bernarr McFadden's magazine, *Fair Play.* Thus Kate O'Hare began her free-lance career, writing for numbers of socialist newspapers. She surveyed working conditions in New York; calling herself Kate Kelley and dressing in shabby clothes in order to gather material for a series of articles, she went "undercover" in a different field each week. She was appalled to observe what she called an army of women marching forth each dawn to bend or stand or strain or lift for so many hours that they would soon ruin their health. She worked with flower-makers "amid the gorgeously colored but poison-laden materials, with the button-makers, where shell dust destroys the lungs, with candy-makers whose [sic] excess heat and steam make ready victims for pneumonia, and with the garment workers, whose consumption lurks in lint and foul air." She also worked as a department store clerk and as a waitress, all the while learning the impossibility of living on the pittance that women were paid. When the O'Hares were not working, they participated in the various social activities of New York's Socialist party. At a bazaar, for example, Frank served as a barker, and Kate was a palm-reading gypsy, drawing on her knowledge of psychology to give plausible readings. Their work was satisfying, but they began to feel homesick for the Midwest, and Kate apparently was thinking about having a baby, so they left New York.

En route to Kansas City, the O'Hares lectured and organized in the Appalachian upper South and in cities in the Midwest. They had selected Kansas City, Kansas, for their home because they knew the area and had socialist friends there. Frank began working as an organizer for the party, even though he had promised Kate he would devote his energies to earning a living. By then, Kate O'Hare had begun to build a reputation in socialist circles. She had accepted the first of what would be many positions as a regular columnist for a socialist newspaper. That year she began to write a column for the *Coming Nation,* a resurrected Wayland periodical run by Fred Warren. Her column was aimed at socialist women and potential female converts. As historian Elliot Shore has recently noted, earlier efforts to reach women in socialist newspapers had tended to be through columns by wives or female relatives of the editors or publishers. O'Hare's feature was the first such permanent fixture in a socialist newspaper by a woman who was developing her own following in the movement. Still, her approach was very traditional; she appealed to her female readers as helpmates to their menfolk. She addressed women only as wives and mothers at this stage of her own cultural evolution, even though she observed and worked with women proletarians during the months she wrote for the *Coming Nation.*

Despite the heavy responsibilities the young couple bore and the somewhat nomadic lives they led, Frank did get a job in a wholesale hardware firm, and they started a family. Their first child, Richard, was born in November 1903. The very next month, demonstrating the continued centrality of the socialist movement to their lives as well as their commitment to maintaining a normal home scene, the O'Hares hosted a Christmas gathering for many of their Girard School classmates. Dick won notoriety even before his first birthday. Kate took her six-month-old infant with her to the Socialist party's national convention in Chicago. He was fussed over by delegates, was the subject of a newspaper story headlined "Woman delegate brings her infant," and was caricatured by a leading cartoonist, Ryan Walker.

Late in 1904 the O'Hare family began what would become a five-year odyssey. They joined thousands of Americans migrating to the Oklahoma territory, then viewed as the last frontier. Frank O'Hare went there first to organize for the party. He felt that party leaders viewed him as a country boy and blocked him from established urban routes; he wanted a chance to prove himself. He liked the settlers he found in Oklahoma, and so he accepted a job on the Chandler *Publicist*. He asked Kate to consider moving the family there, and she agreed. They both worked on the socialist-oriented Chandler newspaper, and Kate became the associate editor after a few months. Frank O'Hare later recalled their stay in Chandler as a "beautiful time," and Kate O'Hare remembered the move as "faring forth to seek the Great Adventure."

They settled into life in the undeveloped Oklahoma Territory, at first in the small town of Chandler, located not far from the Creek Nation and near the center of what would, in 1907, become the state of Oklahoma. After six months they relocated slightly to the east, where they leased a half-section of land in the remaining Indian Territory. Thus, they became farmers. They joined others from Kansas and elsewhere, many of whom had been wiped out financially and were buying or leasing land in hopes of achieving some measure of independence. Fragmentary newspaper and party records indicate that both Kate and Frank continued their activities in the socialist movement. Frank became a state organizer, operating out of an office in Oklahoma City, and tried to create stability for his growing family.

Oklahoma had opened to white settlement with the infamous "land runs," starting in 1889. By 1900, four hundred thousand Caucasians had become residents of Oklahoma Territory; most of them were homesteaders, while the three hundred thousand whites residing in the Indian Territory were renters because land there could only be owned by Native Americans. By 1907, when the territories were merged and Oklahoma entered the Union as the forty-sixth state, each of the combining sections held a population of about seven hundred thousand, and 86 percent of the population was Caucasian. Oklahoma, larger than any state east of the Mississippi River, was experiencing an environmental transformation that undermined its original promise. The O'Hares had arrived barely in time for Kate O'Hare to rhapsodize over "beautiful prairies where succulent grass covers the ground with a carpet of richest emerald, of alluvial valleys, . . . of clear sparkling streams and magnificent forests." Those grasses holding the prairies together were disappearing, along with the forests, and their loss meant the destruction of the balance of nature.

Northwest and north central Oklahoma homesteaders grew wheat while the renters, who were often sharecroppers, of the southeast "Little Dixie" area specialized in cotton. Whatever diversification had initially been used was quickly succeeded by one-crop, labor-intensive farming, especially in the southeastern corner. In less than a generation, the potential of the Oklahoma frontier was lost in rapid modernization. What has been described as a "migratory cultural ecology" evolved. The impoverished tenants and mortgaged homesteaders moved on to new leases, always seeking more productive opportunities. Meanwhile, "grafters," or real estate brokers, enjoyed the fruits of the land. According to Kate O'Hare, the manipulation of the land by a real estate machine dependent on shyster lawyers was leading to the increasing landlessness of the people of Oklahoma, Indians and whites alike. She named her adopted home "The Land of Graft" and predicted that statehood, along with the rising anger of the exploited, would defeat the system, which she compared to the political rings that controlled urban areas.

When Oklahoma was granted statehood at the end of 1907, its constitution was deemed one of the most progressive. In fact, it was denounced as a radical document by President Theodore Roosevelt, who opposed its passage. The constitution's progressive nature was in part due to a coalition of members of the incipient labor movement and an organized bloc of farmers. The unusually detailed document included a bill of rights and featured antimonopolistic measures, initiative and referendum procedures, and protective legislation and restrictions on land speculation, the last of which passed too late for many residents. Statehood was celebrated with great fanfare all across Oklahoma. The O'Hares, at home in the former Indian Territory, no doubt participated in the celebration. As Edward Everett Dale, one of the deans of western history described the events of that November, businesses closed, and everyone turned out except Native Americans, who boycotted the occasion. Celebrants brought basket dinners to the festivities, which included speeches, fireworks, brass bands, and parades.

As a resident at the official start of Oklahoma's history, Kate O'Hare offered a somewhat reserved but not cynical prognosis. The new state lacked an educational system, a state capitol, decent roads, and most public buildings. It was overwhelmingly rural, having only a few towns and many unincorporated villages linked by railroads and dirt roads. O'Hare hoped that statehood would mean a better life for the masses of the people, with less corruption and more self-government. From her perspective the most serious element in the situation was the dependent condition of the farmers; however, she saw hopeful signs on the horizon. The exploited and discontented were beginning to organize themselves; unions were a growing presence in the few cities with populations over five thousand; and the Socialist party had already begun to bring its message to Oklahomans.

The O'Hare family scene underwent changes during their Oklahoma years. Frank's weeks away from home were at first hard on Dick, Kate reported. He needed assurance that Frank would return. But new additions to the family continued to arrive and partially countered his absences. Kathleen was born in 1905, and twin boys, named Eugene and Victor (both after Gene Debs) were born in 1908. The birth of the twins was a special event; only one baby had been expected. Moreover, Kate's poor health during the pregnancy had caused concern over a possible miscarriage. Kate delivered prematurely, and she recalled later that the doctor and a Cherokee nurse who assisted him were her only companions. Normally, Kate was surrounded by family and friends; giving birth on the frontier was typically a female community ritual, an event for which a network of women would gather, and the expectant mother might even stock extra food in case of a long labor. To be alone at such a time was dreaded, but Kate O'Hare made the best of the situation. Frank became more thoughtful with the arrival of the children; he doted on the twins. Nevertheless, he still felt committed to his travel on behalf of the socialist cause throughout the state.

Kate's parents joined them in Oklahoma, Andrew having given up his Kansas City partnership in a hardware store. They bought a half-section fifteen miles north of Vinita near Miles, and when Kate became ill, she went to stay with them. Frank had no aptitude for farming, and he leaned on his father-in-law's expertise. They became close as they farmed together and read and discussed the same books. Kate O'Hare, besides cooking and sewing clothes for the children, maintained a garden. She kept two hundred chickens and marketed the eggs. The family once traded some of their eggs for an Indian pony for the children. Kate viewed the area as a good place to raise a family and believed that it was far better to live in the country than in the city. The O'Hares did not have to worry about grocery bills or rent collectors, and they could go camping occasionally and fish and collect berries, much as in her youth.

Frank O'Hare continued his work as a party organizer and lecturer, and Kate still wrote for the socialist press and began to win a following as a public speaker. In fact, she became a regional figure of some renown in these years. Her public life was beginning to monopolize her time, and she had to find methods to handle her family responsibilities. Somehow, a balance was struck between hired care-givers and family members; she often relied on Frank's sister, Gertrude, an arrangement which apparently was not always successful. Gertie was a difficult woman who lacked wide horizons. Frank O'Hare's biographer believes that Frank came to resent Kate's absences from home, and the children later said that Frank wanted Kate to abandon her travels until they were at least eight years old. Kate herself acknowledged that she did not like leaving the children with hired help. She preferred to have a housekeeper so that she, when present, could handle the children. O'Hare, like most women in public life, struggled to meet her separate commitments, but as the perceived primary parent, she could be faulted for insufficient involvement in her children's lives.

The O'Hares lived among a congenial and growing group of socialist coworkers who were recreating their own Girard. Many of them would share the same aspirations and tribulations over the next fifteen years in the course of their movement activities in various regions of the country. By this time, the party presence in Oklahoma had grown beyond simply circuit-riding organizers and "soldier-salesmen" hawking subscription to the *Appeal to Reason.* A party structure had emerged.

In what Kate O'Hare described as the dusty, blistering, sun-baked, sweltering heat that was Oklahoma for great stretches of each year—so much so that forever after to her, hot weather and Oklahoma were inseparable—the socialist circle grew and seemed to thrive. Most of the major activists were migrants to the area, like the O'Hares. One of the leading organizers, in fact, was an immigrant from Bavaria. Oscar Ameringer was a portly, jovial, Germanic Mark Twain, a troubadour for the cause. Previous to coming to Oklahoma, he had edited trade union newspapers and undertaken socialist organizing in the Midwest and Louisiana. When he arrived in Oklahoma in 1907, he intended to concentrate on organizing the industrial proletariat in Oklahoma City, Guthrie, and the few other towns with an industrial work force. He quickly realized, however, that the class struggle in the new state had to be viewed as between landlords and those who worked the land. He altered his focus and was able to reach out to farmers with success. Despite his heavy German accent, he was popular as a speaker and even as an entertainer whose musical quartet with his three sons performed before and after his talks. A few years later he edited the *Oklahoma Pioneer* and ran a strong race for mayor in Oklahoma City in 1911. His common-sense approach to explaining socialist theory was effective with his audiences, and Ameringer himself was impressed with the simple and direct openness of the farm people who came to hear him. They often turned out as whole families for his talks and he believed that they were "grateful for anything that broke the monotony of their lonesome lives. Of more than average intelligence, they followed the main arguments easily and caught . . . subtle points quickly." Ameringer moved on and spent the years leading to World War I in Wisconsin, which featured the most German-dominated and most electorally successful socialist movement in the country. After that he returned to Oklahoma and edited another socialist paper.

Otto and Winnie Branstetter were other comrades whose lives, like the O'Hares, were framed by their work on behalf of the Socialist party. Otto Branstetter was the state secretary, appointed by the party's National Executive Committee and instructed to organize and streamline activities in the "Sooner State." He sought to centralize party functioning and to organize on the precinct level where possible. He tried to win adherents county by county and to schedule at least twenty speakers in the field at any one time. The Branstetters' backgrounds were remarkably similar to the O'Hares'. Otto had worked as a trade unionist in Kansas City. A few years later, after his Oklahoma stint, he became the national secretary of the party. Winnie Shirley Branstetter and Kate O'Hare had met in Kansas City through their mutual membership in the Socialist Labor party. Winnie became a Socialist Party organizer in Oklahoma and New Mexico, held state-level positions in the Oklahoma party, wrote for its press, did outreach work to area unionists, and a few years later headed the party's National Woman's Committee. Winnie especially kept in contact with Kate O'Hare over the years.

Caroline A. Lowe, Winnie Branstetter's sister, was another party activist. She had been a school teacher in Kansas City, who eventually practiced law as a defense attorney for labor. Lowe became well known on the speaking circuit in the plains states and the Southwest. She was an official of the party's Woman's National Committee, participated in labor education experimental programs, and ran for public office as a Socialist.

These socialists and others who left fewer records of their activities sought to bring the message of socialism to the working people of Oklahoma. That population was characterized by Ameringer as people from another America than what was focused on in the national press. "The population was of many states and many types. From Texas had come cowmen and cotton farmers; from the Old South, share croppers and other poor whites. From the north and eastern states had come corn, cow, hog, and wheat farmers and a good percentage of former wage earners." Most of these Americans were disappointed in their experiences in this final frontier, and some of them began to draw upon a radical strain in Oklahoma's background on which the Socialists hoped to build.

During the territorial era, bricklayers, building trades, and railroad brotherhoods had organized unions. The Knights of Labor led strikes in the coal fields in the 1890s, and within a few years was succeeded by the United Mine Workers. The Twin-Territorial Federation of Labor was established as early as 1903. In 1907 the first state legislature was sufficiently attuned to organized labor that it passed a mine inspection law and established a state mining board and a board of arbitration and conciliation. Even before that, while Oklahoma was initially being settled, the Populist party had enjoyed some successes among the area's farmers, winning one-third of the vote for seats in the territorial House of Representatives in 1894. Some writers note degrees of continuity between populism and the origin of the socialist movement. Historian James R. Green has estimated that about one-half of the most active Socialists in Oklahoma had been Populists, and perhaps an even greater continuity can be traced in leadership. After the Populists faded, some former Populists organized the Farmers' Union to promote agricultural cooperatives. Their newspapers reveal an increasingly anticapitalist, if not socialist, message. The Farmers' Union cooperated with trade unionists in a joint effort to shape the state constitution, as suggested above.

A sociologist, Ellen Rosen, has argued that the working farmers of Oklahoma were receptive to agrarian radicalism much as peasantry may be during a period of uprooting modernization. She has postulated that the intrusion of modern capitalism and its market economy with such startling rapidity in Oklahoma created an impoverished and alienated farming population. People who were not economically secure found themselves increasingly threatened. Rising land values led to decreased acreage per farm and some individuals no longer farmed large enough tracts from which they could earn a living, as Carey McWilliams, the editor of the *Nation,* demonstrated many years ago. By 1910 44 percent of western Oklahoma homesteaders were mortgage holders and 36 percent were tenants, and western Oklahoma was the most prosperous part of the state. The "Little Dixie" tenants and sharecroppers continued to be at the mercy of the price of cotton which, while not as low as in the early 1890s, would not provide a reasonable return until World War I. These economic tensions and vulnerabilities were exacerbated by the distance that separated the farmers from those who appeared to hold local power. Unlike the earlier Populists, who focused their hostility on external agents of control, the so-called eastern interests, these farmers felt powerless before local elites of bankers, merchants, and town officeholders. The towns seemed exploitative of the countryside—the farmers' land was assessed at higher rates than were town properties, while rural schools were inadequately funded, and some public services were totally absent. The Socialists were able to make use of the farmers' resentment by referring to "the parasites in the electric light towns."

The Oklahoma Socialists used summer encampments as an agitational tool. So successful were these summer programs in reaching out to thousands of southwestern families that the leading French socialist, Jean Jaurés, invited Kate O'Hare to come to France and advise the party there on how to attract the peasantry to its message. The idea of the encampment was borrowed from a populist institution, and it had overtones of revivalist tent meetings. Rather than challenging local religious impulses in accord with orthodox Marxism, the encampment drew on them to expand existing feelings of injustices and hopes for a better world. In fact, the Bible was used as a symbol of social protest. Frank O'Hare had attended the first socialist encampment in Grand Saline, Texas, in 1904, and recommended adopting such programs in Oklahoma. For the next several years, the Oklahoma Socialists held an annual series of week-long summer camp meetings in various areas of the state, which attracted thousands for days of socialist speeches, propaganda, songfests, and other activities. Regions began to compete to host an encampment. Crafts, skits, games, and carnival-like attractions, as well as economics and history classes were integrated with musical interludes, featuring familiar secular and religious tunes with new lyrics emphasizing the party's message. Three formal meetings were held each day during individual encampments held in various hamlets across the state.

People came from the surrounding region, traveling for up to one hundred miles for what was the major event of the summer, even the highlight of the year, perhaps the only respite from their routine. They came by foot, on horseback, and in covered wagons. They brought their food and cooking utensils; the party organizers supplied fuel, water, and other necessities. Local businesses and even the Chambers of Commerce underwrote some of the expenses, suggestive of how inherent these events were in community life. Large canvas tents accommodated audiences of up to one thousand for the talks and events, while special programs were held to occupy the children. Outdoor talks drew even larger crowds. The encampments were a combination of an educational experience, a religious-like revival, and a vacation, all in one. Horseback parades through the main street of the nearest town often marked the start of an encampment. Typically, mixed choruses performed at opening sessions. Throughout the week, the Ameringer "orchestra" would perform classical music, preceded by a lecture on the compositions. Talks by major speakers, both regional and national figures, were clearly the major events, and their themes would be rehashed in the evenings in discussions over camp fires.

The leading national figure of the socialist movement, Eugene V. Debs, the perennial party nominee for president, was the star attraction. The encampments were always on his itinerary, whether he was staying in his hometown of Terre Haute, Indiana, or in residence at the *Appeal* in Girard. His talks were always lengthy, but in that era, before the development of the mass media and the concomitant decline of the public's attention span, hours-long addresses were no barrier to a speaker's message. Debs provided the audience with the essence of the party's philosophy, and he discussed current events from a socialist point of view. Another favorite speaker was Mother Jones, who appeared occasionally at encampments. The feisty septuagenarian always received major billing. Whether she discussed a coal miners' strike in which she was involved or some other subject, such as woman's suffrage, the importance of which she minimized, seemed immaterial. It was enough for the audience that Mother Jones was there in person. After Debs and Mother Jones, Kate Richards O'Hare was the crowds' favorite. Unlike the other notable speakers, O'Hare lived on the land. She knew the lives of homesteaders from direct experience. She had experienced the effort to establish a homestead, the struggle with the elements, and the battle with economic forces, which working farmers could not easily overcome. She had known the helplessness and anger of a family when its members realized they could no prevail through hard work. She knew intimately rather than theoretically the issues her audience confronted and the odds facing all of them. At one encampment or another, Kate O'Hare would speak in the afternoon and in the evening. In one talk, for example, at Black Jack Grove near Miles, in early September 1906, she told the crowd that while the American standard of living had improved over the past, the conditions under which working people labored, especially women and children, were so "degrading and demoralizing" that every true American, she said, knew that a change must occur. She implored her audience to study economic issues. In another talk, she outlined the history of the trusts, and she told any shopkeepers in her audience that they were minnows who would be swallowed up as the trusts gained control of all lines of business. Based on her links to the encampment audiences, her renown in the movement grew beyond the fame which her columns had brought her, and her reputation eclipsed Frank's on the socialist lecture circuit.

Oscar Ameringer was also one of the most popular speakers. He was billed as "the Funny Dutchman from Oklahoma." Ameringer, despite his heavy accent, effectively reached his audiences through his judicious use of humor mixed with his detailed knowledge of the agricultural conditions facing his audience. His concept of a rural-based socialism had evolved as he came to view the landless especially as the proletariat of the region. He emphasized the elimination of large land holdings through a taxation policy which would free land for those who were working farmers. Other popular speakers included the O'Hares' former teacher, Walter Thomas Mills, and Caroline Lowe.

The support for the Oklahoma Socialist party, implied by participation in the encampments, can only be conjectured. What is crystal clear, however, is that the socialist vote in Oklahoma grew dramatically in the encampment years. In 1900 approximately fifteen hundred socialist votes were cast in the Twin Territories. In 1904, the year the O'Hares moved to Oklahoma and on the eve of the introduction of the encampment programs, the socialist vote climbed to over four thousand. In 1908 Oklahoma cast more than twenty thousand votes for Debs, the greatest number of votes for him in any state. At that time the party had over eight hundred local organizations and several newspapers in Oklahoma. Frank O'Hare exulted after the vote that "socialist thought is making tremendous strides" among the landless farmers and what he called "toilless [*sic*] laborers." Four years later the vote grew again, and Debs claimed over forty-two thousand votes, 16 percent of the ballots cast nationwide, winning as much as 30 percent of the ballots in some of the southern counties. Before that date, the state party had placed a farm plank in its platform that reconciled the principle of collectivization of land with the idea of the family farm. Without a doubt Oklahomans from 1907 on had seen the Socialists become a major political party. While the party never won a statewide election, it did claim the support of one of five voters over the next few years in some statewide and congressional elections and had more members than did New York. By 1914 it had elected five state representatives, a state senator, and dozens of county and local officials. Its voters were concentrated in the poorest southern tier of cotton growing counties (not in the O'Hares' north-central corn-growing area) and among some wheat farmers in the northwestern counties with relatively low farm values. Support came from cash crop-growing areas, therefore those related to the market and its fluctuations. The structure of local agriculture was central to the pattern of votes.

Frank O'Hare published an article after the 1908 election entitled "The Oklahoma Vote," in which he wrote of exciting prospects for the local movement, and he remarked that party members looked forward to future campaigns with "renewed enthusiasm and great expectations." Ironically, Frank and Kate and their family were not to enjoy the peak years of the Oklahoma socialist movement. Frank's health collapsed shortly after that election. He suffered what was then described as a nervous breakdown. To cope with his temporary disability, the family moved back to the more settled environment of Kansas City, Kansas.

The years from 1901 to 1908 were crucial in Kate O'Hare's development. She discovered her adult self in the socialist milieu of Girard, Kansas. She became a trained socialist public speaker, married a party comrade, and combined her public life with motherhood. She and her young husband, Frank, shared organizing trips to the East Coast and through the Midwest while she began her career as a columnist for socialist periodicals. The couple refocused their efforts when they abruptly moved to Oklahoma for a four-year period. Oklahoma proved to be much more than a detour for Kate O'Hare. There, she further honed her skills and developed a regional following which would serve her well in the future. The family's next move, back to Kansas, provided them with a more central location and marked the start of Kate O'Hare's emergence as a national figure who would become arguably the most significant voice in the Socialist party west of the Mississippi River.

3

MATURE AGITATOR

By the age of thirty, Kate Richards O'Hare had acquired a wide following. Her name was known to Socialists throughout the Southwest and, increasingly, thoroughout the nation. The rank-and-file of the Socialist party listened to her speeches, read her articles, and began to elect her to national party offices. Her growing fame was based on her popular talks on the socialist lecture circuit and on her columns, which appeared in a dozen movement periodicals. Her speaking was the expression of her activism. O'Hare's constant touring defined her life for almost twenty-five years. From 1904 to 1919 and for most of the 1920s, hers was a life on the rails. She was an early twentieth-century circuit rider, itinerate preacher, and drummer selling a secular and ideological message to the public, taking only occasional breaks at home with her family. Kate O'Hare had the ability to address listeners so that they knew shc was one of them, someone who understood their problems and their needs; she was particularly successful with rural audiences. She denied that she could reach urban listeners, stating that she knew her limitations, but she came to be in demand as a platform speaker with urban audiences too.

O'Hare was an attractive woman, especially as she matured. In her twenties she herself remarked that "I will never die of an overplus of beauty." But she gradually came into her own, and her public was certainly drawn to her. Her height, slenderness ("a beanpole," she called herself), and her "lustrous" hair were her strongest attributes. She became a striking figure by adding theatrical touches to her appearance. She would dress dramatically, appearing in flaming red dresses or in ugly prison attire. A forceful speaker, she organized her talks as a series of points, patterned after elocutionists she had heard in her youth. She was also, no doubt, influenced by her mentor, Wayland, who used the same style of highlighting brief points in tight paragraphs in his editorials. She employed this style throughout her career, and in her later years listeners found it old-fashioned. In her heyday, she often spoke three or four times a day. She reached out to audiences, chatting with them before and after her presentations. An imperiousness that she sometimes displayed as she got older showed itself only with coworkers, never with her public.

O'Hare was not initially effective before audiences, and no one would have predicted that speaking was her calling. Her first talks were as appendages to Frank O'Hare's addresses. He would give the major talk, and she would begin to add a ten- or fifteen-minute extemporaneous postscript to his remarks, to beef up his presentation and to build on the publicity that accrued to them as a young married couple on the socialist circuit. They started to bill themselves together because they correctly guessed that the audiences might be attracted to them as a curiosity.

Kate O'Hare's voice itself was initially weak, shrill, and high. Frank much later likened her early public speaking efforts to Eleanor Roosevelt's. He worked with his wife to lower her pitch, but it was not until the couple recorded their voices on a phonograph record, while visiting the St. Louis World's Fair in 1904, that she fully understood his critique. When she heard herself, she was shocked at the high pitch of her voice. Thereafter, they exercised vocally to lower her register by one-fourth. They also practiced on the substance of their speeches, rigorously criticizing each other's message and delivery. Kate O'Hare also had to learn to get the most out of her arguments, for she had a tendency to build to a conclusion and then throw away her major point or punch line. Gradually, she surmounted her initial awkwardness and problems. In her favor as she reached out to her audiences was a natural gift for charming the public. She sometimes seemed to intimidate women of her audiences but was able to transcend that problem once she got into the particulars of her remarks. She was strengthened in her outreach by her photographic eye for detail, an ability to integrate local color in her remarks as the O'Hares traveled across the country, and her own religious and rural background. In fact, she helped Frank to minimize some of his "city slicker" characteristics. She encouraged him to prepare an appropriate grace to use as necessary for meals taken with those they met. She was well served in this regard by her Campbellite influences. She came to be seen as kinfolk, if more educated than many in her audience. Gradually, as she eclipsed Frank on the socialist lecture circuit, she began to give the main addresses. They traveled separately more and more. Before 1910, she had become the featured name and main attraction, while he worked behind the scenes as a party organizer, router, or newspaper staffer. As Frank O'Hare evaluated her efforts, Kate O'Hare soon outdid all other party speakers. Frank remembered years later that everyone else except Gene Debs took a "back seat" to her.

Kate O'Hare was not a soapboxer, except on rare occasions. Her milieu was the rented hall, even at the beginning of her touring with Frank. Audiences were attracted to those halls by handbills the O'Hares printed and circulated. When possible, as soon as she arrived at a destination she would insert an announcement of the evening talk in the afternoon edition of a town's newspaper. Early on, Kate O'Hare developed a basic speech, which she used for years with appropriate variations for time and place. She referred to it as "the trinity of life"; the title referred to life's political, economic, and social variables, which she framed within her socialist message.

Up to 1911, most of her touring was through the lecture bureau of the *Appeal to Reason,* and for the next several years her travels were sponsored by another socialist regional newspaper whose editorial staff she joined, the St. Louis-based *National Rip-Saw.* Her annual tours were organized regionally. She often was scheduled for tours of both the South and the Northwest in spring, the encampment circuit in summer, and a "Yankee" trip in fall. Other, briefer, tours were inserted around the basic itinerary. After a while, specific stops were shaped by demand. Locals who purchased four hundred subscriptions to the sponsoring newspaper were able to book an O'Hare date. The newspapers advertised when she would be available in certain locales and drummed up bookings by encouraging competition among socialist locals for O'Hare. Towns were advised that they were neither too large nor too small for an O'Hare visit but that only two or three locations could be accommodated in a state. Whichever locals were lucky enough to book her, they were told, they would hold an advantage in their next political campaign.

As an example of tour planning, announcements were issued of the broad outline of her schedule. Readers were advised one year that in April, she was to be in Illinois and in and around St. Louis, her home. In May and June she intended to speak in Iowa, Nebraska, the Dakotas, Colorado, Utah, and possibly travel north to Oregon and Washington State. In July and August, her itinerary was set for Arkansas, Texas, and Oklahoma. In September, she planned to be in Minnesota, Michigan, Indiana, Ohio, Pennsylvania, Maryland, and West Virginia. In November, she was to be in Florida, the Carolinas, Virginia, Georgia, Alabama, Mississippi and Tennessee. Finally, in December she intended to visit states she had missed that year and also scheduled some repeat visits to Texas, New Mexico, Arizona, California, Nevada, Utah, Colorado and Kansas.

The enormous scope of her travels can be seen from the final schedule for her winter 1912, tour to the West Coast.

January 21 Springfield, Missouri
January 23 Mooreland, Oklahoma
January 24 Amarillo, Texas
January 25 Hagerman, New Mexico
January 26 Roswell, New Mexico
January 29 Alamogordo, New Mexico

January 30–February 1 El Paso, Texas
February 4 Anaheim, California
February 5 Santa Ana, California
February 6 Huntington Beach, California
February 7 Long Beach, California
February 9 San Jose, California
February 10 San Francisco, California
February 12 Woodland, California
February 13 Sacramento, California
February 16 Chico, California
February 17–18 Medford and Ashland, Oregon
February 19 Roseburg, Oregon
February 20 Springfield, Oregon
February 21 Salem, Oregon
February 22 Portland, Oregon
February 24 Sedro and Wooley, Washington
February 26 Port Angeles, Washington

It was with considerable truth that she was billed as not only the fore-most woman orator but also the busiest woman in America.

Such constant, elaborate touring was astonishing in human terms. Not only were there the routine separations from her husband and young children, but, moreover, the enormous wear and tear on O'Hare herself was extraordinary. Yet it seems clear that she came to thrive on this lifestyle. Nevertheless, criss-crossing the country constantly by train, staying in different hotels each night, managing her "grips," and washing laundry as she traveled meant juggling stressful logistics. Her meals were whatever she could grab on the run or that others would provide for her, so much so that she was later able to convince herself that prison fare could not be worse than some of the meals she had consumed over the years or the water worse than the green-colored liquid she had imbibed in Indian Territory and in lumber camps. While the party faithful who booked her attempted to entertain her as comfortably as possible, still O'Hare was always living by the hands on the clock and the numbers on the train schedule, subject to drafts and chills, heat and humidity, day in and day out.

It was no wonder that she endured occasional physical prostration. As late as 1922 she had to be begged to discontinue a tour and take time off to ward off another collapse. More than one tour had to be terminated because she could not continue, while a few were interrupted, if briefly, by life-threatening illnesses. Once, in Minot, North Dakota, a doctor advised her that a neglected abscess in her left ear could have killed her. A sprained ankle in Portland, Oregon, less dangerous to her overall health, barely slowed her down. Not infrequently, missed or late trains caused stressful schedule adjustments for her. Once in Argenta, Arkansas, for example, she did not arrive for her 2:30 P.M. talk until 4:00 P.M.; despite being frazzled, she spoke for an hour and a half. After a dinner break, the crowd demanded more discussion, which continued until she begged off, in danger of heat prostration. Other times, events of a different nature intruded on her schedule. In Tallapossa, Georgia, a less-than-friendly mayor tried to disperse her meeting, and O'Hare ended up protecting the mayor from a mobbing. Lighter moments occurred, too. She visited New Hampton, Iowa, where Frank had spent some of his childhood. The elderly druggist remembered him and his family, and she took a break to chat with the old man as he served her an ice cream soda.

Her commitment to and appetite for her work did not waiver. She wrote to her sister-in-law, Gertie, who then was caring for the children, "Like all workers, I am not my own master." Another time, she wrote to Gertie that she hoped that Frank remained healthy, as she was "getting along so well in my work that I'd hate to be disturbed now." Frank began to fume, as his letters show, but Kate O'Hare loved road work. She enjoyed the beautiful scenery. Writing from Arizona, she commented enthusiastically about the "wonderful country" in which she was traveling. She mentioned having been taken by her hosts into Juarez, Mexico, to see a bullfight. However, she admitted to feeling sorry at times that she was alone, and she wished on one trip that she had taken eight-year-old Dick along with her. All things considered, she loved her agitational work sufficiently to pursue it from the early 1900s until just before the Great Depression. She was on the road during her pregnancies and until her menopause. While Kate promoted her cause, her children grew from infants to adults, and the buoyancy of those first years of the Socialist Party of America, under Eugene Debs, gave way to fragmentation and decline, under Norman Thomas.

Kate O'Hare's work as a journalist formed the other half of her commitment to the socialist movement. As a writer she commented ably on the world around her from a socialist perspective. She brought the same good eye for detail to her columns that marked her oral presentations; she could be witty and folksy, and she was always able to find an appropriate anecdote to get a point across to her readers. Imaginative and inventive, she could, however, be sentimental and even maudlin in her tales of the human costs paid by the victims of the contemporary social order. She had started by writing occasional columns and features for socialist newspapers in Kansas when she was newly converted to the movement. In 1902 and again from 1904 to 1905, she briefly wrote a regular column, but mostly, in that first decade of the 1900s, her pieces appeared here and there, picked up by one newspaper and then another through the expansive socialist press network. Her work appeared in the Girard or Rich Hill *Coming Nation, Wayland's Monthly, Socialist Woman, International Socialist Review, Wilshire's Magazine,* New York *Call,* Chicago *Daily Socialist,* Chicago *Christian Socialist,* Chandler (Oklahoma) *Daily Publicist, Fair Play,* Kansas City *Socialist Teacher,* Garnett *Kansas Agitator,* and Oklahoma *Pioneer,* among others. Her writings could also be found in the various directly owned Socialist party newspapers, including the *Party Builder* and the *American Socialist.* Additionally, as a well-known social critic and writer, O'Hare was occasionally invited to write pieces for general-circulation magazines, such as the *Arena.*

O'Hare's features appeared most regularly in three socialist papers. She wrote columns for Wayland's *Appeal to Reason* from 1902 to 1911. Her work appeared routinely in 1913 in the St. Louis-based monthly called the *Melting Pot,* a socialist newspaper that focused on theosophy and attacked organized religion in tune with the intellectual idiosyncracies of its editor, Henry M. Tichenor. Finally, she wrote for the newspaper with which she came to be most identified, the *National Rip-Saw*. For more than dozen years, she worked for the paper, first as a featured columnist, then as associate editor for this regionally circulated newspaper based in St. Louis. After it folded, she and Frank revived it under the title *American Vanguard* and published it at a number of locations. O'Hare also wrote and published several booklets, which were printed by some of the newspapers for which she wrote or by the Socialist party itself. They included "Law and the White Slaver," "Church and the Social Problem," "Common Sense and the Liquor Traffic," and the book *The Sorrows of Cupid,* an earlier version of which had been a socialist best-seller entitled *What Happened to Dan.*

O'Hare's writings focused on the ills of modern industrialized society and the substitution of a socialist order for capitalism. She, like many early twentieth-century Socialists, believed that socialism would gradually replace capitalism through a series of reforms. Within that overall framework, during her career O'Hare touched on a wide variety of political, economic, and social issues. She wrote on working conditions, child labor, exploitation of women, political corruption, the Solid South, agriculture, black sharecropping, race relations, religious institutions, female suffrage, organized vice, American foreign policy, current events, and, near the end of her career, on war and prisons.

As a Socialist, Kate O'Hare's fundamental commitment was to the working masses of America. She emphasized the vulnerability of workers who neither owned the tools of production nor received the full fruits of their labor. Accordingly, she wrote about young girls toiling in factories and breaker boys working in mines, about so-called "blanket stiffs," about women tending looms and operating sewing machines, about farmers plowing the fields and their wives raising hens and hoeing gardens, about shop clerks and prostitutes, and about tenant farmers and hired hands. Central to that commitment to workers, she, like her party, supported the American Federation of Labor, despite the fact that she and her comrades tended to criticize the AFL for its narrow approach to labor organizing. The AFL organized workers by craft or trade, rather than by industry. By definition, this approach meant that it organized essentially skilled workers and ignored the needs of the unskilled who, in fact, were increasingly dominating the labor force. It eschewed the needs of the most vulnerable components of the industrial work force: immigrants, blacks, women, and children. The federation also, at least under the entrenched leadership of President Samuel Gompers, was hostile toward Socialism and government intervention and supportive of business unionism and voluntarism. O'Hare and the party attempted what was called "boring from within," encouraging the AFL to become more open to a socialist message. In the meantime, O'Hare was somewhat favorable toward moves toward industrywide labor organizations, such as the Industrial Workers of the World (the Wobblies), which was established in 1905. But she was essentially sympathetic to individual Wobblies; she, like many of her comrades, believed the organization to be anarchistic and violent in its tendencies.

In her view, American workers had to use the fact of universal male suffrage to promote fundamental changes. Because all American male workers possessed the vote, they had the capacity to alter the system, unlike workers in many nations. Therefore, in their own self-interest, workers had to and would embrace the Socialist party, she argued, to bring on the cooperative commonwealth. For the same purpose, as well as other important reasons, women should be granted the ballot, she went on, so that women workers also would be armed with an essential instrument of peaceful change.

While the workers and the Socialist party exploited the electoral process in order to undermine the capitalist system, O'Hare argued that immediate reforms of the industrial system needed to be effected. O'Hare, the reformist Socialist, unabashedly wrote of the immediate need for a shorter work day, an end to child labor, and the implementation of protective legislation for all workers. Many of her columns were devoted to detailed exposés of horribly exploitative working conditions. A lengthy, moving feature, for example, detailed the plight of sweatshop workers

in tenement environments. It ran at the time of the infamous Triangle Shirtwaist Factory fire, a disaster on the Lower East Side of New York in 1911 that claimed the lives of over 140 workers, most of whom were young Jewish or Italian immigrant women. Some of these columns were based on her own investigative reporting of working conditions—not only in sweatshops but also in lumber camps, mining towns, and factories.

Able to praise the exceptional capitalist whom she encountered, she wrote several features applauding Henry Ford in whose plants "not a single worker receives less than a living wage." She was impressed with Ford's having introduced the eight-hour day to his workers. While she was critical of his time-study devices, she was notably untroubled by the broad implications of mass production for workers' skills, autonomy, and individuality. Rather, she emphasized what she saw as concrete gains: the five-dollar-a-day wage, job security, and limitations on the foremen's arbitrary authority. She also positively welcomed the "uplifting" programs promoted by Ford's "Sociological Department." Possibly as a carryover from her Crittenton days, O'Hare, who harbored few of the fashionable prejudices against immigrants, applauded the department's work as promoting assimilation and "progress." Her favorable publicity for Henry Ford contrasted with, for example, her coverage of the management practices of a flour factory, which she exposed for its inhumane conditions and its inadequate piece-work wages. O'Hare participated in a municipal minimum wage study in St. Louis, which demonstrated that women workers received far less than a living wage, and it led her to write acidly that rather than paying workers enough to earn a living, employers paid them only enough to keep them "in good mule condition," just as a farmer fed a mule just enough corn to keep it alive.

Occasionally she covered strikes as a reporter. For example, she visited a major copper miners' strike in the Upper Peninsula of Michigan in the winter of 1913–1914. In a classic company town confrontation, workers and the Western Federation of Miners were pitted against management, with its hired thugs, scabs, and the National Guard. Miners of various nationalities, with Finns especially visible, had struck over abominable conditions. When O'Hare visited Calumet, Michigan, she reported to her readers that she "saw real war up there. I heard heads crack and bones snap. I walked over bloodstained snow. I heard bullets whistle and watched a passenger train riddled with stones and clubs." Striving to convey the feel of events in their most human dimensions, she concluded on an upbeat note: "Men and women have stood solidly together, race and creed lines have been obliterated, and those thousands of workers have acted together like one great body." O'Hare's optimism notwithstanding, the strike was broken months later.

O'Hare's bitterest pieces tended to be about the plight of the unemployed. In 1915, a winter of high unemployment, she wrote, "Vast armies of hungry, poverty-stricken men have drifted from city to city. . . . These men have crept into jails, workhouses and municipal lodging houses like animals to their burrows and whined like famished dogs in breadlines and before soup kitchens. Hundreds of thousands of girls have lost their six-dollar-a-week jobs and have been driven out on the streets to be used by lustful men and made the victims of police brutality." She was determined to focus the public's attention on the numbers of Americans living below the poverty line, and she sarcastically derided media tips on how the unemployed might achieve a balanced diet.

Her articles about American farmers consistently reflected the sure touch of someone who had lived the life she discussed. Not only were her girlhood memories of homesteading still vibrant, but her summer encampment tours reinforced her familiarity with their circumstances. Consequently, O'Hare's was one of the strongest voices in Socialist party debates, urging the formulation of a farmers' program. Most party policymakers focused on the urban proletariat and dismissed farmers as property-owning employers. However, many farmers were simply laborers, whether they owned their land or rented it. O'Hare understood the typical farmers' hand-to-mouth existence: Families hoped they could plants their crops, and then they prayed that market conditions and the generosity of nature, that is, the lack of a natural disaster, would result in an adequate return for their labor. Then they could make the mortgage payments that saved them from foreclosure—and disaster of another sort. She pointed out that some areas, specifically Oklahoma, had a higher tenantry rate than did Ireland. She wrote of farmers' dwellings almost denuded of furniture and described supper tables with nothing on them. Poor farmers and their families were subject to malnutrition if not actual starvation. These Americans toiled day in and day out in an endless struggle. Working in summer's searing sun and winter's whistling winds, they never received an adequate return for their toil because of their exploitation by bankers, merchants, and landlords.

Calling attention to the role of the farming woman, she pointed out to her readers that such a woman also struggled with the elements and economic forces. To O'Hare nothing was more tragic than a woman on a cotton farm enduring the hopeless life of a tenant. Life was at the subsistence level. Not only did such individuals lack material goods, but the harsh environment of the Southwest often meant no flowers or vines "but barren, sunburned, sunbaked ugliness." Moreover, the farmers themselves, because of the economic pressures under which they lived, exploited their families, which O'Hare was initially alone in noting. She reported seeing women working in the fields only hours before delivering babies and returning to hoe and spade within ten days of delivery, not unlike chattel slaves. At each birth, she wrote, such mothers knew that they were only breeding "another slave to walk in their footsteps." The exigencies of the farmers' increasing desperation were, she wrote, making them receptive to socialist teachings. The more they understood fundamentals of political and economic conditions, she predicted in 1913, the more they would demand the full product of their labor. She sensed an embryonic cry from rural America: "We want our Land, our Forests and our Mines."

Another issue that Kate O'Hare addressed in her columns was race. While she seemed to take pleasure in stating that as a Kansan she was reared in "the abolition state of all states," during her girlhood she did not live among African Americans nor were they a strong presence in her life in Kansas City or Girard when she left the family fold. She wrote that contemporary labor exploiters were a greater menace to society than had been the slave-owning aristocracy. In Oklahoma, pockets of black settlement were notable; in 1910 blacks made up 8.3 percent of the state's population. After 1889 especially, ex-slaves entered the Oklahoma Territories, establishing about two dozen all-black towns. Three-fourths of African American Oklahomans were rural-dwellers who typically were required by landlords to grow cotton, while a minority grew corn, and some even herded cattle. Their numbers were not as sizeable as in the Deep South, and race was therefore less of an explosive issue; nevertheless, it could be and was divisive. O'Hare attempted to defuse the issue of race, but she herself was capable of stoking up racial animosities and fears. While she never wrote with the contempt for blacks that marked the columns of a fellow socialist journalist, J. L. Hicks of Texas, her writings were not as far removed from his as she imagined.

The Socialist party of Oklahoma was divided on the subject of race. The party's official position favored civil rights for all Americans and welcomed all workers, regardless of race, into the movement. Policy held that all working people were wage slaves engaged in the class struggle. African Americans were eligible to join the Socialist party, making it one of the few institutions in American life at the time that did not maintain a color barrier. However, the party did not actively recruit African American members, and it always viewed the race issue as less important than, and subsumed within, the labor struggle. Evidence suggests that numbers of Oklahoma party members not only did not recruit black members but were, in fact, far from enthusiastic about promoting black rights.

O'Hare believed blacks to be inferior to whites. While not totally unsympathetic to their precarious situation, she was essentially concerned that their exploitation was a means of preventing working-class solidarity. Moreover, she argued, African Americans could endure a lower standard of living. "Every chain of economic servitude" shackling blacks adversely affected white workers, whose wrists were also bound by those very shackles. She told of black men replacing white men in packing-houses and in mines and, inviting deep concerns, she described white working women "forced to associate with [black men] in terms of shocking intimacy" on the job. Becoming even more ominously suggestive, O'Hare wrote, "The white daughters of white voters drag the cotton sacks down the cotton row next to 'nigger bucks.'" She maintained that she favored equality of opportunity for blacks for the sake of all American workers and so that the blacks had a chance for self-advancement, but the opportunity she wanted for them was to be separate. Indeed, she unequivocally condemned the idea of social equality. She favored party propaganda efforts among African Americans, but she pledged to work to solve the so-called race question in some future socialist America by assigning blacks a separate section of the country where, if they were capable of seizing opportunities, they could develop their own civilization. If not, they could choose to idle their time away.

O'Hare's views on race were no different from many Americans of her time; she was certainly not in the racial vanguard of her party, which actively welcomed black membership. She was not among those Socialists, such as William English Walling, Mary Ovington White, and Charles Edward Russell, who joined with W. E. B. DuBois in organizing the National Association for the Advancement of Colored People (NAACP) in 1909. There is no record of O'Hare joining with those Oklahoma Socialists who unsuccessfully opposed efforts during the first state legislative session to establish segregation. Shortly after the O'Hares left Oklahoma for Kansas, Oklahoma's legislature debated a referendum to incorporate a "grandfather clause" into the constitution to disenfranchise African American voters. The O'Hares' close socialist comrades Oscar Ameringer and Otto Branstetter were in the forefront of the unsuccessful effort to oppose black disenfranchisement. Reflecting national party policy in favor of black suffrage, they filed suit against the measure, but, simultaneously, they had to deal with criticism from party members in the "Little Dixie" region of southeastern Oklahoma. Thus, white supremacists and civil rights advocates coexisted in the party, and Kate O'Hare did not align with the latter during her Oklahoma residence.

The most notable non-Caucasians in Oklahoma were, of course, the Native Americans, who made up 4.5 percent of the state's population in 1910. O'Hare's views on these Americans are crystal clear. She demonstrated enormous sympathy for the plight of the Native Americans at the hands of the whites, describing each Indian as "ready prey." Possibly because she lived near them in Indian Territory, she found it easier to view them as individuals than she did blacks. She discussed the expropriation of the Indians' lands in terms of misrepresented and violated treaties and intrusive and cheating white settlers. A year prior to Oklahoma's achievement of statehood she predicted that the Native Americans' final separation from the land was imminent. She wrote, "With his tribal organization destroyed, his blood impoverished by his Christian brother's 'fire water,' and long idleness from his accustomed labors, . . . demoralized, expropriated, helpless, the inebriate asylum, the penitentiary and the insane asylum will be his refuge, the natural destination of incompetents. The Cherokee, the Choctaw, the Creek, the Seminole and Chickasaw tribes will live only as a tradition in the memories of old men."

While O'Hare could state that Native Americans were "not fond of work," she nevertheless discussed their situation in rather balanced terms. She described them as neither the noble red men of legend nor the bloodthirsty murderers more typically presented in the press. She explained the Native Americans' plight as due to the fact that while they were not savages, they were not yet civilized. They were, she announced in an echo of many nineteenth-century scholars of evolution, "in the childhood of the race," making it easy for whites to trample them out of existence. She assumed a social Darwinist perspective and noted that the Indians' dilemma was the result of the survival of the fittest. Their evolutionary stage was primitive compared to that of the whites; consequently, full bloods were disappearing, and mixed bloods were becoming assimilated. O'Hare sympathized with efforts to restrain the exploitation of the Native Americans, but, fundamentally, she believed that their fate was sealed by their slower evolution compared to that of their competitors.

Jews were another distinctive group to which O'Hare reacted. She did not view them as clearly separated from her as she did African Americans and Native Americans. In the course of her career, especially through her travels to urban centers, she became acquainted with and even close to many individuals of Jewish background. She viewed Jews sympathetically as a people with a history of deep oppression. She came to enjoy aspects of Jewish culture as she got to know about them, holidays and foods particularly. Many of her admired comrades were Jewish. She was capable, however, of making negative generalizations about those of Jewish background without realizing it. For example, while she embraced a new Jewish son-in-law, she described him as being "Russian and Jewish with the good qualities of both, and let us hope few of the bad ones. . . . " In a discussion once of the need to round up volunteers for chores, she wrote, "It's rather hard . . . for some of the . . . office men, but they are doing their best—even the Jews."

O'Hare, who claimed to be the granddaughter of a preacher, devoted more of her attention to religion than she did to race. She was often scathing in her attacks on organized religion. Because of the youthful religious commitments she had discarded, her criticisms of and even attacks on Protestantism as well as Catholicism sometimes had the ring of a personal vendetta. Indeed, she was a convert to a secular ideology who held only contempt for the type of institutional loyalties that she had abandoned.

Her quarrel with organized Christianity was three-fold. First of all, she believed that Christianity perverted the message of Jesus. Secondly, it ignored the social problems and needs of the masses of the people. And, thirdly, it supported the wealthy while bilking the people of desperately needed resources. She believed in the religion of Jesus Christ and the prophets, she wrote, rather than in the churches she saw around her or, as she phrased it, "the religion of John D. Rockefeller." The master classes, she argued, traditionally had used religion to divide workers from each other. Her work on behalf of socialism, she declared, reflected loyalty to the teachings of Jesus and her effort to create a world in the image of those teachings. She maintained that the cornerstones of her belief system were the Sermon on the Mount, Leviticus 23–25, Deuteronomy 24–26, and Nehemiah 1–14. She challenged Christians, especially clergy, to consider how they could view themselves as individually righteous but be what she termed "collectively unrighteous." However decent a person as an individual, his or her support for the existing system amounted to participation in the sins of capitalist society. She told a group of Kansas ministers whom she invited to a public debate that the socialism she endorsed "simply means the actual tenets and teachings of Christianity applied here and now to the everyday affairs of political, economic and spiritual life." O'Hare castigated clerical indifference to the poor and the unemployed, as seen in the refusal by the churches of St. Louis to allow the homeless to bed down in their cloisters during the economically hard times of spring 1914. She argued that it was not so much that ministers were indifferent to or lacked knowledge of the plight of the masses of people, but that ministers felt beholden to the capitalist class. She denounced responses to industrial accidents by ministers who tended to conclude that the loss of life was the will of God. She was angered by their blaming God "for every catastrophe from war to syphilis. . . . Blame it on poor God. He can't help Himself and it's so much easier to sit down and twiddle our thumbs and mumble, 'God's will be done,' than it is to stand up like men and women, give God a square deal and rebuild society in a decent, sane, humane manner." She reserved her special derision for famous, fundamental Protestant preachers like Billy Sunday, but her longtime nemesis was Archbishop John J. Glennon of St. Louis. After the O'Hares settled in St. Louis in 1911, she encountered the archbishop. He was then presiding over the construction of what was to be perhaps the largest and most magnificent cathedral in the Midwest and even in the world, rivaling in architectural style and brilliant mosaics St. Mark's in Venice and St. Sophia in Constantinople. St. Louis Cathedral symbolized to O'Hare a wealthy and smug institution that was amassing even greater ostentatious riches on the backs of its poor parishioners while ignoring their very real needs. While she applauded the archbishop for his comments calling attention to the unemployment rate or decrying the military as paid assassins, for the most part O'Hare attacked him. She emphasized what she termed Glennon's and the Catholic church's failure to promote maternity compensation bills, the abolition of child labor, adequate wages, or solutions to other social ills. But when she once interviewed Archbishop Glennon at length for a column, she successfully encouraged him toward stating that he agreed with the Socialists insofar as they were attempting to help working people.

She undertook direct battle with southern Protestant ministers in periodic debates. Some persistent preachers at times followed her around on her annual tours, attacking her presentations. They would speak in towns after her lectures, drawing audiences based on O'Hare's fame, but they rarely accepted her challenges to confront her directly from the same rostrum. Some preachers would invite her to debate and then either fail to appear or arrive late, which O'Hare assumed to be a ploy to tire her, as she would have already delivered a talk. Such public verbal jousting, she insisted, was never about religion as far as she was concerned, and she maintained that she and most other socialist speakers knew better than to lock horns with seminary graduates on theological matters. The debates tended to be framed by her opponents' attacks on socialism as promoting atheism and free-love and her defense of the ideology as standing for collective ownership under democratic control. Audiences were drawn to these spectacles. On her autumn 1916 tour, O'Hare debated two different ministers in back-to-back presentations in the villages of Center Ridge and Conway, Arkansas. O'Hare reported that hundreds of people arrived in every type of vehicle, from a "tin Henry" to an oxcart. They came for these entertaining sideshows, which broke up the monotony of long days of labor, much as rural folk attended the encampments in the summers. O'Hare described one of the debates as side-splitting fun. Audiences seemed to respond to these events, and hamlets that O'Hare termed "wide spots in the road" might draw up to five thousand people for such encounters. Kate O'Hare relished them herself.

Issues concerning women were constant topics in her lectures and columns. She was interested in what could be termed the sociological study of women. She addressed such subjects as women as workers, both in the labor force and as unpaid workers, the sexual entrapment of women, reforms to alleviate women's plight, and finally, how a new socialist order would liberate women. In her overall approach, O'Hare drew on the substantial socialist literature on the "Woman Question" and also on her own observations and judgments. She was familiar with European Marxists' writings on women. Karl Marx and Frederick Engels themselves had explored the situation of women in nineteenth-century capitalist societies in their work published in 1844, *The Condition of the Working Class,* in which they emphasized the impact of industrial capitalism on women and the family. In 1883 Engels published a book entitled, *Origin of the Family, Private Property and the State,* which was an extensive examination of gender relations as affected by socioeconomic systems over time. He argued that the oppression of women had occurred with the development of the institution of private property. Engels, influenced by early anthropologists such as Lewis Henry Morgan, believed that matriarchy had tended to be the norm when societies were organized communally. However, with the emergence of private property, the nuclear, patriarchal family evolved. Such views were echoed by the German Social Democratic leader August Bebel, who published a book (also in 1883) titled *Woman Under Socialism.* Bebel emphasized that the oppression of women through the institution of private property meant that the liberation of women could occur through the collectivization of property. Socialist Party teachings worldwide on the plight of the masses of women were framed by the arguments of these books. O'Hare's remarks often referred to these socialist classics.

O'Hare wrote that women workers were exploited by the same fundamentally harsh conditions under unregulated industrial capitalism as were their male colleagues. They were exposed to unhealthy and dangerous working conditions while being forced to labor longer hours than were humanly feasible. Their wages were lower than those of male workers. Women were always paid less and assigned to the most menial jobs, given that they were virtually shut out of the labor movement and, therefore, had no organized voice to represent them. O'Hare was able to flesh out that general picture of the exploited woman worker because she had managed to walk in the shoes of such women. Her investigative journalism had given her the feel for what others only observed. Having been employed in various sweatshops and other similar work environments, and also having formally conducted investigations of working conditions and interviewed women in different lines of work, O'Hare, better than other commentators, knew what women experienced in the factories of the large cities.

She pointed out that women working was not a new phenomenon, that women had always worked, and in fact, always in the same areas. They wove, dyed and sewed the clothes for their families, and grew, processed and cooked the food for their loved ones. But such occupations under modern capitalism had become very different from their traditional forms. She wrote, "Priscilla of old owned her loom and spinning wheel, and though she wove but little it was all hers. Priscilla's loom to-day is owned by a capitalist and though she weaves much it is not hers, but belongs to the man who owns her loom, who gives her only a very little in return and calls it wages. . . . When butter was made by hand there was butter for the bread of all who were willing to work for it, and now the workers eat unwholesome, unclean oleomargarine [*sic*]."

The changed dimensions and particulars of work had destroyed the meaning and satisfaction of work. She wrote, "[L]abor is a joy when we perform it for those we love and reap the fruits of our industry, but it is a curse when we labor for a master and the wealth we create means added misery for us and our loved ones." Women could neither take satisfaction in nor develop any sense of accomplishment for work that was without autonomy or reward, she observed.

O'Hare publicized the plight of poorly paid working women. Their desperate conditions typically drove them into accepting any marriage possibility. They did not have the luxury of choice since they could not afford rooming house rents or adequate contributions to their families' maintenance. But what O'Hare characterized, at least at first, as loveless marriages were never the escape that the women anticipated, for their wage-earning husbands could not support their families. So such women continued in the work force, and working-class families had to scrape by on too little to the detriment of their health and often of their emotional well-being. Rising separation and even divorce rates testified to the numbers of increasingly dysfunctional families among American workers. O'Hare also noted, almost uniquely among commentators, how the impoverishment and pressures on working-class families were leading to a generation of unhealthy and poorly educated children, who would recreate the cycle of poverty of their families of origin. She fretted about the children who typically entered the work force at an early age, thereby sacrificing their health, education, and any chance of a better future.

O'Hare's columns and lectures described even worse scenarios for women of the working class. In one of her most famous essays, entitled "Wimmin Ain't Got No Kick," which was published by the Socialist party and circulated widely in pamphlet form, she feelingly discussed the issue of prostitution. Women had three responsibilities assigned to them by society, she wrote: The first was to serve as cogs in the industrial machine of the nation. The second was to reproduce another generation to follow in their footsteps. The third was to be the essential ingredient in prostitution rings, which flourished across the country. O'Hare was perhaps the foremost public speaker to link the subject of ill-paid working women with the issue of prostitution. Interested in the phenomenon since her youth, she railed against a system that unfeelingly reduced almost three-quarters of a million women, she estimated, to such a fate. Attacking public indifference and official complicity (including that of the church she had attended in Kansas City), vice rings and police departments, she also focused on the topical issue of white slavery in an essay entitled "Law and the White Slaver." She bitterly condemned society's authorities for accepting such an outrage and for conspiring to ignore the situation and, therefore, to perpetuate it. O'Hare noted that the victim rather than the white slaver was prosecuted by the court system. While at least the Mann Act was being prepared to prevent the transportation of women across state lines and into the country for illicit purposes, nevertheless, the scope of the tragedy was not acknowledged by society. Nor was the nation committed to altering fundamental conditions that entrapped women into prostitution.

Consistent with her general promotion of reform legislation, O'Hare suggested and publicized various measures to improve conditions for women. First of all, she supported woman's suffrage. As a socialist, she did not believe that the enfranchisement of women would liberate them and achieve equality as did some pure-and-simple suffragists. But for her, the vote was a weapon needed by the powerless of society. She saw the ballot as a means of self-defense for women, just as it was for workingmen. Working women, and indeed all women, would be better served in their efforts to defend and help themselves by possession of the ballot. They would be better armed in their struggle with exploitative employers if they were voters. Also, echoing many nonsocialist suffragists, the most famous of whom perhaps was Jane Addams, she wrote that enfranchised women would be positioned to protect the best interests of the American family and home.

In her promotion of female suffrage, O'Hare violated the spirit if not the letter of the policy of the international socialist movement. Socialist policy favored universal woman's suffrage and at least officially promoted it, although not as a primary goal. Socialists were warned against campaigning for woman's suffrage in collaboration with nonsocialist, middle-class suffragists. O'Hare believed that her efforts were sufficiently distinct from so-called bourgeois suffrage campaigners, and she, in fact, worked in tandem with such suffrage groups in Kansas City, Kansas, and in St. Louis. Simultaneously, she participated in socialist suffrage campaigns in, for example, Terre Haute, Indiana, and in many other cities where she spoke. She traveled to New York City in 1914 specifically to join a massive but unsuccessful statewide suffrage effort. There, she worked under the auspices of the Socialist Suffrage Campaign Committee, leafletting on the Lower East Side of Manhattan and lecturing to crowds in Carnegie Hall, at the McKinley Square Casino in the Bronx, and in the Brownsville section of Brooklyn. She shared the podium at the headlined events with Gene Debs and Meyer London, then serving his first term in the United States House of Representatives. She spoke five times a day from soapboxes and automobiles as well as in halls. Before these New York audiences she expressed the hope that she sustained "the reputation of the West in general and my sex in particular to the best of my ability" The campaign committee sent O'Hare across the Hudson River to address a crowd in Jersey City, New Jersey. In Washington, D.C., a year earlier, she had participated in the largest suffrage parade ever held in the United States, and she served as grand marshall of the socialist component of the march, the largest segment of the parade. She actively cooperated with the National American Woman Suffrage Association, the umbrella organization, and worked with its members on municipal- and state-level suffrage campaigns. She also conducted highly publicized debates with antisuffrage speakers. Within the Socialist party, she was not among those women members who attacked it—in what became a highly charged issue—for not promoting suffrage and other so-called women's issues sufficiently. However, she did sometimes criticize workingmen for denying women the right to vote when they went to the polls. The energies that she devoted to suffrage campaigns clearly demonstrated that the issue was one of her priorities both within the context of the Socialist party and outside it.

The education of girls and young women was another subject of importance to her. O'Hare had a lifelong interest in educational reform, and, indeed, at various times in her career she administered and taught at innovative schools for working people. She faulted contemporary public school education, which, she insisted, failed to expose the masses of youngsters to liberal arts and vocational subjects. She wanted girls as well as boys to enjoy opportunities to be literate, to develop wide horizons, and to obtain training in a craft or manual skill. She herself, by happenstance, enjoyed that background, and she was convinced such education was necessary to have a full life with a promise of autonomy.

For girls who were fortunate enough to remain in school beyond a tender age rather than being thrust into the workforce, O'Hare bewailed their segregation in a curriculum of the frivolous and unessential. She berated educators for the valuable time schools wasted on inculcating social graces and charm in young women. She, like many progressive reformers of the era, wanted them trained in what were called the domestic arts. Her most emphatic educational preference was for a heavy dose of study in a subject that a few decades later would be offered in classes on marriage and the family. "Home" she believed to be "the logical location of womanly activity" because of what she termed the natural division of labor and of biology. And yet girls grew to adulthood tending to have limited knowledge of household management and of their own physiological development. They needed to be trained for homemaking, their life's work, but she also argued from a more contemporary-sounding perspective, that the entire responsibility of the home should not rest on the shoulders of women. O'Hare wanted men to be educated "to be helpers and sustainers" of the home. Moreover, discussing topics that few public speakers, other than Margaret Sanger and Emma Goldman, broached, O'Hare pinpointed the sexual naiveté of most young American women and sometimes offered lectures on sex education. She deplored that aspect of the double standard where young boys absorbed unwholesome versions of physical relationships and young girls were denied all such knowledge so that they were emotionally unprepared for intimacies.

O'Hare favored the options of birth control, abortion, and divorce. As a Socialist, she believed that the institution of marriage within capitalist society discouraged healthy relationships between men and women and destroyed the family. Therefore, it was necessary for the emotional and mental health of Americans that these reforms be introduced in order to allow some flexibility within the system. Birth control measures must be legalized to allow options to families which could not support children. Moreover, young couples should be encouraged to delay having families until they were emotionally mature, waiting until perhaps their mid-twenties. She argued that abortion needed to be available legally in order to save the lives of young women and also to offer a solution to the problem of "sub-normal" infants, another tragedy which she rested at the door of exploitative capitalism. But O'Hare held serious reservations about what she called a rising tide of "infanticide." She remained concerned about identifying herself too closely with the issues of birth control and abortion. She feared stoking fires that encouraged others to charge socialists with promoting free love and atheism. So she left the front lines of the battle to Sanger and supported her efforts, attacking Archbishop Glennon and others who prevented Sanger from lecturing at St. Louis's Victoria Theater in May 1916, including the police who did not even allow Sanger to speak to the crowds outside on the sidewalk. But O'Hare decided against even assisting in distributing Sanger's literature.

On the subject of divorce, she became reluctantly convinced of the need for its legalization everywhere. She argued that the existing social system placed enormous strains on people who, consequently, might need such an option for the sake of their mental health. As early as 1905, she published an article considering whether the legalization of divorce was a step backward or forward for society. She never believed in the preservation of a marriage at any cost, but divorce remained an issue with which she struggled. Unlike bourgeois reformers, she did not assume that wives were supported by husbands but rather that the wages of both were required. While a woman alone was economically vulnerable, she needed the option of divorce for her mental and emotional well-being. These morality issues were certainly not the primary focus of O'Hare's work, and she could even be called erratic in her promotion of these causes. But O'Hare was distinctive as a socialist leader in her involvement in these significant cultural issues.

O'Hare envisioned a vast improvement in women's lives once the socialist society emerged. They would no longer bear the double burden of class and sex. Women would not have to toil around the clock, working lengthy shifts on the job and staying up all hours managing the home. Women would be able to choose whether or not they wished to work outside the home. If they chose outside employment, they would enjoy reasonable hours under safe conditions and would receive the full fruits of their labor. If they instead confined themselves to homemaking, they would be compensated for the socially important work of rearing the next generation. Consequently, they would be economically independent, healthy members of society who had an equal stake in the system. Under those changed circumstances, the marriages they decided to enter would be more rewarding, stable, and fulfilling, and the social problems endemic in the presocialist society would be much minimized. She felt quite sanguine that women would at last fulfill their biologically determined destiny, no longer confronting arbitrarily erected social impediments to healthy family life. Moreover, O'Hare felt no concerns that a future collectively controlled system might regiment family life or spawn an interfering bureaucracy through whatever prenatal programs, maternal subsidies, national nurseries, and all-encompassing educational systems it might establish.

O'Hare's view of women was not so radically different from that of middle-class reformers. She believed that a woman's place was naturally in the home. She never recommended any measures as revolutionary as the feminist economist and sometime-Socialist Charlotte Perkins Gilman, who favored kitchenless homes and communal dining halls. Gilman wished to minimize parental responsibilities in favor of what she described as all adults having opportunities to assume more socially useful roles.

One feminist activist in the Socialist party whose writings certainly would have been known to O'Hare—more assuredly than Gilman's were—published views that reflected the latter's ideas. Meta Stern Lilienthal of New York published a booklet called "Women of the Future." In it, she transcended both capitalist and socialist traditional views of a sexual division of roles and responsibilities. She envisioned a socialist society with community and family institutions structured to liberate women for personal development. She, unlike all her party comrades, dared to predict that socialism would indeed destroy the home and family, as its critics charged. It would uproot those institutions, as they existed based on women's economic dependency, and redesign them on the basis of individual freedom.

O'Hare, in contrast, fundamentally believed that the liberation of women was essentially, perhaps almost entirely, a question of the socialization of property. While she did refer to some minor adjustments beyond that, she lacked a feminist consciousness in this area, which, admittedly, only a minority of activist women then held. But judging her in the context of her own times, she certainly did not consider herself a feminist. The "Woman Question" was never as important to her as the basic "Social Question." O'Hare proved to be very much the traditionalist, as she envisioned freeing women so that they could address themselves more easily to their historical role assignment within the existing nuclear family.

As a socialist woman, O'Hare identified, discussed, and emphasized aspects of women's lives that most of her male colleagues did not recognize, minimized, or discounted. She, unique among the top party leaders, pointed out the intimate ways in which industrial capitalism affected and threatened women. She wrote of the loneliness and vulnerability of young working women and the double burden borne by women wage-workers who also managed households. She pointed out their lack of social and economic opportunities, noting the various ways in which society miseducated them. Finally, she discussed sexual issues, which the Socialist party hierarchy preferred to ignore.

When Kate O'Hare addressed the subject of the role of women in society, she did so from a distance. She viewed women's issues as pertaining to others, at least until later in her life. The exploitation of women as workers and their subservience as wives formed the context of the lives of other women. When O'Hare was aware of the unequal treatment that she sometimes received as a woman, she dealt with it without internalizing it as an issue. As demonstrated, O'Hare believed that a woman's most important roles were as wife and mother, but she did not seem to assign those priorities to her own life. She seemed, rather, to have become so male-identified that she could write of issues that affected women while remaining comfortably uninvolved. Such identification has not been uncommon for accomplished women in male-dominated professions. In O'Hare's case, when she discovered her life's work, she joined what was essentially a man's world, and she bonded with it. By so doing, she avoided seeing herself as an outsider in the Socialist party. She became a leader in a movement that, in its first generation of existence, had never had a woman in a leadership position. The quixotic Mother Jones, who certainly was pivotal to O'Hare's moment of decision, did not function within the party itself but was a labor leader separate from all its institutions. Perhaps it is not coincidental that it was Jones who helped provide O'Hare with a sense of direction, for Jones never identified with women. She viewed women as appendages whose role was to help their men. So O'Hare did not think of herself as really of the world of women about which she wrote and spoke so sympathetically. Had she embraced or, at least, recognized her own status as an outsider, which some of her male comrades certainly did, she could perhaps have used that awareness as a positive force for herself and others. But as an honorary male, O'Hare never identified herself as the "other" in Simone de Beauvoir's terminology; therefore, she remained the distant commentator.

By this time in her life, O'Hare had become an accomplished speaker and writer who had developed set views on the major issues which the United States confronted. As a revisionist socialist she believed in encouraging legislative reforms and promoting electoral campaigns to move society peacefully from a capitalist to a socialist system. She supported American workers in their various efforts, especially the American Federation of Labor. She recognized and tried to speak for distinctive groups of working Americans, particularly farmers. She sympathized with the plight of both African Americans and Native Americans, but she displayed social Darwinist attitudes toward them and was particularly harsh toward black Americans. She gave perhaps her most detailed attention to the problems besetting American women, but she never seemed to be able to identify herself with their lot.

𝓨 4

ST. LOUIS WOMAN

I n 1909 the O'Hares moved from Oklahoma to Kansas City, Kansas, where they hoped, after eight years of marriage, to finally sink roots. They needed an urban environment, where Frank could find dependable work and earn a solid income, and where they could both continue to participate in the socialist movement. Also, they wanted to provide the children with a more normal home life. They would soon be forced to move again, this time on to St. Louis, where the family would have their happiest, most stable years together.

Returning to Kansas seemed like a logical move for the O'Hares. Not only were Kate Richard O'Hare's roots there, but the couple had discovered their life work in Girard, Kansas. The couple might have chosen to settle back into the Girard socialist circle; most of their close friends were among its members. However, such a small town could not provide a means of support and the solid educational institutions necessary for a family with four children, so the O'Hares chose nearby Kansas City, Kansas.

Even in 1909, Kansas City, Kansas, was a city existing in the shadow of its neighbor. For a time during the nineteenth century, Kansas Citians on the west side of the state boundary had dreamed of annexing their eastern brethren, but the realists knew that was impossible. While the Kansas side claimed more manufacturing at first, possessing, at the turn of the century, a smelter, at least one of the area's packing plants, and most of the flour mills, in every other measurable way the Kansans lagged behind their Missouri competition. In 1900 the cities' combined population was over two hundred thousand, but only fifty-one thousand residents lived in Kansas. By 1910 the population had increased to eighty-two thousand out of a third of a million in the metropolitan area.

During the two years the O'Hares stayed in Kansas City, they lived modestly at 811 Troupe Avenue, one block from busy Seventh Street. Their's was a working-class neighborhood, not far from where the Missouri River divided Kansas and Missouri and just north of the central business district. The children enrolled at local schools, and Frank resumed his old occupation of hardware sales, which he intended to give his full attention.

For the first time since their marriage, Frank O'Hare seriously cut back on his participation in political activities while Kate devoted more time and energy to the local socialist movement. Consequently, Kate O'Hare became the socialist leader of the family, and from then on she overshadowed Frank in party fame and influence. Their reversed status was unique among the many couples in the first or second rank of party leadership. Married couples whose work for the party was also the core of their lives together were not uncommon. The O'Hares knew several couples who devoted their energies to the advancement of the Socialist party: Victor and Meta Berger of Milwaukee; Otto and Winnie Branstetter, who had originally worked as organizers alongside the O'Hares in Oklahoma; A. M. and May Simons, who worked as journalists in Kansas, Chicago, Milwaukee, and elsewhere; and George and Grace Brewer, who worked on the *Appeal* in Girard. Usually, the husband was seen as the party leader; this was most clearly in the case of Berger, who was one of the most significant figures in the national party. Kate's growing fame did not seem to trouble Frank; he emphasized how much they continued to function as a team.

Kate O'Hare's work in Kansas was within the framework of one of the most dynamic branches of the Socialist party. Backed by the editorial influence of the *Appeal to Reason,* the country's most popular socialist newspaper, the state organization boosted multi-layered party activities. On the lecture circuit where O'Hare was the most prominent speaker, Socialists toured the state and adjacent areas. Women's socialist groups were organized across Kansas in larger numbers than elsewhere. The women were even able to hold a statewide conference, and the *Socialist Woman,* the only major socialist paper for women, was initially published there. In Fort Scott, near Girard, the People's College was about to be organized as a correspondence school inspired by Mills's school.

Although Kate and Frank O'Hare had moved back to Kansas with the intention of providing a more stable life for their children, Kate apparently never seriously considered abandoning public life. She advocated traditional motherhood, but she did not assume that role herself. Rather, she constantly improvised to find others to take on primary responsibility for the children. Frank O'Hare supported Kate's decision to travel; as she lectured throughout Kansas, they both begged Frank's sister, Gertie, to come and stay with the children, as she had done in Oklahoma. Perhaps, as a cerebral woman, Kate was less able to nurture, but there is no clear evidence that that was true. O'Hare's remoteness from her children can more definitely be attributed to physical distance: she was either on the road or, later, in the office rather than at home. Her solution to the problem of balancing roles, which all working mothers face, was to involve her children in the socialist movement. Thus, she attempted to synthesize her independent professional life with her private life. The socialist network was an extended family for the O'Hares. Both Kate and Frank lived their lives within it, and their four children were cared for by the older children in party youth groups. Everyone spent much of their leisure time in movement demonstrations and rallies, and the O'Hare youngsters belonged to this party's children's groups. As they got older, they joined the adults in substantive party activities that were educational as well as recreational. They even helped their parents produce newspaper issues, and sometimes they traveled with them on the incessant speaking tours. Whether or not Kate O'Hare's decision to balance her public and private life satisfied her family, and there is evidence that they resented her constant absences, it allowed her to have an unusually long and successful career.

Kate O'Hare first ran for public office in 1910, when she was nominated by her party in Kansas's second congressional district. She told an interviewer during the campaign that she wished she could remain at home with her family ("I long for domestic life, home and children with every fiber of my being.") but because only socialism would protect the home, she felt she had to run for office and promote the cause. She was the first woman to run for Congress in Kansas, but women had been elected to municipal and school board offices in the state since the 1880s. Women still did not enjoy full suffrage in Kansas, and would not acquire it until 1912, but residents were used to seeing women in public office. O'Hare took her nomination seriously and spent three months campaigning vigorously across the district, which included Kansas City and nine counties in eastern Kansas. She spoke in Kansas City and in small, rural towns, and she spoke at the University of Kansas, Baker University and other institutions of higher education. While she had addressed farmers and workers for years, this marked her first focused effort to interest students in socialism. Since the party had established the Intercollegiate Student Society, which was then organizing dozens of chapters on campuses across the country, she could safely assume that she faced a potentially receptive audience. O'Hare initially stressed the ethical aspects of socialist doctrine, which, she believed, appealed to young people, rather than its economic aspects, which were less readily grasped by students. She must have been impressive; one group held a conference after her appearance to debate the points she had raised.

The Kansas state party had been running slates in congressional elections for several years. In 1911, three small towns, including Girard, elected Socialists to office, and three Socialists served in the state legislature. They introduced legislation to nationalize the coal mines and railroads, to set mine safety standards, and to establish a minimum wage for women. Had O'Hare been elected to office, she would have become part of a small but supportive network of socialist colleagues.

Kate O'Hare's campaign for Congress was unsuccessful, but she made a credible showing for a socialist candidate. Her strongest support came from workers in Kansas City and miners in the southeastern part of the district. She won over two thousand votes, 5 percent of the forty-five thousand votes cast in the four-candidate race. While other socialist candidates for state-level offices had amassed an average of sixteen thousand votes, her totals and her very strong showing in some wards and precincts were encouraging.

By the time of Kate's campaign the O'Hares had established a new routine: Frank devoted most of his time to business, and Kate lectured and wrote under the auspices of the *Appeal,* often in connection with Gene Debs. Just as they had settled into it, they received a plea from a publisher-comrade, Phil Wagner. Wagner had taken over as editor of the *National Rip-Saw,* a regional socialist monthly published in St. Louis, and he desperately needed writers. He invited Kate O'Hare to become an assistant editor and Frank to assume the duties of business manager. After apparently same soul-searching, the O'Hares finally decided that this would be a good move for them, so the family packed up and moved to St. Louis in 1911. Frank thought of St. Louis as his hometown, and he and Kate had often visited. They had been through on Socialist party activities, and of course they, like millions of Americans, had attended the St. Louis World's Fair in 1904. At the beginning of the twentieth century St. Louis was the fourth largest city in the country and falling behind its rival, Chicago, in population and industry. Like most large cities of that time, St. Louis was plagued by political corruption. A pattern of bribery had been revealed to the nation in Lincoln Steffens's 1902 article "Tweed Days in St. Louis," Joseph W. Folk, the circuit attorney and soon-to-be governor of Missouri, had waged a campaign to wipe out the graft in city government. At the same time Mayor Rolla Wells and his administration had made a herculean effort to resolve some of the city's most serious physical problems—transportation, street paving, air and water, and other weaknesses in the infrastructure—in the two years before the fair. Supported by a Civic Improvement League city beautification campaign, St. Louis had made great strides by the day of the opening of the fair.

The fair was hosted by St. Louis in an effort to regain the status it had lost to Chicago. It was one of the most successful international expositions ever held by most objective standards. Situated in the city's vast Forest Park and spilling over onto the campus of Washington University, the fair featured the latest scientific and technological advances; audiences were especially thrilled with its electric light displays. Past, present, and future presidents (Grover Cleveland, Theodore Roosevelt, and William Howard Taft) and a Hohenlohe Prince visited. Several major events took place in St. Louis at the same time, including the Democratic National Convention, the quadrennial Olympics, and a number of national conventions of professional organizations. When it was all over, St. Louis was less corrupt and better maintained, but Chicago clearly had eclipsed it in population and economic significance. A 1909 fair commemorating the centennial of the incorporation of St. Louis and recalling the city's lost importance was held not long before the O'Hares arrived.

St. Louis was an ethnically diverse city and suffered from the tension created by a population that lived together but rarely interacted. One-third of the Roman Catholic parishes in St. Louis officially used two languages. Immigrant mutual aid societies proliferated, and social groups, such as the Germans' turnverein organization, kept traditional cultures alive. Large, early established groups of immigrants—the Germans and the Irish—were being displaced by the relatively small numbers of new immigrant groups moving into St. Louis, particularly the Italians. Other new groups included Jews, Greeks, Poles, Bohemians, Hungarians, and South Slavs. Most of them worked in unskilled labor, especially in the garment and shoe industries, and they lived near the Mississippi River just north of and south of downtown. A relatively small number of African Americans were also moving into St. Louis. The Missouri constitution mandated a system of segregation, but blacks successfully opposed its expansion. They prevented the segregation of streetcars and railroad coaches, blocked the enforcement of a segregationist housing ordinance, and preserved their right to vote. Tensions surrounding their presence and activities were, however, palpable.

In these years, St. Louis was struggling with the same issues that pre-occupied the rest of the country. In addition to political corruption which the city confronted, the media spotlighted inequitable utility taxes and corporate arrogance. Public ownership of utilities was debated, and pro-tective legislation and direct democracy measures were also promoted. Charter revision was focused on and dramatized by Socialists and also progressive forces as a battle between the people versus the interests. The other significant local issue, and one which remained unresolved for over a generation, was a proposed free municipal bridge across the Mississippi River. Tolls kept prices high for soft coal from Illinois, and the free bridge symbolized graphically the struggle between economic groups. From all these conflicts, the "Missouri Idea" emerged. Both Governor Folk and his successor, progressive Republican Herbert S. Hadley, used the idea to place Missouri in the vanguard of antitrust, civic-minded forces.

The city of St. Louis unrolls from the Mississippi River with boule-vards flowing toward the west, and many of its residents have tended to move from their first homes, near the river, west, toward Forest Park. This was true of the O'Hares. They initially lived on Cook Avenue, near the office building on Olive Street that housed the *National Rip-Saw,* where both Kate and Frank worked. Their house was directly beyond the central core of the city, in an area changing in language and com-plexion with each incoming new group. Cook Avenue was, in fact, the site of riots occasioned by the reaction against African American teach-ers and Pullman porters purchasing homes there. These events were fol-lowed by a successful petition drive for a segregationalist ordinance in St. Louis, the first such ordinance passed by an initiative petition anywhere in the country. White support for this measure was lowest in those German-populated wards where socialist sentiment was strong.

The O'Hare clan quickly outgrew its Cook Avenue home. The children (Dick, who was eight, Kathleen, six, and the twins, Gene and Victor, three) needed more space, good schools, and fresh air in which to grow and play. The O'Hares moved slightly south to the more fashionable Castleman Avenue, where they lived in a larger house only a half-block from Tower Grove Park. The park's main attraction was Shaw Gardens, established in 1859, the oldest botanical gardens in the United States (later renamed Missouri Botanical Gardens). While the rare and exotic plant areas were certainly off-limits to children's games, the proximity of the park was a great boon for the O'Hare children. Indeed, the open space was an outlet for the adults, too, especially on the hot, muggy summer evenings so common to St. Louis.

The additional space was even more handy for the O'Hares than they might have anticipated. Kate's parents soon came to live with them, just as earlier they had followed them to Oklahoma. Andrew and Lucy were now in their declining years. Andrew was in his seventies and would not live out the decade. (He died in 1916.) While they might have chosen to retire to Kansas, which was more familiar, they wanted to live with Kate, who was still her father's daughter and apparently the leader among the five siblings. Andrew had become accustomed to city life since he had been forced off the land, nevertheless, he had remained very much a man of the soil. To his son-in-law, Frank, Andrew seemed a displaced person in the city. Since Andrew was a reader, the O'Hares provided lots of books to occupy him, and he made himself handy around the house. Lucy seemed to settle down without any notable difficulties.

The children were exposed to both public and private education at different times, attending schools run by various religious groups and those of an experimental bent. Frank was the product of a Catholic up-bringing, and Kate had been exposed to a variety of Protestant currents, and both were determined to prevent narrow and parochial notions or bigotry from taking root in the minds of their children. While they did not rear the children in any particular faith, the twins, for example, were sent for one year following the primary grades to a Catholic boarding school so that they would not be, as Kate O'Hare wrote, "warped by the stupid, vicious prejudice against their fellow men who chanced to be of that religion." They attended the Chaminade Preparatory School in St. Louis, which was run by Marianist priests who taught Catholic principles and moral values. Serious plans were made to send all of the children to a Quaker school for the calm temperament and thoughtfulness that Kate O'Hare believed a Quaker environment might impart. All the children attended more than one experimental workers' school so that they would be educated liberally and also have some manual skills, as did their parents.

Kate and Frank settled into the office of the *National Rip-Saw*. Phil Wagner had taken over running the paper from its erratic founder, the self-styled "Colonel" Dick Maple, whose real name was Seth McCallen. In 1914 Gene Debs left the *Appeal to Reason* in Girard to tour for the *Rip-Saw* and write a column for it, and the O'Hares were happy to be reunited with him. Oscar Ameringer, Henry Tichenor, and soon James O'Neill and Scott Nearing, who would later become nationally known figures on the left, all joined the staff. The O'Hares were part of arguably the finest socialist editorial staff in the world, and they had a home base again that provided an intimate microcosm of shared values.

The *National Rip-Saw* was a regional monthly that tried to attract farmers especially, so much so that it has been mistakenly described it as a semi-Populist newspaper. It became a friendly competitor of the *Appeal,* which was itself in transition: Walter Wayland had taken over as publisher following the suicide of his father, J. A. Wayland in 1912. The *Rip-Saw* achieved a circulation of one hundred fifty thousand, far less than the *Appeal's* half-million circulation (which included many of the same readers) but, nevertheless, drawing one of the largest readerships among socialist periodicals. It printed advertisements for over-the-counter medications and other products, demonstrating little interest in their integrity. O'Hare, Debs, and others promoted the paper on their tours, and the paper used their drawing power to the fullest: arranging daunting schedules for weeks and months of too many lectures on time-tables that were at odds with realistic train travel. Subscriptions to the *Rip-Saw* were sold at summer encampments by the thousands. The paper's audience was clearly found among those whom O'Hare knew best—the farmers and rural inhabitants of the Midwest, plains states, and the Southwest.

As the paper's business manager, Frank O'Hare oversaw the clerical staff and daily operations and booked the tours of the lecturers. He held responsibility for the paper's publicity and business correspondence, including the heavy load of letters to and from locals on the details of hosting one of the speakers. He also wrote a folksy column called "Circulation Chats," in which he discussed his activities and encouraged subscribers to sell "subs" to others, a circulation method borrowed from the *Appeal to Reason*. Because Frank was always in the office or at home while Kate was out on the lecture circuit, he became the primary parent, much to his increasing distress.

The St. Louis branch of the Socialist party, to which the O'Hares now belonged, was a vibrant organization with strong ties to the local labor movement. It was closer to local labor than perhaps any other branch of the party except Milwaukee with its fabled union-party alliance. St. Louis had been the national headquarters of the Socialist party for the first three years of the party's existence. It was a compromise site selected partially because of infighting over the possibility of choosing Chicago as party headquarters. The first national secretary of the party was Leon Greenbaum, a St. Louis trade unionist, and other St. Louisians served on the party's first National Executive Committee. The St. Louis party had been able to build strong support within the central body of the city, the Central Trades and Labor Union, and the Missouri Federation of Labor. In fact, many local labor leaders, including the first president of the state federation, David Kreyling, were Socialists. Reuben Wood, who served for over twenty years as the president of the state federation, was also a party member, as was Louis Phillipi, who became president of the Central Trades and Labor Union in 1910. Thus, an overlapping of personnel helped form a partnership between the unions and the party, even though the majority of unionists in St. Louis and Missouri were not Socialists.

The state federation and the St. Louis central body chose to participate in politics, even though the policy of the American Federation of Labor fundamentally opposed that strategy. Missouri labor leaders hoped to legitimize labor in the eyes of the public so that it could become an acceptable interest group and claim a place in the public dialogue. Deciding early in the twentieth century that both major parties, the Republicans and Democrats, were pro-business and anti-labor, the unions tried to run their own local candidates in the 1906 elections. Failing even to get on the ballot, organized labor thereafter moved closer to the local socialist movement. The unionists backed the St. Louis Socialists when they ran for public office, and union members themselves were often the candidates. Trade unionists owned stock in the local socialist newspaper, a daily called *St. Louis Labor,* and its German version, the *Arbeiter Zeitung.* Thus, close ties evolved without benefit of formal affiliation.

German workers were the nucleus of the party-union nexus. While the Germans of the city were neither politically cohesive nor radical as a group, the workers of the German wards, the eighth to the fourteenth, could be depended upon to provide socialist candidates with their best showings at the ballot box. German workers were the artisans who, it has been said, built Missouri, and the cigarmakers, especially, and the typographical unions were solidly aligned with the socialist movement. These workers believed in the importance of a labor-identified party in politics and in government protection from economic exploitation, both of which German workers had been familiar with in Bismarck's German Empire. Accordingly, they were drawn to the Socialist party, and provided it with an ambience of Old World beer gardens and turnverein-like activities.

Leading German unionists in the party were Otto Pauls and William M. Brandt, of the cigarmakers, Otto Kaemmerer, of the garment workers, and G. A. Hoehn, the editor of the newspaper *St. Louis Labor.* Hoehn and Brandt both served in party offices and ran as candidates for public office. G. A. Hoehn (1865–1951) was the embodiment of the St. Louis Socialist party. Hoehn had been a young cobbler in the German Empire who, after immigrating to Baltimore, was drawn to labor issues and socialism during the eight-hour day movement of the 1880s. He began to write for the German-language labor press, and he took over editing the *Chicago Arbeiter Zeitung,* following the removal of its editors after the Haymarket Affair. At odds, however, with the paper's anarchist philosophy, Hoehn settled in St. Louis in 1891, and for the next sixty years he was the voice of labor there in both German and English. He often headed the St. Louis County Socialist party and ran for a number of public offices in the city on the socialist ticket. Hoehn was a member of the original National Executive Committee of the Socialist Party, was in frequent correspondence with Gene Debs, and was, in sum, a national figure of the second echelon. William M. Brandt (1870–1942), the other key local figure, was an American-born itinerate cigarmaker. He helped organize his trade in St. Louis and held high union offices. He became a Socialist in the 1890s and ran many times for public office; his best race occurred in 1911 for the city council, when he lost by thirteen votes in a disputed election. He was the longtime secretary of the central committee of the St. Louis County socialists as well as secretary of the CTLU.

Kate and Frank O'Hare joined the front ranks in the St. Louis branch of the party, showing themselves as comfortable in a German milieu as they had been in a rural southwestern environment, but they never became the mainstays running the party. Kate especially was seen as a "star." Her aura was that of a celebrity, and it was an added attraction, and perhaps a curiosity, that she was a native-born woman. Her main contribution to the local movement was her public lecturing. Kate O'Hare spoke during election campaigns and at other times as well. Her topics included socialism in general, women and socialism, and farmers and the socialist movement. She addressed all-city meetings, appeared before branch party meetings of women's committees and other groups, and was often called on to substitute when a visiting speaker was delayed or absent. Additionally, she routinely spoke in surrounding hamlets and county seats and was especially popular as a main speaker for all-day countywide picnics sponsored by the party. In essence, she built on her role as an encampment speaker at these local events, and proved to be popular with the St. Louis area rank-and-file. But she was viewed as an outsider, evidence suggests, by local leaders such as Hoehn.

During this time, she elaborated on a device she had used earlier with audiences, developing it into a popular ploy in her talks. She would challenge any lawyer or Republican or Democratic politician in the audience to step up and share the platform with her. She would put up money to have them debate her statement that local public officials were the private property of the wealthy. She would taunt her foes that "Here is a chance to pick up $100. You fellows are smart, while I am only a woman with not enough sense to vote. Why don't you come on?" According to the records, no one ever took up her challenge.

Kate O'Hare ran for public office a few time in these years. She was a candidate for the board of education in St. Louis. Had she won, she would have followed in the footsteps of Meta Berger, the wife of Victor Berger, who was the first socialist woman elected to a school board. O'Hare became the first woman to campaign for a seat in the United States Senate, when she was nominated by her party in Missouri in 1916. As earlier in Kansas, when she ran for the state legislature, she drew support from worker wards but from few others. She won only fourteen thousand votes out of the three-quarters of a million cast. Frank O'Hare was active in the CTLU, held a few party positions, and also ran for public office on the socialist ticket. In 1914 he was the party's nominee for the state senate and the next year for the office of Railroad and Warehouse Commissioner. He also occasionally gave talks to the St. Louis faithful.

The St. Louis Socialist party, with its trade union backing, offered a detailed program of immediate demands and practical reforms. Its platform planks included municipal ownership of public utilities, ice plants, and railroads, creation of public farmers' markets, municipal lodging houses, the initiative and referendum, an end to contract labor on public works, public employment for the jobless, protective legislation, such as an eight-hour day for all workers, an end to child labor, a system of pensions, employer liability laws, free legal services and employment offices, and compulsory, free public education, free textbooks and hot school lunches. The party campaigned for democratic charter reform in city government, and it favored ending tolls on traffic and freight crossing the Mississippi River. It opposed nonpartisan and at-large elections, both of which were fought by Socialists throughout the country because they undermined minor parties.

The Socialist party was strong enough to embellish its members' lives with a full complement of cultural and recreational activities. Citywide meetings were held monthly, and locals met weekly. Seasonal dances were sponsored, with the Fourth of July all-day picnic the major event of the year. Winter festivals, fall bazaars, and Labor Day parades were supplemented by neighborhood-sponsored parties. Mass meetings were held, such as the annual March commemoration of the Paris Commune. Foreign-language branches—German, Jewish, Italian, Bohemian, South Slav, Lettish, Polish, and Hungarian—offered their members a full slate of events in their own languages. Women's committees, which were at the time established in the party nationally as an effort to interest women in socialism, were well represented in St. Louis.

Party leaders from elsewhere toured the area. Gene Debs was, of course, a favorite and, demonstrating the importance of St. Louis to the party's national ticket, he opened and closed his most important campaign for the presidency in 1912 in St. Louis. Other Socialist speakers included Karl Legien, of Germany's General Federation of Labor Unions, Keir Hardie, a Member of Parliament in England, Winfield R. Gaylord, a state senator in Wisconsin, Emil Seidel, Mayor of Milwaukee, and Oscar Ameringer. Socialist singing societies, Sunday schools, and other organizations helped round out the activities of local party members. Both newspapers, *Labor* and the *Arbeiter Zeitung,* as well as an election broadside called the *People's Voice* (which was printed and delivered free on Sundays whenever an election was in the offing), thus kept the membership informed. It was not unusual for the party to distribute hundreds of thousands of pieces of election broadsides the week prior to an election, using a "bundle brigade," which it had adopted from the Milwaukee Socialists. The local movement was sufficiently expansive that, although membership figures are not extant, it is clear that party members could live their lives within its framework: developing friendships within its confines, marrying within the party, and exposing their children to its ideology through organized activities and branches of the Young People's Socialist League.

The party vote increased in these years, thanks to expanded and disciplined organizational activity. For example, in the municipal election of November 1910, the Socialists won eight thousand votes in the city, in the spring 1911 election, about twelve thousand, and in the November 1911 election, they won sixteen thousand votes. In at least one election, they were able to displace the Democrats as the second-strongest party. The vote grew in the state of Missouri, too, where the Socialists also nominated full tickets. In 1908 Eugene Debs pulled fifteen thousand votes in the state; in 1912 he received twenty-eight thousand. In the meantime, crowds turned out for the party's major events and fundraisers, and a nationally known speaker, if it were Debs, could draw ten thousand listeners.

The St. Louis Socialists hovered on the brink of electoral success. A Wisconsin socialist state senator predicted during a visit to St. Louis that the Mound City would be the next American metropolis to follow the Milwaukee example and gain control of its city government. Such an idea could not be easily dismissed; Socialists across the country were winning municipal and other offices. Milwaukee was the greatest electoral success story, with Socialists in the mayor's office and other city and county posts for two years before one took the mayor's office for a twenty-four year reign. But in 1911 more than seventy American cities elected socialist mayors. It was not impossible to imagine that St. Louis, with its tightly organized party cadres, its solid relationship with the local labor movement, its labor and socialist newspapers, and its rising numbers at the polls, might move into the socialist electoral column.

However, it did not happen. The peak year of socialist electoral success in St. Louis was 1912. Thereafter, a new city charter undercut the party's potential. As elsewhere in the country, the so-called streamlining of municipal politics—through the introduction of nonpartisan elections, the increasing numbers of at-large or appointive offices, and the redrawing of ward lines—served to strengthen the grip of Republicans and Democrats on the electorate. The Socialists and their labor allies had fought to open up the political system and for a while they had successfully opposed charter revision, which would have lessened neighborhood representation. However, they could not win. Symptomatic of the new thrust, in 1913 progressives established the Public Service Commission to set railroad rates, thereby empowering experts rather than elected officials and sacrificing the principle of representation. The charter revision initiative was revived, and it passed in 1914. The new charter reduced the number of elective offices, thus minimizing the political power of central city neighborhoods, where socialist strength was most pronounced. Whereas the Socialists had made a very strong showing in the election prior to the new charter, thereafter they were never serious contenders.

As Socialists had elsewhere, the St. Louis party confronted the existence of old party loyalties of the electorate, the strong, organized antipathy of the local Roman Catholic Church, and the hostility and disdain of the mass daily newspapers. As an example of the latter, the *St. Louis Post-Dispatch* often did not even report socialist election results but merely tabulated the totals of the Republicans and the Democrats. The Socialists also faced the more concrete problem at elections of clerical errors and undercounting of their votes. In the face of such challenges, the party did not do poorly. To win over a majority of the voters, they probably needed a charismatic figure at the national level. They did not have such a figure, and Kate O'Hare, the one national figure residing in St. Louis, neither controlled the party nor did she often run for public office. Moreover, as a woman, she might not have been accepted in the guise of a party leader and boss. Without such a major leader of daily party affairs, the charter revision wiped out any chances for electoral success. Thereafter, the link to organized labor began to wither as local unions moved toward a more nonpartisan posture.

During the years Kate O'Hare was immersed in St. Louis's socialist movement, she focused on issues and causes such as intolerable working conditions, mass unemployment, inadequate housing, and the denial of women's suffrage. She was a well-known local figure, striding up and down Market Street to rally support for a particular issue, sitting on committees beside civic reformers such as Roger Baldwin, who would later found the American Civil Liberties Union, testifying before municipal hearings, addressing workers, and publicizing her causes in various columns and articles. As a journalist she covered the hearings of the Missouri State Senate Minimum Wage Commission at the Planters' Hotel in 1913. Dismayed at the legislators' apparent unwillingness to recognize the actual cost of living, O'Hare herself investigated costs. She visited working-class rentals, and she talked to landladies and managers of boarding houses, rooming houses, and furnished rooms, reporting her findings in an attempt to influence the outcome of the hearings.

The next year, 1914, she was appointed by Republican Mayor Henry Kiel to a municipal committee on unemployment. The committee included a colleague Nellie Quick, of the National Woman's Trade Union League, with whom she had collaborated before, a union representative and two others with ties to labor. The committee met over several months and concluded that unemployment affected as much as 40 percent of the work force. It recommended that a program of municipal relief be established at once to provide clothing, food, and fuel for the most needy. It also recommended that the city hire all those laid off, placing its work force, including administrators, on part-time duty as necessary. The committee urged the establishment of a permanent commission on unemployment to observe the response of other localities to such problems. In several of their recommendations, O'Hare and her colleagues were apparently using the programs of the city of Milwaukee as its model.

For the long-range problems of workers, the commission recommended that model tenements be built to replace decaying housing. It called attention to the example of municipal housing programs in Manchester, England, where tenements were rented at a rate to cover interest, upkeep, and a sinking fund, with financing of the operation handled through liens on the improved properties. The committee's long-range recommendations were immediately filed and forgotten. O'Hare, on her own, informally continued the commission's work; the next month she contacted the city about hiring the unemployed to shovel snow when property owners, despite an ordinance requiring it, failed to do so. She even filed a formal complaint with the city attorney to begin proceedings.

O'Hare worked with local women's suffrage proponents, promoting and speaking on behalf of the enfranchisement of women. Despite party policy against collaboration with non-Socialists on issues of mutual concern, both she and the St. Louis party supported the efforts of the local branches of the Equal Suffrage League and the National American Woman Suffrage Association. Under both joint and separate auspices, she held public debates with local antisuffragists.

After only a few years in St. Louis, O'Hare, the daughter of displaced homesteaders, had become a woman of stature in the community. Called upon by mayors, quoted in the metropolitan dailies, and elected to office in civic organizations, she shared anecdotes with local politicians, debated with Archbishop Glennon, and was one of the most well known and respected women in town. While her ideological posture as a socialist speaker, candidate, columnist, and party leader meant that she was critical of many public policies and officials, nevertheless, hers was a voice to be heard beyond the city limits. Known throughout the Midwest, she was becoming one of the most famous women in America.

5

PARTY LEADER

F
rom St. Louis, Kate Richards O'Hare took to the
national stage. Each year the Socialists seemed to
win more adherents and gain additional public offices from coast to coast, and as she worked for the party
O'Hare became a familiar, even famous, figure on a corner
of the political landscape. Had there not been a Socialist
party, O'Hare would undoubtedly still have pursued work
devoted to public policy, but against a less-visible back-
drop. But, as it happens, in her era a movement emerged
that promoted a social and economic transformation of
society, one that—unlike the Communist party later—was
able to operate in the public arena and was not automatically branded an illegitimate or un-American institution.
Because of O'Hare's own intellectual growth, the influences upon her, and her psychological needs, she came to
devote her energies and her time to, and even to risk her
family's well-being for the cause of international socialism. In effect, everything came together: O'Hare had the
desire to participate in public life, she had a party that
enabled her—even as a woman—to do so, and the climate
of opinion in the country at the time was hospitable to
movements supportive of change and reform.

In the second decade of the twentieth century the Socialist party appeared to have an exciting future. By then
it was ten years old. It had developed and honed a party

hierarchy that functioned in most of the states of the union. By 1910 the Socialists had one member in the U.S. House of Representatives in almost every Congress, either Victor L. Berger, representing Wisconsin's Fifth Congressional District, or Meyer London, representing the Lower East Side of New York. Socialist mayors were elected in dozens of American cities, including Milwaukee and Manitowoc, Wisconsin; Schenectady and Lackawanna, New York; Berkeley and Daly City, California; Butte, Montana; Coeur d'Alene, Idaho; Ashtabula and Lima, Ohio; and Minneapolis and Crookstown, Minnesota. Both large cities and tiny hamlets were among the over one hundred fifty municipalities that elected socialist mayors between 1911 and the era of World War I. More than one hundred Socialists served in state legislatures. Even states that tended not to elect Socialists because of the location of voter clusters or the pattern of ward lines sometimes had strong socialist followings. Oklahoma, for example, had proportionately the largest party membership of all the states, but the party did not win many elections. Further, a widespread movement media existed, most of which was not owned by the party but which supplemented its efforts. Monthlies, weeklies, and dailies were published throughout the United States, both in English and in many foreign languages. In 1913, for example, at least one hundred socialist newspapers and periodicals were published in the United States.

In order to reach and engage Americans, the Socialist party organized many subgroups. Beyond its basic locals, it had foreign-language locals, young people's groups and campus organizations, and women's committees. The Socialists spawned a bureaucracy of lecturers and organizers who traveled constantly throughout all the states and territories and into Canadian provinces as well. To support such organizational activities, the party printed and circulated millions of pamphlets designed to appeal to groups such as workers, housewives, immigrants, and farmers, indeed every group the party could imagine, other than bourgeoisie.

This vibrant and dynamic national party was a branch of the international socialist movement, linked to similar parties overseas; it was,

therefore, supported by a worldwide effort that appeared to be everywhere on the march. American Socialists participated in congresses and
other meetings of the Second International and were expected to adhere
to its policies while, at the same time, receiving support from the International and gaining a sense of solidarity and prestige as an inherent
part of a larger whole.

The Socialist party's domination by revisionists rather than by orthodox Marxists meant that party policy encouraged social and economic
reforms so that American workers might live and work in a more humane
environment. Such reforms were intended to modify the existing economic system toward the collective control of the means of production
and distribution. Policy also promoted democratic reforms of the political system so that the masses of the American people might use direct
elections, primaries, referenda, recall, and the initiative as tools through
which they themselves could control the political system. Nominating
candidates with such views was held to be a means of gradually educating the public to acceptance of socialist ideology. The successful promotion of such ideas could obviate the need for a bloody upheaval to
transform the system from capitalistic to collectivist. Socialists of this
perspective, led by Victor L. Berger, who was seen as the boss of the
Milwaukee socialist movement, and urbane intellectual Morris Hillquit
of New York, had controlled party machinery and offices since the founding party convention, and they set policy.

The orthodox Marxists had to content themselves with struggling
against party directions in usually hopeless efforts to reverse policy.
This faction opposed the practice of nominating slates of candidates for
public office and, hence, usually chose not to accept nominations themselves. Rather, these Socialists focused their criticisms and attacks on
those who held office and made policy. They opposed ongoing political
action in favor of direct action at the moment of revolution. Appearing
to be obstructionists, they helped limit their own following and, in the
meantime, lacked more than a few names who might have galvanized a
following within the party. Their greatest asset was Gene Debs, al-

though his most notable biographer, Nick Salvatore, does not label Debs a party leftist. Debs ran for public office while refusing to become involved in party factionalism and infighting. He simply would not challenge individuals who were his friends and comrades, and as a result, he often sat out controversies. Indeed, while he was the most well known and most popular Socialist with the membership and the American public, he played virtually no policy-making role, seldom attending conventions or committee meetings or accepting a party office. Accordingly, Debs did not strengthen the orthodox Marxists, with whose policies he usually sympathized, in their struggle against the revisionist direction of the party.

In this spectrum of opinion, Kate O'Hare's views, as demonstrated in all of her activities, were reflective of the majority revisionist, or reformist, position. Her whole career was devoted to trying to enhance the lives of working people in the here and now. Whether she was investigating factory conditions, writing the about the plight of tenant farmers, or testifying on the need for female enfranchisement, she promoted improvements within the existing system. To O'Hare, it was unforgivable to wait for the coming of the revolution to guarantee decent housing, wages, and protective legislation. No direct actionist, she preferred step-at-a-time political reforms, which would help the workers at once. The future revolution would transform the system, she believed, but until that time a gradual improvement of conditions through the political process was the mandatory goal for any Socialist of humane instincts.

However, O'Hare was not usually seen as a revisionist. Her reputation suggested, in fact, the opposite of her record. No doubt due to her closeness to Gene Debs, she was often seen as an adherent of the obstructionist or "impossibilist" faction with which his name was linked. There is no debating that she saw Debs as a father figure. They were both midwesterners and colleagues on both the *Appeal to Reason* and the *National Rip-Saw,* and they corresponded with one another. Debs wrote to her frequently when she was in prison in Jefferson City. The two shared the onerous routine of itinerate speakers, and while they were routed separately by Frank O'Hare and other booking agents, they often appeared together on the same platforms at the summer encampments and occasionally elsewhere. She viewed him on a platform as a Jesus of Nazareth and saw herself as a disciple at his side. Both speakers knew what it was like to relate intimately to crowds of people and luxuriate in the waves of fellow-feeling that would ripple across the auditorium or tent. Each basked in the love of thousands of rank-and-file party members. They had many of the same friends—Mills, Wayland, Ameringer, and other journalists and organizers. It is perhaps no wonder that they were casually assigned to the same ideological camp by some party members and, subsequently, by many historians. As a result of that fact, O'Hare has been referred to as a revolutionary within the party context, or as "Red Kate."

A second reason for her distorted reputation relates to the personal prejudices of the leaders of the dominant reformist bloc. The leadership was eastern or at least urban and sometimes immigrant. Those who did not fit that profile, the western, rural and native-born, were often labeled ignorant and unlearned, wild and unreliable or, in short, hayseeds. The stereotype was applied to O'Hare by the dominant leaders and was symptomatic of a deep division within the party between western agrarians and eastern or urban-based Socialists. Many struggles over strategies, tactics, and goals arose from this split, with all westerners sometimes falsely called direct actionists by their opponents, and all easterners at times charged by their opponents with being out of touch with the rank-and-file. O'Hare might have been well positioned to bring together the two mutually suspicious factions. While she was a westerner who was as deeply attached to the land as the thousands of Socialists who farmed, her path had taken her to the city so that she, beyond most of her colleagues, knew the struggles of those who worked the land and those who toiled in the sweatshops and factories. As an adult she lived in Kansas City and St. Louis, and she knew the working and living conditions of the workers in New York, the shop girls in St. Louis, and the Germans with whom she associated in her local party organization. But the suspicions in the highest party echelons against O'Hare as a westerner were so strong that she never had a chance to try to mend the party split. It is significant that Frank O'Hare felt sufficiently stigmatized by the dominant party leadership that, in 1904, he decided to move his family from Kansas to the virgin territory of Oklahoma, where he could strike out on his own as a party organizer. The eastern establishment of the Socialist party viewed the O'Hares as outsiders who represented a competing outlook. Neither her votes on internal party issues nor her closest associates in movement activities, other than Debs, suggest ties between Kate O'Hare and the orthodox or Marxist faction. Despite her erroneous title and the animosity of some of the eastern national leadership toward her, she was very comfortable in the revisionist camp.

O'Hare was not a consistent participant in the rough and tumble of party policymaking and frequent infighting. Indeed, no women was, which indicates that even those women able to operate as political activists ultimately found the party inner sanctums to be a man's world. The essence of O'Hare's party life was her relationship to the membership. O'Hare was the darling of the midwestern and western rank and filers. She was often nominated for party offices, and she was always assured of a heavy vote in Kansas, Nebraska, Missouri, Oklahoma, and the surrounding states where she was known best. She usually won election when she ran for a nomination for party or public office or for convention delegate. She held national offices, including service on the party's executive committee, sat on ad hoc committees, and was one of a handful of the nationally known Socialists to represent the party abroad at international meetings. She was once nominated to be executive secretary of the party. O'Hare ran for the party's national ticket in 1916 for the vice-presidential nomination. On that occasion she came in second to a fellow Kansan, George R. Kirkpatrick, who was not a major party leader. But he was at the time popular as one of the most vigorous antiwar pamphleteers active in the preparedness controversy.

O'Hare attended four of the five party conventions or congresses held between 1904 and 1917. Her first socialist convention was held in 1904 in Chicago, although she was not a delegate that time. In 1910, at another convention (officially termed a Congress since an election slate was not being nominated) held in Chicago, she played a crucial role in one of the major debates of the proceedings. On the eve of the 1912 convention in Indianapolis, she and Victor Berger were chosen as a delegation to the mayor to request permission to carry the red flag in the opening day parade, a socialist custom. In 1917 at an emergency convention in St. Louis, called at the time of American intervention in World War I, O'Hare presided over the debates and shaped party policy on American participation in the war.

At the 1910 national gathering, where O'Hare was one of the three delegates representing Kansas, she was in her element. She casually greeted old friends, swapped gossip with comrades, and visited again with those party members who had played host to her one time or another on her tours. Longtime friends were also there as delegates, including Oscar Ameringer, Caroline A. Lowe, Winnie E. Branstetter, and George D. Brewer from Girard. Because of her constant touring, she inevitably knew many of the delegates at party gatherings. She was active in debates, participated in votes, and was elected to one of the important policy-making committees. Major policy debates at the Congress in 1910 took place on the topics of immigration, industrial unionism, female suffrage, and a proposed farm policy. O'Hare was not vitally interested in the subject of immigration. The party, however, was caught up in what was a potentially damaging issue. International socialist policy, as enunciated in 1907 after a debate at a Congress in Stuttgart, Germany, in which American Socialists had participated, opposed barring any national group. The American Socialists, however, were anxious to avoid antagonizing organized labor, which was increasingly restrictionist-minded on the subject of immigration. The reformist leadership, thus, wanted a policy that would appear to be faithful to the intent of the International and yet harmonized with the sentiments of the American Federation of Labor. After a spirited debate in which some support was voiced for the exclusion of Asians from entering the United States, a policy already applied to the Chinese by U.S. Congressional actions, convention delegates rejected full exclusion of Asians, phrased as exclusion of "backward" rather than racial groups. The compromise, which was finally accepted, condemned the principle of outright exclusion of groups but opposed the deliberate importation of laborers. O'Hare, who did not ask for the floor during the debate, opposed the blatant principle of exclusion. She also voted against a modified exclusionary motion, which would have excluded Japanese not as Japanese but as representing a menace to the American standard of living. At the conclusion of the debate, O'Hare joined those who opposed the successful compromise measure as a violation of the spirit of the International's position.

By 1910, the Socialist party, having failed in its effort to bore from within and persuade the American Federation of Labor to its point of view, followed a policy of cooperation with the mainstream labor movement. However, ever since the establishment in 1905 of the more dynamic and militant Industrial Workers of the World (IWW), controversy had raged about formally supporting the Wobblies. In fact, some party members did so as individuals, including Debs for at least a short period. Moreover, Big Bill Haywood, the most influential Wobbly leader, was at this time also a leader of the Socialist party. The IWW's form of organization, industrial unionism, enjoyed some support in the party as more appropriate than the craft-based skilled unionism of the AFL. The delegates debated these issues once more at the national party Congress in Chicago, arguing over a motion to endorse industrial unionism. Opponents, including O'Hare, successfully argued that the form of labor organization was up to the workers themselves, and that the party was correctly on record as supporting all workers. Thus, the more militant Wobblies had not won over O'Hare and the majority of the membership.

This debate was a prelude to a subsequent one at the next national convention in 1912 at Indianapolis, at which O'Hare was present but not an official delegate. Had she been, she might have voted with the majority which opted to insert a clause in the party constitution prohibiting a member from advocating sabotage. This was directed at the Wobblies and their sympathizers for their alleged use of industrial sabotage. The anti-sabotage clause created a great controversy, and was followed within several months by the recall of Haywood from the National Executive Committee of the party based on the charge that he endorsed the use of sabotage. The ouster of Haywood was accomplished by unconstitutional procedures but was endorsed in a referendum by more than two to one. If Kate O'Hare was at all disturbed by the manipulation of party machinery in order to get rid of a leader of a troublesome and militant minority, no evidence of that exists.

Another debate at the Congress was focused on the correct methods of conducting female suffrage campaigns. O'Hare was one of those who took a leading role in this debate, along with Caroline Lowe (1874–1933) her old friend and one of the other Kansas delegates. Other major participants were Theresa S. Malkiel (1874–1949), a former garment worker from New York with whom O'Hare would soon work quite closely in the New York suffrage campaign of 1914, and Ella Reeve Bloor, affectionately called Mother Bloor (1862–1951), a party organizer who would later be a heroine of the Communist Party of America. O'Hare was anxious to clarify how Socialists could cooperate with nonsocialist suffrage advocates without running afoul of party principles. She frankly stated that she held membership in nonsocialist groups, such as the Women's Trade Union League, and believed that she could argue on behalf of suffrage within W.T.U.L. debates, for example, without compromising her socialism. Responding to opponents who argued that such efforts would inevitably mean sacrificing the class-base of her arguments, O'Hare maintained that whoever her audience and whatever the subject, she was able to "always bring it right back to the Socialistic base. I don't care whether they talk on the marriage question, or on the comet, I will bring the comet back to the Socialist proposition." She suggested if others had problems in that regard, perhaps different sections of the country required different approaches. She maintained that in the regions which she knew best, the west and the southwest, it was possible to participate in middle-class women's suffrage campaigns without sacrificing her socialist framework. She stated that she always emphasized, "that only through the Socialist movement can we have a universal suffrage that will mean anything, that won't shut out, as it does in many parts of the South the poor white man who can't pay his poll-tax." She was cogently drawing on her exposure to the disenfranchised in the South and also demonstrating her exclusive focus on white enfranchisement. She pointed out that European Socialists joined any struggle on behalf of expanding the franchise in their countries, and so she, similarly, wanted to be free to participate in any struggle for expanding the ballot in Kansas or Oklahoma or wherever she went, no matter which party or organization initiated the campaign.

O'Hare's efforts were at least partially rewarded. She and others were not forbidden from joining other suffrage movements nor were they even discouraged from doing so. The party position held that a member could participate in nonsocialist suffrage campaigns as individuals but that the party officially could not be represented as cooperating with such efforts. On an issue that O'Hare saw as related, white slavery, a long-standing concern of hers, she convinced the delegates to adopt a resolution to publish propaganda on the economic causes of prostitution. Soon thereafter, O'Hare herself wrote the pamphlet that circulated as the party's basic document on that subject.

A most important debate in which O'Hare took a central role was over whether or not the Socialist party would at last develop a program through which it could explicitly appeal for the support of farmers. O'Hare was elected as an additional member to a sitting committee to recommend policy. She was an obvious choice and received more votes than any of the other dozen nominees for the six positions to be added to the committee. For years she had argued that American farmers were workers and that the party must reach out to these workers, too. But the party leadership found it difficult to recognize any group other than industrial workers as a proletariat. Moreover, the party had to confront the crucial question of whether a socialistic farmers' program, by definition, had to involve the collectivization of the land. On the one hand, if the program endorsed collectivization, then automatically the party undoubtedly would lose any chance it had to attract most farmers but, on the other hand, if it did not endorse that position, in the eyes of many it would be sacrificing its principles. Thus, it was not due to absentmindedness that it was a decade into its existence before the Socialist party established a farmers' program.

While O'Hare and Ameringer, who was also elected to the Farmers' Committee, had long been the most persistent voices demanding a party policy on farmers, even some urbanites, such as Victor Berger, had agreed with them. A. M. Simons, who had written for, among other newspapers, the *Appeal to Reason,* was another such voice. All of them believed that it was necessary to reach out to the small farmer who was not disappearing (despite Marx's prediction), but without endorsing the principle of private property. Further, as Ameringer had argued in Oklahoma, large landholders, that is, incipient agribusinessmen, could be eliminated through tax policies, which would mean more land could be made available to the farming proletariat.

The previous convention in 1908 had not reached a consensus on a farmers' program. This time, O'Hare was active in the debate and she, the most famous party leader identified with agrarian America, told her fellow delegates that socialist speakers would have to abandon organizing in rural regions if they were not finally given a policy. She recalled being asked a few months before by a farmer in St. John, Kansas, how the socialist position on the land question compared with that of the Republican party. She felt that she had to dodge the question because she had nothing to offer the seven thousand farmers in her audience. She pleaded with her party comrades in these words: "I must work among the farmers because it is the farmers' psychology that I know. . . . I can talk to people who were born on the Western ranches as I was, I can talk to those who have lived the life of a farmer's daughter, and a farmer's wife, and as I say, I want to work among them; and so I say, when I go back among them, give me something to talk on, something that I can take a stand on." She asked for no more study groups, committees, or elaborate debates that ended up with tabled programs. She demanded that a program addressed to farmers be developed and accepted at the convention.

However, the Farmers' Committee was charged by the Congress to develop a program by the time of the next party convention in 1912. In those two years, Kate O'Hare remained adamant on the need to frame a program. But no committee meeting was called, and she was busy with her own lecturing and writing schedule. Anxious as she was to have a program in place, not just by the next convention but before the encampment season of 1911, she wrote to other members of the committee and suggested that those few who lived near each other meet to develop the program, and she would do her best to attend. She was apparently aghast that all that was being considered was circulating a translation of the German Social Democratic party's policy on the agrarian question. She pushed Ameringer especially as the individual most able to develop a program with American cotton farmers in mind.

The report of the Farmers' Committee to the 1912 convention was not formally signed by O'Hare. By then, she was a member of the party's executive and too swamped with a number of official duties to participate in finalizing the farmers' program. However, she approved that program which, in the face of much criticism, won the convention's endorsement. The farmers' program of the Socialist party sidestepped the issue of the collectivization of land. Instead, it emphasized that the means of transportation, storage, and machinery upon which the farmer depended be "socially owned and democratically managed." While the committee members denied that they were influenced by the work of Henry George, they endorsed the idea made famous by George of taxing land not in cultivation, and that actual use and occupancy "be the only title to the land." The beleaguered committee had attempted to design a synthesis of agrarian property ownership with revisionist Marxism. For what it was worth, Kate O'Hare at last had a farmers' program to present to her audiences, but she and the other supporters of that program found themselves harangued as defenders of private property who had forgotten that the party was of the working class and not of farmers.

The two years following the party Congress of 1910 saw O'Hare at the peak of her party influence. In that period she won election to the National Executive Committee of the party, was selected as the first women to represent the Socialist Party of America abroad at a meeting of the executive body of the Second International, and also was elected to the Women's National Committee. Elected to the N.E.C. early in 1912 for the usual one-year term, she was only the second women to sit on the executive committee. Her enthusiastic support from the west was illustrated by the fact that she received more votes in Oklahoma than did any other candidate.

Her participation in the N.E.C. occurred during the year of confrontations over the issues of direct action and syndicalism as symbolized by the presence of the Wobbly leader, Big Bill Haywood, on the committee. During that year, the N.E.C. went on record as supporting the Wobbly-led strike of immigrant workers, mainly women and children, in the mill town of Lawrence, Massachusetts, but did not follow through on Haywood's suggestions to telegraph protests to President William Howard Taft and the Governor of Massachusetts, Eugene N. Foss, over the treatment of the strikers. The N.E.C. offered less than lukewarm support—only some meager financial aid—to west coast so-called free speech efforts by Wobblies. Led by the vociferously hostile Victor Berger, who described as a brawl the I.W.W. campaign of civil disobedience to win the right to speak on street corners, the reformist-dominated N.E.C. referred the matter to the California State Committee of the party. The subsequent decision by the party's convention delegates to condemn sabotage and opposition to political action as grounds for expulsion, reflected the views of the majority on the N.E.C., as did the later ouster of Haywood.

No evidence suggests that O'Hare argued against the anti-Wobbly efforts of the dominant faction on the N.E.C. led by Berger and Morris Hillquit. But she remained, in fact, consistently sympathetic to individual Wobblies, admiring those rugged militants who challenged the most onerous working conditions, and her relations were always cordial with Wobblies whom she met on the road. But she did not support any institutional efforts through which the I.W.W. might appear tied to the Socialist party.

O'Hare was certainly not a shaping influence during her term on the N.E.C. She could not be a dominating force, even with her inherent leadership qualities, in the face of an entrenched leadership that perpetually served on the committee and viewed her as an outsider. However, she was willing to stand up for her views, as when she challenged Hillquit on his ramming through of a controversial appointee as campaign manager for Debs. But, given the environment, she was not influential on the N.E.C. and was not reelected two years later. Shortly after her term was over, she was interested in joining a party delegation to the West Virginia mine fields during a lengthy and violent strike. Martial law had been declared, unionization efforts flaunted, socialist newspapers raided, and Mother Jones, present to support the strikers, arrested. O'Hare wanted to cover the strike as an investigative reporter, but she came in fourth for the three-member delegation.

In 1913, O'Hare had a chance to pursue further the party's efforts to disassociate itself from any hint of I.W.W.-related direct actionism. O'Hare was elected by the party membership to represent it on the executive body of the international socialist movement, the International Socialist Bureau. She became only the second woman to serve in its twenty-four years, her predecessor being the legendary Rosa Luxemburg. She had defeated Berger and Hillquit, who had tended to view the party's seat on the I.S.B. as their private property, and also Ernest Untermann, like the previously mentioned, a European-born intellectual, and even Debs himself, among nine other candidates. Her election was taken as a personal insult by Berger and Hillquit. She was resented as an outsider, as a westerner, as a woman, and as an American who could not even converse with the internationally celebrated German, French, Russian and other leaders with whom she would rub shoulders. Berger and Hillquit assured each other that O'Hare's election was the result of a misunderstanding. The latter shuddered over the prospect of O'Hare at the I.S.B. meeting. He confided to Berger, "You can imagine what impression [the party] shall make on the comrades of Europe if she comes as the sole representative of the Socialist party." Berger basically held strong reservations about the receptivity of women to the message of socialism, and did not think it was "necessary" even to have a woman on the party's executive committee.

Kate O'Hare was delighted by her election to the I.S.B. and, accordingly, to have her first opportunity to travel to Europe. In order to finance her passage, the national office of the Socialist party arranged a speaking tour for her to the east coast. From there she traveled to London where her reception by the bureau members at the December 1913, two-day meeting was cordial. She was specifically applauded as a woman whose election signified the progress of the American socialist movement, but it seemed to her that some of her colleagues were startled to see a woman as an equal, especially perhaps the British. At both the formal meetings and the social gatherings, O'Hare reported courteous and warm treatment. She felt almost star-struck as she met the various famous European leaders and intellectuals whose names she had known for years. But she reflected thoughtfully that perhaps a few younger party leaders ought to be selected for the meetings rather than just the grand old men of the movement. She regretted her inability to converse spontaneously with the majority of her colleagues, but one of the French delegates, Jean Longuet, a grandson of Karl Marx and the editor of *L'Humanité,* often pitched in as her interpreter.

The bureau meeting had been scheduled in order to draw up the agenda for the next International Socialist Congress, planned for August 1914, in Vienna. The Socialist party had charged O'Hare with the responsibility of placing on its agenda subjects of special interest to the Americans: revolutionary syndicalism, sabotage, and direct action. The party wanted reinforcement from the prestigious International in its struggle to discredit the IWW. While O'Hare tried to be convincing, she could not persuade her international comrades to accept these agenda items. Probably the I.S.B. veterans, Hillquit and Berger, could not have won their acceptance either. The Europeans lacked interest in these issues, since they did not at the time feel threatened by such potential disruption in their movements as did the Americans. They saw no reason to invite unnecessary debate on theoretical matters which could turn acrimonious. O'Hare's proposal was opposed by both the preeminent German leader, Karl Kautsky, and the French leader, Jean Jaurés. Jaurés particularly voiced great respect for O'Hare as able to influence American farmers toward socialism while the French could not reach their farm population. Jaurés even invited her to France to help the movement there with its propaganda but nevertheless he did not support her. Only the English offered her proposed agenda items any support.

O'Hare had also been charged by her party to convince the bureau to unseat the rival American party, the Socialist Labor party, which would mean that the Socialist party would be assigned both American seats on the bureau. There, too, she was disappointed as the matter was referred to the forthcoming Congress which, as it turned out, was never held because of the outbreak of war. But this disappointment, as with the previous issue, did not reflect negatively on her effectiveness because her predecessors had also tried unsuccessfully to unseat their competitors. O'Hare's performance was apparently acceptable; it certainly was not embarrassing to her party as Hillquit had feared, so in 1919 she was again elected to the international post.

During O'Hare's brief visit to the British Isles, she took advantage of opportunities extended to her to speak to crowds of working people. She was asked to attend a convention of the Trades Union Conference in London which was discussing a strike in Dublin of the Irish Transport and General Workers' Union for union recognition. From there, she went to the strike site itself, and addressed two mass meetings of ten thousand people. Moved by her experience, she later wrote,

Never to me again perhaps will there come so great a moment as when the crowd recognized in my speech the voice of brotherhood from across the sea and accepted me as of the clan. Never again will I be so deeply moved as when two hundred Irish policemen stood with lifted helmets to make a path through the seething mass of people through which two stalwart Irishmen carried me on their shoulders to the jaunting car in which I rode to my hotel while the thousands marched beside me as a guard of honor such as perhaps no woman ever had before.

She was fascinated by Ireland, struck by the beauty of its landscape but appalled by the impoverishment of its people. In addition, she was revolted by the religious fanaticism that divided the Protestants and Catholics of Ireland and increased the burdens borne by her economically and politically exploited people.

The other office which O'Hare held in the Socialist party was her one-year membership on the Women's National Committee, the executive body of the women's sector. The W.N.C. was established in 1908 at the behest of those women party members who believed that the Socialist party needed a special office in order to make an explicit appeal to women and address their needs. Concerned about an autonomous socialist woman's organization then emerging, the national convention of 1908 set up a women's sector with its own hierarchy. From the local to the national level, the W.N.C. developed a network that began to thrive with branches in most states. It pushed for the establishment of a woman's committee in every local, and it sent out its own organizers and issued propaganda geared to interest women in the cause. Not without its many critics who argued that the struggle to achieve socialism should not be diluted by excessive attention to the Woman Question, the woman's sector expanded dramatically until its much-debated abolition after seven years.

All three of the women who headed the W.N.C. were well known to O'Hare. The first to hold that position, and the one who was probably the key individual shaping the women's sector, was May Wood Simons. She and her husband, A. M. Simons, were midwestern Socialists with whom Kate and Frank O'Hare had often crossed paths. The Simonses were journalists more than public speakers; nevertheless, they took to the encampment lecture circuit in addition to their writing for various socialists' periodicals. May Wood wrote articles for the *Socialist Woman* and other newspapers, as well as pamphlets for socialist publishing houses. For a while she and her husband resided in Girard when he worked for the *Appeal*.

The others who led the Women's National Committee were very old friends of O'Hare's: Caroline Lowe and Winnie Branstetter. Lowe and Branstetter (1879–1960) were sisters who had shared with O'Hare organizational work in the Oklahoma territories, and they met over the years in various places and remained close friends. Others with whom O'Hare worked in the woman's sector included Grace D. Brewer (1881–1975), who for many years was a mainstay on the *Appeal to Reason* along with her husband, George. Brewer, an Iowa native, had attended Ruskin College in Trenton, Missouri, and she was an editor of the *Appeal* and was in charge of its expansive subscription army. She also arranged for O'Hare's and Debs's speaking tours when they traveled on behalf of the *Appeal*. Theresa S. Malkiel of New York was a comrade for whom O'Hare felt real affection. She was born in the czarist empire and had immigrated to New York City. Like other adolescent, Jewish girls on the Lower East Side, she worked in sweatshops and, not atypically, was radicalized by her experiences as a worker. She organized a union for her coworkers, and from there entered the socialist movement.

These were among the several women comrades whom O'Hare worked alongside of for fifteen to twenty years. And yet it cannot be said that she was close to the majority of them. Her surviving correspondence, limited as it is, reveals proportionately few letters to most of these women. While there are sparks of affection here and there, by implication it seems clear that O'Hare did not tend to maintain meaningful friendships with women comrades. Many of these women, for example, Simons, Branstetter, and Malkiel, shared with O'Hare the pressure of trying to balance work and family responsibilities. Unlike Lowe or some other women activists who did not have children, these three women were all caring for families as well as handling their commitments to the party. They were all professional women whose lives were affected by the fact that they had young children. Logically, they might have together constructed a support system through which they could draw strength from each other. But in O'Hare's case, this was definitely not so. She limited herself to her family resources. The fact that her husband was a party activist, which was also true of the other women cited, meant perhaps that the interaction of family and work resulted in a tightly integrated life so that she did not think of reaching outside for support. Perhaps there simply was little space for others in her life.

O'Hare felt close to one of her sisters, Jessie, who along with her husband was a Socialist. But O'Hare's closest friends were her male comrades. Wayland, Mills, Wagner, and of course Debs figured as much more important in her life. This hypothesis may be reflective of her ambivalent feminism. Indeed, her record during her one year of service on the Women's National Committee also suggests an ambivalence. Moreover, that she failed to contact the International Conference of Socialist Women when she was abroad for sessions of the International Socialist Bureau reinforces this thesis.

Her service on the Women's National Committee could hardly be argued to have had much impact, especially since she was such a major party leader, and she faced no barriers to leadership on this committee. O'Hare missed a number of meetings because of her heavy travel schedule. She failed to mail in her ballots some of those times. She did not attend state-level women's party conferences or nonparty socialist women's events. She did, however, at one point, contribute proceeds from ten of her speaking engagements to the women's sector, and by that gesture she underscored her own belief in the value of the women's sector.

O'Hare was not the only woman activist who had an uneven relationship to the women's sector of the party. The very establishment of such a special bureaucracy was criticized by many women as well as men, including even women activists who emphasized the needs of working women. Such individuals were not persuaded of the appropriateness of campaigns on behalf of particular groups. The future cooperative commonwealth and its socialization of property would emancipate everyone. Fundamentally, O'Hare as well as these other Socialists did not consider themselves feminists, and the Woman Question definitely was subsumed within the Social Question.

O'Hare's overall importance in the Socialist party and her contributions to its growth before World War I should not be minimized. She was frequently elected to high offices; at one time or another she held virtually every major party position. She was a convention delegate, was a member of the National Executive Committee, was elected as the party's representative to the International Socialist Bureau, and served as member of the Woman's National Committee. Although a revisionist in tune with the direction of party policy, as a woman and a westerner she was seldom able to exert great influence in the highest party circles. Her greatest contribution to the Socialist party was as a publicist rather than as a party official. But she did have some impact, especially at party conventions where her renown with the delegates gave her resources that she could not summon in meetings with the top party leaders. She was nevertheless a person to be reckoned with as the party continued to strengthen its hold on segments of the American public. O'Hare's fame would continue to grow in the next, darker years for her and her party. In some ways she was about to become one of the most infamous women in America.

South Main Street of Ada, Kansas, the closest town to the Richards homestead
Courtesy Kansas State Historical Society

Kate Richards in 1897
Courtesy Phillip Ray Carney

"Mother" Mary Harris Jones, the legendary union organizer, who was a direct influence on Kate Richards after their first encounter in Kansas City
Courtesy the Archives of Labor and Urban Affairs, Wayne State University

Julius Augustus Wayland, Girard,
Kansas, April 10, 1908, publisher of the
Appeal to Reason, and one of the most
significant figures in Kate Richards's life
*Courtesy J. A. Wayland Collection, Pittsburg
(Kansas) State University*

Grace and George
Brewer in 1904. Kate
worked with them on
the *Appeal to Reason*
and in the Socialist
party. Grace Brewer
was one of Kate
O'Hare's few close
women friends.
*Courtesy the Archives
of Labor and Urban
Affairs, Wayne State
University*

Kate and Frank O'Hare
with their four children
*Courtesy of the Tamiment
Institute Library, New York
University*

(left to right) Walter G.
Treacher (from Bom-
bay, India), Eugene V.
Debs, and Frank P. O'Hare
*Courtesy J. A. Wayland
Collection, Pittsburg (Kansas)
State University*

Guy H. Lockwood, drawing of Socialist women, 1903. The youthful O'Hare's growing fame in socialist circles is evident in this cartoon of well-known activist women.

Reproduced from the Appeal to Reason, no. 405 (September 5, 1903), courtesy J. A. Wayland Collection, Pittsburg (Kansas) State University

Kate O'Hare in the office of the *National Rip-Saw,* St. Louis, about 1915
Courtesy of Perkins Library, Duke University

118

Frank P. O'Hare in the office of the *National Rip-Saw,* St. Louis, about 1915
Courtesy Missouri State Historical Society

Kate O'Hare at home in a crowd
Courtesy Perkins Library, Duke University

120

Victor Berger, one of the two most influential figures who dominated Socialist party policy. He and O'Hare frequently worked together, often with some misgivings.
Courtesy State Historical Society of Wisconsin

Morris Hillquit, the other dominant Socialist party leader. O'Hare viewed him as a negative influence on the party, as a European intellectual who perhaps never understood the American environment.
Courtesy State Historical Society of Wisconsin

Socialist Party Emergency Convention, April 1917, St. Louis. O'Hare is seated in the center of the front row, wearing a black suit and white blouse. A young Fiorello LaGuardia is seated two to her left, and Walter Thomas Mills, O'Hare's teacher, is seated two to his left. Frank P. O'Hare is standing in the second row, the sixth from the right in the photograph.

Courtesy Socialist Party Papers, Western Historical Manuscript Collection, University of Missouri–St. Louis

122

Judge Martin J. Wade,
Federal Judge of the
Southern District of
Iowa, who presided at
O'Hare's trial. The
previous year, he had
published a critical
pamphlet entitled
"What Socialism
Breeds in Davenport,
Iowa."
*Courtesy State Historical
Society of Iowa–Des
Moines*

The yard of the
Missouri State Peni-
tentiary at Jefferson
City where O'Hare
was incarcerated for
fourteen months in
1919–1920
*Courtesy Missouri State
Archives*

Emma Goldman on the eve of World War I, soon to be incarcerated at Jefferson City where she and O'Hare would become good friends

O'Hare with former Warden Thomas Mott Osborn of Sing Sing, meeting in the office of the *National Rip-Saw* in St. Louis in 1922
Courtesy Missouri State Historical Society

O'Hare addressing an audience of neighbors at Commonwealth College
Courtesy Picture Collection, Special Collections Division, University of Arkansas Libraries, Fayetteville

Upton Sinclair at the Centinella Bowl in Inglewood, California, on July 1, 1934, during his EPIC gubernatorial campaign when O'Hare worked on his behalf, Permission granted by Bertha Klausner International Literary Agency, Inc.

Thomas R. Amlie,
Progressive Party rep-
resentative of the First
Congressional District
of Wisconsin. O'Hare
served on his staff in
1937.
*Courtesy State Historical
Society of Wisconsin*

6

DANGEROUS WOMAN

The year 1914 was one of momentous change in O'Hare's life. The signs of impending disaster were barely discernible in late spring. While the arms race and regional nationalistic rivalries of Europe were clearly menacing, both seemed to be long-term phenomena. They rumbled on, seemingly without any violent disturbances, except for localized outbreaks as in the Balkans two years earlier. In St. Louis, O'Hare's life went on as usual. Residents were preparing for the typical long, hot summer—sweltering days at work or home followed by uncomfortable evenings on front porches or stoops. St. Louisans had just indulged themselves in another of the historical-minded celebrations that the city staged in those years. A pageant was held during the last few days of May in Forest Park, marking the 150th anniversary of the founding of the city and attracting visitors as well as residents, but in nowhere near the numbers that had attended the World's Fair a decade earlier. More prosaically, St. Louisans that June enjoyed themselves by taking excursions on the Mississippi River, by picnicking in the parks, or by attending major league baseball games, either watching the Browns at Sportsmen's Park on North Grand or the Cardinals at Robinson Field out on Natural Bridge Avenue.

The Socialist party of St. Louis was gearing up for its usual round of outdoor summer activities in which every local or branch held a picnic at Linns Grove on north Broadway or one of the city's other large parks. The German Women's branch was one of the first to hold its picnic that year, and the Jewish Branch advertised what was expected to be one of the major events on that year's summer calendar because Gene Debs was their speaker. The all-city socialist picnic was, as usual, scheduled for the Fourth of July, and the speakers were announced as Dan Hoan, the socialist city attorney of Milwaukee and John H. Walker, president of the Illinois State Federation of Labor, with a representative of the Austrian Workingmen's Federation as an added attraction. Speeches were to be given in over a dozen languages, and food would be sold, especially wurst and sauerkraut, at "workingmen's prices." In the meantime, the Socialists focused on what would ultimately be an unsuccessful struggle to prevent the proposed charter revision, while still enjoying their recent triumph in convincing the board of education to open the public schools to evening community meetings.

The local German-American community was also preparing for its summer routine. The state of Missouri claimed the tenth-largest German population in the United States. Of a population of 687,029, St. Louis Germans numbered over 200,000 in the most recent census, counting both the city's foreign-born and their children, and including those of Austrian background. They continued to maintain their gymnastic clubs, singing societies, veterans' organizations, and fraternal and benevolent groups. But with some German-Americans by then moving away from that cohesive culture, only the Turners were strong enough to maintain a citywide organization. German was still taught in the high schools, although it had been almost thirty years since it had been offered in the elementary schools. Nevertheless, parts of St. Louis were described as being as German as Berlin. Many wealthy St. Louis Germans maintained homes on the Rhine River, for example, the family of Adolphus Busch (to whose funeral in 1913 the kaiser's son, Prince Adalbert, had sent a wreath). The Catholic Central Verein of America was headquartered in St. Louis, as were a few other major German-American organizations. All in all, the German-American community, like the local Socialists, had no reason to expect anything but a normal summer in 1914.

When war erupted in Europe during the first week of August, St. Louis's German residents reacted as did those of other large German communities in the United States, such as Milwaukee and Cincinnati. Those who were reservists in the German or Austrian armies contacted the consulates in St. Louis about returning to join their units. A mass meeting at the central Turner Hall was held on August 8 to demonstrate support for the German Empire and to demand fair play for the Fatherland. The crowd denied that the Central Powers were responsible for the war, and they criticized the anti-German editorial stance of the *Post-Dispatch*. The meeting concluded with a standing rendition of "The Watch on the Rhine." In the following months as the fighting continued, the organized German community joined with the local Irish and formed a neutrality league. The Germans staged bazaars to collect contributions for German war victims. The largest such event in this series, which continued into 1917, was the October 1915, charity effort, which raised one hundred thousand dollars for wounded German and Austrian soldiers.

Kate O'Hare was in the midst of her usual spring and summer tours when the war began. In May and June, she had traveled from St. Louis to the states just to the west of Missouri, speaking in Iowa, Nebraska, the Dakotas, and Colorado. In July and August, she was slated for her basic summer territory, Arkansas, Texas, and Oklahoma for the encampments, always the high point of her year. She maintained her schedule that summer and added some additional states. She not only addressed the farmers and others in her audiences on the usual subjects, but she also discussed the war in Europe. O'Hare had already dealt with the issue of war in her columns. Her occasional writings in that vein had led the Women's National Committee of the Socialist party to invite her to write a pamphlet on war, which the committee planned to distribute widely, although somehow the project never came to fruition. O'Hare had published columns of some length on the subject of war in Mexico out of her concerns that that nation's revolution and subsequent internal strife and guerilla warfare might be exploited and manipulated by American business interests. O'Hare, in fact, had been south of the border in Juarez when a revolt broke out that helped lead to the overthrow of the Diaz regime, and after that she retained a keen interest in events in Mexico. She wrote that business interests, which she called the "Plunderbund," in the United States and elsewhere "know[s] no race, creed or national lines" and was anxious to get a death grip on Mexico. She stressed to her readers that the American press was screeching for intervention. The result might well be a war that would soak that country "with blood and dot her mountains and plains with the rotting carcasses of working men." But she warned that the capitalists would have to do their own fighting without proxies: "We of the working class . . . , have no stolen lands, mines or oil fields in Mexico to spill our blood for." Later she wrote of the "farce comedy invasion" that chased Villa out of the border states, expending lives, disrupting families, and costing the United States millions of dollars, which should have been spent on social needs.

These same themes were soon echoed in O'Hare's columns and talks, which focused on the European battlefield. Seven months into the war, she began to demand that the United States Congress exercise its power to stop the slaughter in Europe. It could bring the war to a halt almost instantaneously by preventing the exportation of food and ammunition to the warring nations, she wrote. In a reflection of the phrase of the novelist Émile Zola, from some twenty years before, she composed a stirring column entitled "I Denounce" in which she attacked the policies of the federal government. The unemployment in the United States that first winter of the war was the responsibility of a government that refused to wage "a war on poverty and unemployment" because of its obscene pursuit of profits for capitalism at any price. She declared, "I denounce them [the governing class] and declare their guilt and I challenge them to answer."

Three months later, in June 1915, O'Hare asked, "Shall our sons become cannon meat?" Almost two full years before the official American intervention in World War I, she predicted, "War is striding in seven-league boots across the Atlantic" and soon, she predicted, the newspapers would bear the headline, "Extra! War Declared on Germany!" The war would come to the United States, she explained, because Europe had been "skinned and picked to the last bone, but America is fat and juicy for the slaughter" with its investment capital, its young men, and raw materials. She pondered whether women could make a difference in heading off the march toward war. She urged American women to become antiwar activists. If not, they might find themselves bereft of their loved ones and, as in Europe, she wrote, then might face government demands for another generation of war babies.

Kate and Frank O'Hare together composed an antiwar play to dramatize the issues. A three-act play, it was published in booklet form by the *National Rip-Saw,* and it was performed on the socialist lecture circuit in 1915 and 1916 all across the country. Its popularity inspired a similar play that was produced in St. Louis by the local Woman's Council, and Kate O'Hare charged that their play had been plagiarized. Entitled "World Peace," it was an unimaginative didactic work, but its straightforward and uncomplicated message was popular with audiences. On the stage, the European heads of state—the kaiser, the czar and the other rulers—are shown being manipulated by businessmen and armaments manufacturers. The workers initially hesitate over marching off to kill the workers of other nations but are soon convinced that they must fight for God and country. War then erupts, and soon the United States, despite the misgivings of some, ties its economy to those of the warring parties. To the concerned who encourage peace missions, American business interests respond with disdain.

"Drummer: I should say not! . . . Not when our factories are running twenty-four hours a day, not when we are getting a hundred per cent advance on our shoes, not when unemployment here in the United States makes it possible to work our employees twelve hours a day and cut wages to the bone."

Crowds of citizens of the warring nations, including children, listen to a dialogue, which features a distraught "Columbia," while the character "America" reinforces the argument that war means opportunity. Bankers and drummers back up the views of "America" until a character called the "Messenger" is sent by the Europeans and tries to persuade "America" to discontinue its trade with the belligerents. Finally the character "Democracy" appears:

"Democracy: . . . Remember, this is a Republic. When the people speak it is in the voice of command. The people are demanding . . . differences between nations . . . be settled by mediation and that war . . . be driven off the earth. Declare an embargo on the exportation of war munitions, issue an official demand for mediation and, like dew from Heaven, peace shall bless the earth."

Eventually, characters named "Red Cross" and "Medical Science" care for the wounded, while "Charity" and "Religion" offer bread, and workers enter with hammers to rebuild, having realized that they were foolish to join in the petty squabbles of the ruling class. "America" recants and speaks to "Columbia":

"America: You are right. The blood-stained gold of war is not good business."

In chorus, "Mediators" shout out: "Hear! Hear! World Federation is the next historic step in the onward march of human progress. What say you all?" The European rulers seated on stage look doubtful while the people rally around a flag of brotherhood.

The O'Hares developed a number of themes in the play that fit into the framework of at least twenty-five years of international socialist doctrine on war, imperialism, and economics. International wars were viewed as capitalist induced for the sake of markets and trade, and Socialists believed that workers had no interest in fighting against one another for the advancement of capitalism. In fact, they argued that workers would refuse directives to slaughter one another. Building on various interpretations of Marx's views, Socialists saw workers as without a country, and organized socialist parties assigned themselves the task of encouraging the potential international solidarity of workers everywhere. They hoped to undermine the arms race, to prevent wars, and—should they nevertheless be declared—devise strategies to interfere with their prosecution. Many Socialists, however, believed that they had to keep in step with the views of organized labor in their respective countries on this issue. The fullest antiwar policies adopted by the Second International occurred at two consecutive Congresses in the half-dozen years preceding the war, at Stuttgart in 1907 and Amsterdam in 1910. The International adopted a policy of encouraging concerted action against any imminent outbreak of war. Once a war began, Socialists were instructed to use it to promote the fall of capitalism. Wrangling occurred over what the "concerted action" might involve—debate, agitation, general strikes, or insurrections—and no consensus emerged. The Socialist Party of America's contingent voted with the majority against an explicit endorsement of the general strike. Basically, the American Socialists endorsed the principle of opposition to wars by all, albeit, unspecified, means, and their fundamental party policy regarding war was the promotion of arbitration and disarmament.

When the European war began, to the dismay of American Socialists the majority of the Socialists sitting in the parliaments of various belligerent countries supported their national war efforts and voted to finance them. The Socialist Party of America issued a proclamation that it "in conformity with the declarations of the international Socialist movement, hereby reiterates its opposition to this and all other wars . . . war being . . . destructive of the ideals of brotherhood and humanity to which the international Socialist movement is dedicated."

Six months later the Socialist party recommended detailed policies for dealing with the war in Europe. Initially, in August 1914, a routine statement was issued, condemning the ruling classes for the war. Within months, the party—as had O'Hare in her writings—opposed American exports to aid the warring parties and called for antiwar demonstrations. Party statements expressed concern for the American food supply, as exports began to flow toward European markets, and recommended the nationalization of the food industry. That next winter, the party executive announced a series of peace proposals. It recommended a peace without indemnities or forced annexations, an international court to settle disputes and an international league to maintain peace, worldwide disarmament, the internationalization of strategic waterways, neutralization of the seas, and the extension of political and industrial democracy. The proposals were not without controversy, as many party members criticized one point or another, especially that the program differed little from nonsocialist peace proposals and that its preamble's condemnation of offensive wars suggested an acceptance of defensive wars. The membership, in a referendum, accepted the peace program and amended the party's constitution to provide for the expulsion of any Socialist holding a public office who voted for war or war appropriations. The members also voted against a controversial measure calling for a national referendum before war could be declared.

The Socialists of St. Louis assumed the same general stance toward the war. Their newspaper, *St. Louis Labor,* demonstrated perhaps more foresight about the possibility of the war spreading to the United States than almost any other paper in the country when it raised that alarm the very month the war began. The party sponsored an antiwar meeting on August 16 at New Club Hall that attracted two thousand people. Speeches were given in thirteen languages, with one of the main speakers, G. A. Hoehn, emphasizing that the war amounted to a conspiracy of the rulers and the capitalists against the people of all of the countries involved. The crowd passed a series of resolutions that evening, including one demanding that no American loans or foodstuffs be sent to the belligerents. Meanwhile, the leaders of the local labor movement moved in tandem with the Socialists. William Brandt, who was at the time the Socialist party secretary, drafted the statement of the Central Trades and Labor Unions expressing its solidarity with the people of all the belligerent countries and condemning the ruling class for the war. Rueben T. Wood, the head of the State Federation of Labor and still a Socialist, called the war a capitalistic adventure.

O'Hare's attention to the war intensified as various events, especially, for example, the sinking of the British Cunard liner *Lusitania* in May 1915, with the loss of 1,153 lives (including those of 128 Americans), alarmed the public and began to suggest the possibility of American involvement. O'Hare contemplated a race for the United States Senate, which would mean greater media attention to her remarks. By the time that she accepted her party's nomination, the preparedness controversy of 1916 had overwhelmed other issues so that the war was almost the only topic of her campaign, as indeed it was in the national party's campaign for the presidency. Defections from the party by some of the reformist leadership, particularly the native-born, began to occur as individuals started to waiver over the preparedness issue. O'Hare herself remained faithful to party policy. She began to attack nationalism explicitly, despite the dangers in such a climate, and wrote a column in which she took to task those who were proclaiming that they were Americans first in their loyalties and Socialists thereafter. She labeled that perspective cant and argued,

I am a Socialist, a labor unionist and a follower of the Prince of Peace, FIRST; and an American, second. I will serve my class, before I will serve the country that is owned by my industrial masters. If need be, I will give my life and the life of my mate, to serve my class BUT NEVER WITH MY CONSENT WILL THEY BE GIVEN TO ADD TO THE PROFITS AND PROTECT THE STOLEN WEALTH OF THE BANKERS, FOOD SPECULATORS AND AMMUNITION MAKERS. . . . The world is my country, the workers are my countrymen, peace and social justice are my creeds, and to these and these alone I owe loyalty and allegiance.

In St. Louis as elsewhere, groups, often led by business circles, began to organize to promote public acceptance of economic ties to England and France and of preparedness. As early as 1915, the Navy League organized a branch in St. Louis to encourage preparedness, followed by the establishment of a branch of the National Security League. Mayor Kiel appointed a committee on national defense consisting of one hun-

dred well-known municipal leaders, including Augustus A. Busch and
Archbishop John J. Glennon. It sponsored banquets, pageants, and women's auxiliary groups. President Woodrow Wilson came to St. Louis on
February 3, 1916, during his national speaking tour on behalf of preparedness. He addressed a responsive crowd of perhaps eighteen thousand at the Coliseum, with about as many people milling around outside
cheering him.

Some Socialists circulated through the crowd in front of the Colesium distributing antipreparedness circulars declaring that preparedness was another name for militarism. The party as well as the Central
Trades and Labor Unions continued to issue statements imploring the
president to do everything possible to keep the country out of war. The
Socialists continued to hold antiwar rallies, bringing in speakers from
the national party, such as James Maurer, a Pennsylvania state legislator
and the head of that state's Federation of Labor. They supported nonsocialist opponents of preparedness who spoke in St. Louis such as progressive Republican Amos Pinchot, economist A. A. Berle, and Rabbi
Stephen S. Wise. They also supported the work of a new local group
called the American Neutrality League. All in all, organizational activities on both sides of the preparedness argument competed frantically for
public attention.

A preparedness parade of almost sixty thousand marchers was held
on June 3, 1916. Local labor declined an invitation from the National
Security League to participate. Three months later in September, the
state convention of the Missouri Federation of Labor condemned the
war for extending militarism to the United States. But as war issues increasingly swirled about it, local labor began to waiver and, despite the
arguments of Socialists, endorsed Wilson for a second term. Woodrow
Wilson had been nominated for his second term in St. Louis where the
Democratic Party held its convention in June. He won not only the federation's endorsement but more votes in the German wards than he had
in 1912, although the city's German vote went to the Republican candidate, Charles Evans Hughes. Wilson carried Missouri. The state's vote

for the socialist presidential candidate was only half of what it had been in 1912 but, more than any other factor, that significant drop in support was probably due to the fact that the party's perennial candidate, Debs, did not run for the presidency in 1916. The candidate, Allan L. Benson, was an antipreparedness journalist who was hardly known in the Socialist party. Most of the residents of the state of Missouri, as of the nation, were moving toward acceptance of war. Even so, some of the state's Congressional representatives played major roles in opposing Wilson's preparedness measures in the first months of 1917, as well as his request to the Congress for a declaration of war. Opponents included Senator William J. Stone of Missouri, the head of the Senate Foreign Relations Committee.

Kate O'Hare was not a member of the Socialist party's National Executive Committee during that harried spring of 1917 after the German government resumed its policy of unrestricted submarine warfare. Therefore, she was not involved in its efforts to counter the trend toward public acceptance of intervention, but she supported the committee's activities. The committee encouraged socialist comrades in Europe to hold an international conference to help end the war; it telegraphed President Wilson demanding that he impose a full embargo on belligerents; it arranged mass demonstrations in cooperation with other antiwar groups; and it asked party members to demand that their Congressional representatives support peace initiatives. Finally, the party executive committee, realizing the odds against the success of the antiwar forces, decided to call an emergency convention to plan policy for possible wartime conditions. The convention was scheduled for April 7, 1917, at the Planters Hotel in St. Louis. As it turned out, the convention was gaveled to order the day after the United States Congress declared war on the German Empire.

In St. Louis and on the road, Kate O'Hare had, during those busy months, been churning out her columns for the *National Rip-Saw*. With war a reality and the delegates to the convention gathering in St. Louis, she began to develop an appropriate socialist response to the new situation. O'Hare was a delegate to the convention, and hers was one of the leading voices that determined party policy at that fateful time. An opening rally was held at the Odeon before an audience of two thousand. The party's executive secretary, Adolph Germer, greeted the audience as "comrades, friends, and secret service men," for it was clear that federal agents were present to observe the proceedings. Major party leaders spoke, and Frank O'Hare was the presiding officer. The convention's sessions at the Planters Hotel were lively and even cantankerous as the almost two hundred delegates met under the American flag and the red banner for over an eight-day period. While they remained almost unanimous in their opposition to American involvement in the war, given that Socialists with contrary views, such as A. M. and May Wood Simons and Charles Edward Russell, were abandoning the party over the issue, nevertheless, strong differences of opinion existed over what degree of opposition the party should mount to national policy.

Kate O'Hare was one of three St. Louis delegates present, along with Brandt and Hoehn, the "big three" of the host party, and Frank O'Hare served as sergeant-at-arms. Kate O'Hare was totally involved in the proceedings—presiding at sessions and contributing motions. In some ways, that exhilarating week was one of the high points of her life. She was selected to chair the proceedings on the second day, an honorary post which circulated daily. The delegates later that day elected the convention's major policy-making body to formulate recommendations to the entire convention, and O'Hare won more votes than anyone else to that committee of fifteen, supported by seventy percent of those voting. No one had any doubt of where she stood, for her columns were widely read by party members. She at once resigned her honorary post, and presided for three tumultuous days of nonstop sessions in which the committee heard statements from any delegate who wished to present his or her views. O'Hare supported the majority report. In its opposition to national policy and in its support of international solidarity, the committee was more consistent with the longtime socialist policy of international brotherhood than the European socialist parties had been. In words which baldly challenged government policy, the report declared that "in modern history there has been no war more unjustifiable than the war in which we are about to engage. No greater dishonor had ever been forced upon a people." The report encouraged workers of all nations to refuse to support their governments at war.

O'Hare was enthusiastic about the majority report, but she opposed the two minority reports, one which merely echoed the successful report and the other which equivocated. The majority report was endorsed by an overwhelming vote of the delegates, and O'Hare and the others cheered a telegram from Debs, absent from a convention as usual, in which he urged them to continue their opposition to the war. One of O'Hare's own proposals to toughen the preamble to the report was accepted. It offered a warning to the workers of America against the "snare and delusion of so-called defensive warfare." Demonstrating no fear of antagonizing the American government, she announced that the government would not dare to move against the Socialists there because St. Louis, she declared, was so antiwar. She also supported a successful motion placing the party on record as demanding that any federal conscription program must be preceded by a national referendum. In all of the debates, in committee, and in plenary sessions, O'Hare played a major role and was one of only two delegates who were granted additional time to present their views. The so-called St. Louis Proclamation recommended a course of action to the party. The membership was to continue to pursue the class struggle by opposing the war and any military or industrial conscription, food exports or war taxes, it was to resist any encroachments on the Bill of Rights or on labor's activities, and it was to encourage the nationalization of major industries and natural resources. The passage of this program completed the major work of the convention, and the delegates went home to face the future.

The hectic eight days of lengthy sessions from morning to night was followed by misgivings on the part of some delegates. Some regretted that the antiwar policies had not gone far enough because of the convention's effort to retain as much of the membership's support as possible.

They had wanted a stronger statement condemning all wars and damning the European Socialists for their support of the current war. Others condemned the policies as immoderate and inviting the antagonism of the American people. O'Hare showed no concerns, for party positions harmonized with many of those which she had staked out since 1914. Following the close of the convention, she proceeded to speak in St. Louis and on tour in support of the party positions. Within a week of the convention, she told an audience in Atlanta that the working class had nothing to gain from American involvement in the European war. She attacked food speculators, ammunition manufacturers, and oil and coal trusts, and endorsed the idea of nationalization of areas of the economy significant to the war effort. O'Hare invited those who wished to fight for special interests to feel free to do so but, she was quoted as telling her audience, "We should fight conscription." And, in a sentiment she had often before expressed, she stressed that American women would bear the greatest burden—the loss of loved ones.

On both the lecture circuit and in her writings, she criticized the new selective service system, undaunted by the fact that many St. Louis residents were organizing parades to escort young men to register. She wrote that a few million young men were being conscripted "to fight the battles of the Bank of England" and that soon young women also would be conscripted for industrial work at cheap wages. O'Hare condemned war policies established without a national referendum. She also attacked the U.S. Congress for allowing wartime inflation to push up food and fuel costs.

O'Hare spoke out against the emerging jingoistic fervor that was being stoked by President Wilson's newly appointed Committee on Public Information and by various unofficial state-level loyalty leagues. She criticized the Espionage Act, passed by Congress in June. Under that legislation, anyone reporting inexact news which sought to interfere with the armed forces, or cause military insubordination, or obstruct conscription was susceptible to punishment of fines or twenty-year prison terms or both. Any periodicals carrying such reports could lose their second-class mailing privileges and, hence, their ability to reach out to the reading public. Within a month of the passage of the Espionage Act, various socialist, foreign-language, and even progressive periodicals began to run afoul of the Office of the Postmaster General, which implemented the legislation. Various party newspapers, as well as movement papers, including *The Appeal to Reason* and the *National Rip-Saw,* lately renamed *Social Revolution,* could no longer circulate issues to their readers through the mails. Many of these newspapers soon ceased publication, and their editors were indicted.

In the meantime, the city of St. Louis underwent the same influences as the rest of the country. Its branches of various preparedness groups evolved into national security associations in one form or another. In general, public opinion had seemed to be swayed toward acceptance of war by the events of late winter of 1917. Almost alone among St. Louis English-language publications, a few days before the declaration of war *St. Louis Labor* had insisted that Americans were strongly opposed to intervention and demanded a referendum. On March 30, a large meeting to rally the peace forces was held at Sheldon Memorial Hall. Sponsored by the Socialist party, a so-called Emergency Peace Committee, and a group calling itself the Women's Party of St. Louis, it apparently attracted only members of the sponsoring groups.

The night before President Wilson signed the war resolution, a large Loyalty League rally was held in the Coliseum to demonstrate support for his expected action. It was sponsored by the local branch of the National Organization for Universal Training and was endorsed by Mayor Kiel (who had only two years before appeared at rallies in support of the German war effort) who asked that American flags be flown throughout the city. One week later schools and stores were closed as residents were encouraged to turn out for a parade on behalf of the war effort. Later in April, various organizational efforts to support the war were unleashed. A state Council of Defense to promote mobilization was formed. A Women's Committee of the Council was established to win women away from remaining peace groups. The metropolitan dailies supported these various campaigns, and the influential *Post-Dispatch* railed against "luke-warmers." Following this first flush of enthusiasm, both spontaneous and artificial, local German-Americans began to experience the hostility of other St. Louisans. German instruction was dropped from the public school curriculum, only native-born teachers were to be hired, symphonies and libraries no longer allowed German music and literature, the city ceased printing its proceedings in the German language, and it began to rename Germanic-sounding streets.

Against the din and clamor of the war supporters, organized antiwar voices could hardly be heard. The local Socialists were on the defensive and had few, if any, allies in their lonely opposition to the war. In early summer, the various journalists associated with the handful of socialist publications, *Social-Revolution, St. Louis Labor,* the *Arbeiter Zeitung,* and the recently established paper called *Pro-Humanity,* were all visited by agents of the Justice Department. Phil Wagner, Henry Tichenor, William Brandt, Gustave Hoehn, and Otto Vierling, with whom in one way or another O'Hare had worked, were called before a U.S. Attorney. They received vague warnings from agents to "behave themselves" after no evidence of ties to the German government were found, and their "cases" were referred to the Post Office Department to determine whether the mails should be closed to them. The Missouri Federation of Labor, despite its skepticism, rallied to the war effort. President Wood himself, only a few months after having condemned the European war as a capitalistic adventure, accepted a seat on the Missouri Council of Defense. The Federation aligned itself not with its socialist comrades as it had done so routinely in the past but with the American Federation of Labor and its support for the war. The Central Trades and Labor Unions, having a few months earlier voted three to one against American intervention, maintained as much silence as possible now on the subject of the war.

Nevertheless, Kate O'Hare plugged along, continuing to support the party's antiwar policy. She still traveled across the country, addressing the public as always. In the first three months following American entry into the war, O'Hare honed and scripted a speech with greater care and precision than had been her habit. Eschewing her usual off-the-cuff approach, and intent on making the most persuasive talk that she could concerning the war, she gave essentially the same lecture wherever she went. She later said that she presented her talk under the title "Socialism and the War" seventy-five times throughout the country, but media reports suggest that she might have given it twice as often. The point of her talk was that while the socialist movement had no role in the onset of the war, its events were clearly moving the world forward to a higher plane of international solidarity and socialism. While the socialist movement had so often been attacked as leading to bloodshed and confiscation, in fact, she said, capitalism had led the public into the brutality of war and the confiscation of property and lives. Socialists, she wrote, were the only ones who had stood against war. It was the Socialists, she told her audiences, who opposed the war for which they were "cursed and reviled; they were called seditious, traitorous enemies of their country."

O'Hare mourned what had occurred on the European battlefields. She spoke of "festering in the July heat the bodies of millions of men. I know that, scattered there, are the bodies of the boys with whom I worked in Dublin; there are the miners who sang for me in Wales; there are the Scottish Highlanders and the London newspaper men." She spoke movingly of war's immorality, pointing out the appalling reversal of normal ethical standards whereby anyone plunging "a bit of steel into the heart of another" in spring 1914, would have been branded a murderer, but in summer such a man received medals. Women were subject to similar reversals of standards. In spring 1914, a woman who gave herself to a man without benefit of marriage became an outcast and her baby cursed, but thereafter with millions being killed, "if a woman gave herself to a man . . . she was a perfectly honorable heroine and her child was a patriotic 'war baby.' "

She explained to her audiences that the war was a matter of trade and profits. Was ours really a war effort dedicated to democracy and humanity, as President Wilson maintained, she asked her audiences? O'Hare said she wished she could believe that. But it would be easier to give the war whole-hearted support "for democracy in Germany, if we had a little [more] of it at home." Basically, war had come because the German U-boats had threatened international trade, she argued.

O'Hare noted with grim satisfaction that each nation involved in the war had found it necessary to turn to "at least a modified form of Socialism." It had occurred in the European nations, and the United States was following that same path. A form of state socialism where the state operated or owned important industries was adopted for the sake of efficiency. This system was not social democratic because the masses of the people did not control the government but nevertheless the inefficiency, if not the heartlessness, of capitalism had been understood. She denied that Socialists were hindering the successful prosecution of the war or of the draft. While they opposed the war, if this war was the path that had been chosen to reach socialism, the Socialists ultimately accepted it, she said.

In the course of her hour-long talk, she offered a sub-theme which was later to be viewed as the most significant aspect of what she said. It was one of the only times in her address that she might have departed in any way from her prepared remarks. O'Hare was aware that agents of the Justice Department were in the crowd. For just as every issue of each newspaper that might be critical of the war was being screened, so every public speaker was being observed and his or her words noted and transcribed. She had developed the habit of sending complimentary tickets for her talks to local law enforcement agents. In her talk, when she referred to the role to which war was reducing the women of Europe, she had maintained that women now held "the status of breeding animals on a stock farm." What she was later charged with having stated was that American women were now "nothing more nor less than brood sows to raise children to get into the army and be made into fertilizer." These remarks were said to have been delivered in the county seat of Bowman, North Dakota, a village in the southwest corner of the state bordering Montana and South Dakota which O'Hare later described as

". . . a little sordid, wind-blown, sun-blistered, frost-scarred town on the plains." They were embedded in some form in the talk which she had already given scores of times in places as varied as San Francisco during the emotional days of the Tom Mooney case and in the vicinity of Bisbee, Arizona, at the time of the Wobbly banishments. In Bowman, which claimed a population of almost five hundred, O'Hare delivered her usual remarks before over one hundred people at the Cozy Theater on July 17, 1917, and her talk led to her arrest, trial, conviction, and imprisonment under the Espionage Act.

The day after her talk, July 18, 1917, M. S. Byrne of the U.S. Navy, who had been on furlough and in the audience, sent a telegram to his superior officer in Minneapolis. He wrote, "Kate Richards O'Hare, former editor of *National Rip-Saw,* spoke here last night. Highly unpatriotic tending to discourage enlistments and resisting draft. States among other things that it was a good thing that those who did enlisted [sic] did so as they were no good for anything but fertilizer anyhow. What action can be taken. People highly indignant." A naval recruiter at once notified the Justice Department which, in turn, asked North Dakota U.S. Attorney, M. A. Hildreth, to investigate the charges of discouraging enlistments and advising draft resistance. The Justice Department wanted Hildreth to determine if, in fact, O'Hare had merely criticized the law or had actually advised resistance to the draft. Twelve days after her Bowman appearance, O'Hare was arrested on July 29 at Devil's Lake, North Dakota, and taken the next day to Fargo for arraignment.

Ostensibly free on her own recognizance, O'Hare thereafter lost whatever privacy she had ever known. She later said that "Since the day I made that speech, no Queen of royal blood has been so carefully cared for as I have been by the U.S. Department of Justice. . . . They are always on the job." She reported that agents went everywhere with her, without any effort to conceal their presence. They checked her luggage, her habits, her associates. The satirical aspect of the situation did not escape her nor did her sense of wry humor desert her, for she even was known to help the agents transcribe her remarks by offering corrections.

The reasons behind the arrest apparently related more to the situation in Bowman than to any purported remarks of O'Hare's. The state of North Dakota was at the time torn between factions for and against the Nonpartisan League, then spreading across the Upper Midwest. The league, representing the grievances and goals of some of the farmers ever since its inception in 1915, had been supplanting the local Socialists as a growing protest movement. The state of North Dakota had claimed the strongest socialist presence in the Northern Plains, electing a few mayors, a state legislator and at least one county official. The center of its strength was in and around Minot, in the north-central part of the state, and in the counties to its west and north. The league was spearheaded by former socialist organizers, especially Arthur C. Townley. A non-socialist organization, the league demanded state ownership of grain elevators, packing houses and other commercial enterprises which impacted on farmers. The Nonpartisan League came to dominate state politics and elected a governor, Lynn J. Frazier, in 1916, who swept each county and received the greatest majority any gubernatorial candidate had ever attained.

In Bowman, the local leaders of the Nonpartisan League were Edward P. and Lillian Totten. Edward Totten, a judge of the County Court and previously Bowman County State's Attorney, published the *Bowman Citizen,* and his brother, George A. Totten, Sr., a former minister, was a controversial appointee to the State Board of Regents. O'Hare was very enthusiastic about the league; rather than seeing it as a competing organization to the Socialists, she viewed it as a "revolutionary" social phenomenon. During her visit to Bowman she socialized with the Tottens. Lillian Totten was the postmistress who, it appears, was being subjected to a vendetta by her predecessor in that office, and an unsuccessful effort to indict her had been made. It was anonymously reported that Lillian Totten had attended O'Hare's talk and had supported her remarks. Thereafter, anti-league forces, according to Robert L. Morlan, the major historian of the Nonpartisan League, "immediately heralded far and wide" the incident, and "North Dakotans were never given the opportunity to forget the charges." The state of North Dakota had been strongly anti-interventionist but during the war it zealously filled its liberty loan quotas. The Nonpartisan League, which tried to walk a narrow line of criticism of war profiteering while accommodating itself to the war effort, was painted by its opponents as disloyal. In short, Kate O'Hare had innocently entered an arena ripe for charges under the Espionage Act. Her case did not even sufficiently satisfy some local appetites. An indictment against Lillian Totten failed, but almost one year after O'Hare's address, her old teacher, Walter Thomas Mills, then about eighty years old, was indicted and tried for a speech which he made in Fargo in June 1918. At his subsequent trial, the judge, Charles F. Amidon, a league sympathizer, deciding that the emotional climate made balanced deliberation unlikely, directed the jury to return a verdict of not guilty.

Between July when charges were pressed against Kate O'Hare and her trial in Bismarck in December, she and Frank were understandably worried. The strain of frequent separations and conflict over family responsibilities were evidently exacerbated at this time by the growing tension. Kate continued to travel and speak to focus publicity on her case, while Frank tried to write her cheerful letters. He told his sister that he wished he could take some of the strain off his wife by touring in her place, but the public needed to see her. Kate O'Hare began some of her talks that fall by telling the audience that they were looking at an indicted person. Increasingly, she addressed subjects other than the topic of the speech for which she was indicted, speaking broadly on international developments.

The O'Hares had left the staff of the *National Rip-Saw* at the beginning of 1917, and their home base for much of that year was in the vicinity of Tampa, Florida. Both Kate and Frank had retained their interest in labor education and cooperative living, ever since each had separately enrolled at the socialist training school in Girard. They wanted to reestablish themselves in a congenial rural setting, with Kate even contemplating giving up her field work. The O'Hares had long watched with interest the industrial school and collectively owned colony that had been organized a few years earlier at Ruskin, Florida, on the west coast of that state. The school first had been established in 1909 embedded in a Christian socialist colony by an idealistic minister, George Mc.K. Miller. It was opened on the site of a collapsed cooperative colony at Trenton, Missouri, which had encompassed stores and factories as well as agricultural and other miscellaneous enterprises. Miller's ideas on worker education had been familiar to Frank O'Hare since he initially met Miller in 1901. The school was moved by Miller from Trenton to Glen Ellyn, Illinois, and finally to Florida. He established Ruskin on twelve thousand acres as a socialist society, with five- to ten-acre farms offered for sale to like-minded buyers. The small school which was set up as part of the colony was called Ruskin College and required the students to work on behalf of the colony. The O'Hares, believing that a change of scene would be good for the family, moved to Ruskin in the spring. Kate still had to travel as her lecture schedule required, while Frank remained there. He put in a garden and worked on colony projects. The children moved from St. Louis to Ruskin when the school year concluded. In fall, Dick attended Ruskin, while Kathleen and the twins enrolled in public schools in the area.

The bulk of Frank's time at Ruskin was devoted to efforts on behalf of Kate O'Hare's defense. The couple had decided to handle fundraising and publicity themselves rather than leave those efforts to the Socialist party's National Office. That was probably a wise decision because in the first year of the war many of the leaders of the party were indicted under the Espionage Age. Kate O'Hare's indictment was followed by conspiracy charges against Victor Berger and Adolf Gerner, a mine organizer who was then the executive secretary of the party. Also indicted were William F. Kruse, director of the Young People's Socialist League, the Rev. Irwin St. John Tucker, former head of the party's Literature Department, J. Louis Engldahl, editor of several party newspapers, and Rose Pastor Stokes, a very popular public speaker, as well as other prominent party members, including a full year after O'Hare, Gene Debs.

Later the O'Hares resented the National Office for not having paid sufficient attention to her case, and they felt that her indictment, compared to others', had been virtually neglected by the socialist press. They were bitter about what they perceived to be the party's failure to get the facts out to the public. They came to agree that Kate's sense—which she had long tried to shake and which Frank had scoffed at—was correct that she, as a woman, was snubbed by the male leadership. But both of them were sustained by their belief that the rank and file of the party was behind her, and others of the public were certain to rally behind her.

Kate O'Hare went to Bismarck for her trial directly from three months on the road. Frank remained at home at Ruskin with the children and, consequently, she did not have his support during those difficult days as she stayed alone in a hotel. Just before the trial opened, O'Hare went to Bowman, a distance of 150 miles, to spend a day lining up her witnesses. A blizzard was developing as she finished arranging for twelve witnesses, mostly non-Socialists who had attended her talk, when she was notified abruptly that her case had been put forward on the docket. Frantically, she found someone to drive her through the night to a railway line that could return her in time to Bismarck for the trial. Exhausted and isolated, O'Hare faced the opening of proceedings on December 5, 1917. She was confronted with two counts of violating section three of the Espionage Act, intending to obstruct recruitment and enlistments in the armed forces. Her attorney, V. R. Lovell, a well-known local attorney, and a Democrat, moved for dismissal at the beginning, in the middle, and at the end of the trial, at each point arguing that O'Hare was guilty of no offence and that none had been proven.

The very opening scenes of the trial convinced O'Hare that she was not likely to be found innocent. From a list of sixty possible jury members, twelve men were impanelled; all of them were nonleaguers and established businessmen in a region swarming with card-carrying league members who were depressed farmers. In addition, the jury membership was heavily Roman Catholic, which O'Hare well knew suggested an antipathy to the subject of socialism. The judge, Martin J. Wade, was a sudden substitute assigned to the case two weeks before the date of the trial in place of the sympathetic Judge Amidon. Judge Wade had already made anti-Socialist statements, and his Roman Catholicism further convinced O'Hare that he could not see that she received a fair trial. Also, he had made remarks expressing disapproval of women in public life, which reinforced her perception. But O'Hare's efforts to have him removed were to no avail.

Testimony affirming O'Hare's "brood sow" remarks as demonstrating an intent to interfere with the war effort was given by five witnesses, only two of whom had heard her talk. Of the twelve witnesses O'Hare had lined up for her defense, all of whom had been present at the Cozy Theater, eight were allowed to testify, and they all swore that she had not made those purported remarks. Further, her witnesses took pains to try to explain that, as their affidavits expressed it later during the appeals process, "a bitter political feud existed" in Bowman County between the Republican county leader, James E. Phelan, and the Tottens of the Nonpartisan League, and that O'Hare "was used simply as a lever to attack the Tottens." But this background information was not allowed to be fully developed for the jury. When Kate O'Hare took the stand in her own defense, she explained that the nature of her talk was a presentation of socialist ideology, and she denied having any purpose or intent of obstructing enlistments or recruitment. She maintained that she had dropped her opposition to conscription as soon as conscription became law and that she did not oppose Liberty Loan drives or Red Cross activities. She also denied using words and phrases like "fertilizers" and "brood sows" in the manner charged in the indictment. O'Hare told the court that she hailed from a family which had been in the United States for generations and had fought in all of this country's wars. She declared that "[T]he great objective of my lecture was to prove to the people that we all hated war and that my belief was that the way to kill war was by eliminating the profits from war."

The prosecutor told the jury that O'Hare was not a criminal but a dangerous woman, dangerous because she was "shrewd and brainy," which led O'Hare to tell audiences later that she had been indicted because she was brainy. The prosecution's main argument was that the remarks which were attributed to O'Hare directly undermined the patriotism of the American people, that they were made willfully in order to obstruct enlistment and recruitment and, in short, were in violation of the Espionage Act, while the defense attorney argued that the evidence did not sustain the charges. Judge Wade, a professor of constitutional law who was at the time a member of the U.S. District Court of Iowa, instructed the jury to ignore as irrelevant any testimony that had referred to the Tottens. The judge also advised them that the existing right of free speech, guaranteed by the U.S. Constitution and by the constitution of the state of North Dakota, did not extend to violations of laws passed by the Congress. Further, he invited the jury to take into consideration any general knowledge available to them, including the fact that a nation at war must mobilize soldiers, either through enlistment or conscription, and that the government has the right to protect itself against any who might interfere with those activities. He also expressed the hope that anyone who violated the laws in question would be convicted, which the defense attorney tried unsuccessfully to delete from the charge as prejudicial, inasmuch as the judge had not also expressed the hope that anyone who was innocent would be acquitted.

The jury of businessmen had no trouble deciding the case. They deliberated only briefly while Kate O'Hare chatted with the reporters covering her trial. Unlike other well-known radicals tried under the Espionage Act, O'Hare did not have a husband or family gathered around her at this critical time, and so she endured that hour, as she spent so much of her life, in the company of strangers. The reporters predicted a guilty verdict with a six-months sentence, joking that it was such a foregone conclusion that they had already filed their stories. The jury returned with the expected unanimous decision of guilty.

O'Hare later published articles indicating that she really had no wish to be a martyr. Her strongest hope after the verdict was to move promptly to the sentencing so that she could leave town on bail and arrive home in

Florida for the Christmas holidays. A week delay did occur, however, while Judge Wade procured further information on O'Hare from Justice Department officials in St. Louis to help him decide on a sentence. That delay occasioned the only anger that O'Hare showed during the entire ordeal. When the court reconvened for sentencing, O'Hare was allowed to make a lengthy address, her first chance to demonstrate her flair for words and the eloquence of which she was sometimes capable. O'Hare maintained, as had she and her attorney during the trial, that a person could not be tried for something which she or he had never done, but she said in fact there was a charge that recurrently emerged that had not been stated in the indictment but which was at the heart of the case against her. She explained,

> This crime that was charged by inference in the trial was the same crime, was the same charge that was brought against the first slave rebellion, against the first serf revolt. It was the charge that was brought against Moses and Spartacus, Watt Tyler and Cromwell, George Washington and Patrick Henry, William Lloyd Garrison and Wendell Phillips, and it was the same crime that was charged against Jesus of Nazareth when he stood at the judgment bar of Pontius Pilate. The crime is this: "She stirs up the people." And, Your Honor, if by inference I can be charged with that crime, and tried for it, then, Your Honor, at this point I plead guilty of that crime, if it is a crime. For twenty years I have done nothing but stir up the people.

She told the court,

> I am dangerous to the invisible government of the United States; I am dangerous to the special privileges of the United States; I am dangerous to the white slaver and to the saloonkeeper, and I thank God that at this hour I am dangerous to the war profiteers of this country who rob the people on the one hand, and rob and degrade the government on the other; and then with their pockets and wallets stuffed with the filthy, bloodstained profits of war, wrap the sacred folds of the Stars and Stripes about them and shout their blatant hypocrisy to the world. You can convince the people that I am dangerous to these men; but no jury and no judge can convince them that I am a dangerous woman to the best interests of the United States; and at this hour will

my conviction, with my incarceration behind the bars of a prison have the tendency to cement and hold together the great mass of people in this nation, or will it have the tendency to create hatred and bitterness, . . . and make these [one hundred thousand] people who know me . . . feel that this whole case is nothing but an attempt on the part of the war profiteers to eliminate me and get out of the way a woman that is dangerous to them?

She continued in a prophetic vein:

It may be that down in the dark, noisome, loathsome hells we call prisons, under our modern prison system, there may be a bigger work for me to do than out on the lecture platform. It may be that down there are the things I have sought for all my life. All my life has been devoted to taking light into dark places to ministering to sick souls, to lifting up degraded humanity; and God knows down there in the prisons, perhaps more than any other place on earth, there is need for that kind of work. So if, as it was necessary that Jesus should come down and live among men in order that he might serve them, it is necessary for me to become a convict among criminals in order that I may serve my country there, then I am perfectly willing to perform my service there.

Sounding contrite at this point, she apparently reined herself in from charging that her trial was akin to the witchcraft trials of the seventeenth century. But she published a piece shortly thereafter in which she likened Bismarck to Salem, and that she, like those against whom the cry of witchcraft had been made, was charged with being "shrewd" and "intelligent" and "powerful" and casting an "evil eye" on others. But while she had held off from such a counterattack, Judge Wade was not mollified. In fact, he was angry, and in his long statement before passing sentence on her, he drew on information which he had obtained from a special agent of the St. Louis office of the Federal Bureau of Investigation. The agent informed him that both Kate and Frank O'Hare were radicals who had associated with members of the German-American Alliance, the People's Peace Council and "anything and everything that would give aid and comfort to the enemy." The agent enclosed the Socialist party's resolution on war and militarism from the emergency convention, and he concluded by stating that "Nothing would please this office more then[sic] to hear that she got life."

Judge Wade in his remarks attacked O'Hare for her criticisms of American policy, her failure to praise its institutions, and her prewar play, "World Peace", which he interpreted as sowing the seeds of discontent and even anarchy. He found her to be not only unrepentant but clearly, as the prosecution had maintained, a threat. Accordingly, instead of the six-month prison sentence that had been reported to be his intention, he sentenced her to five years.

O'Hare's ordeal as a defendant at the bar had ended only to be succeeded by the ordeal of a political prisoner. With that thought undoubtedly in mind, she entrained for Ruskin, arriving just in time for Christmas with her husband and children to spend what appeared to be the last holiday season with her family for the foreseeable future. The next few months saw both Kate and Frank O'Hare try unsuccessfully to unwind. They should have remained at home together in order to relax. However, the tension over her possible imprisonment and the necessity to publicize her case pushed them to travel and brought them near the breaking point. Meanwhile the strain on their marriage was palpable from this point onward. They set up a committee called the Liberty Defense Union, consisting of socialist comrades such as Theresa Malkiel, Scott Nearing, and Helen Phelps Stokes, along with Progressives such as Amos Pinchot and O'Hare's old associate Roger Baldwin. The goal was to organize one hundred subsidiary committees across the country, with other separate groups to be organized as well. The National Office of the Socialist party simultaneously was pressuring the O'Hares to develop a general defense strategy for all party members accused under the Espionage Act instead of only highlighting Kate's struggle. Growing tensions between the O'Hares and the National Office and even between Frank and the normally tranquil Debs embittered the O'Hares. Financial stress plagued them, too. They had to repay Phil Wagner for funds he expended for the expenses of the trial. Eventually, the party executive contributed a few hundred dollars specifically for Kate O'Hare's appeal process but basically the couple had to orchestrate whatever efforts they could. She remained bitter about what she saw as the party officials denigrating the importance of her case and, as late as 1928, threatened to bring up the matter at a socialist convention.

Kate O'Hare undertook a nationwide lecture tour, always with government agents sitting in her audience. Her route took her across the northeast, and her billing featured a series of questions: "Shall the Sentence Stand? Which Shall it Be? A Criminal or Joan of Arc?" In Buffalo the mayor prevented her from speaking because she refused to submit her text in advance. In rural Pennsylvania a district attorney prohibited her appearance at a public school which the local Socialists had arranged. A young colleague, W. E. Zeuch went to Bowman, North Dakota, interviewed dozens of residents and publicized his findings that a fair trial had not been possible in that environment. Independent groups, including the Political Action Committee of the Chicago Church Federation, argued her innocence and attempted to convince President Wilson to intervene in the case.

Crowds of supporters and of the curious came out to see her wherever she was allowed to appear. In the meantime, Judge Wade and U.S. Attorney Hildreth, as well as North Dakota's Senator P. J. McCumber demanded that the Department of Justice see that O'Hare was put behind bars without delay. In fact, the Justice Department received letters and telegrams demanding her incarceration while others insisted that she was innocent. Justice Department officials themselves divided over the case with at least two members of its War Emergency Division arguing that her guilt had not been proven and that, moreover, it appeared to them that she had been convicted by perjured testimony and sentenced by a biased judge.

Those long months as winter faded into spring and then summer saw Kate O'Hare traveling, talking to crowds, and working with the pressure groups that she and Frank had organized. Nevertheless, on October 28, 1918, the Eighth Circuit Court of Appeals confirmed her conviction, and almost six months later, on March 3, 1919, the Supreme Court denied her appeal. At that point, the reality of her sentence had to be faced. She had to serve five years in prison.

On March 25, Kate O'Hare set off on a farewell tour of over a dozen cities en route to Fargo, North Dakota, where she was to surrender to federal marshals. The mass media reported on her tour and described her as vigorous, serene, and seeming to feel that she was starting on an adventure. Thousands came to see her, and many were moved to tears. In her old hometown, St. Louis, where an overflow crowd of five thousand turned out to hear her at the Odeon Theater, an argument between the Police Chief and the Police Board over the propriety of her addressing the crowd nearly led to the cancellation of the talk. In Chicago, the audience filled Orchestra Hall. In New York City, the crowds were sufficiently large that she spoke on two dates while, in contrast, she was not permitted to speak in St. Paul, Minnesota. During the farewell tour, she refrained from concentrating exclusively on her conviction. Instead, she criticized President Wilson directly, which she had avoided earlier, and she urged votes for Socialists in the 1919 elections. She encouraged her audiences to work toward a revolution without bloodshed.

In closing her farewell talk, O'Hare looked to the past and the future and spoke in a personal vein: "I am content. I gave to the service of the working class . . . my girlhood, my young womanhood and my motherhood. I have taken babies unborn into the thick of the class war; I have served in the trenches with a nursing baby at my breast. I leave my children now without my care and protection, but I know that I have only done my duty . . . millions of devoted comrades will never see my children want for anything."

However much Kate O'Hare had prepared herself, the sentence facing her had to seem catastrophic. She was used to a virtually nomadic life. She needed to travel to avoid feeling confined, as someone who, she often remarked, had really enjoyed the outdoors since her earliest years on a homestead. As a woman in her middle years, she was facing the onset of menopause, or as Frank described it, she was at that "time of life . . . when peace and rest and loving care must be hers." Rather than having the leisure to deal with her physiological and psychological needs as they arose, she was confronted with regimentation and confinement.

The significance of the world war for O'Hare should be clear. When that war began in Europe in 1914, she upheld her socialist and internationalist principles, unlike some of her comrades. She condemned the war as an imperialist adventure, and she opposed American intervention in 1917 as economically motivated. She led her socialist comrades in convention in their continued opposition to the war and she toured the country condemning the war as against the best interests of working people. After three months of such speeches, O'Hare was arrested and tried in North Dakota under the Espionage Act. At her trial she somewhat toned down her hostility to the war effort, but the core of her views remained unchanged. For her outspokenness, she was about to pay a steep price.

❧ 7

POLITICAL PRISONER

W hen Kate O'Hare entered prison on April 15, 1919, she became a member of a perhaps not-so-select twentieth-century group. She joined the ranks of those millions of individuals who have been incarcerated for their beliefs, values, or statements. While the phenomenon is not new in world history, it has been an unhappy hallmark of this century. The unrelenting pattern of repression has been repeated in prisons and concentration camps throughout the world: in czarist Russia and the Soviet Union, in Nazi Germany, South Africa, China, and Latin America. In the United States, despite the most explicit guarantees of the Bill of Rights, waves of arrests have occurred in each generation, followed by indictments, trials, and, sometimes, imprisonment, all for the voicing of unpopular opinions. This pattern has been pronounced following each of the world wars. Thus, O'Hare had plenty of company, figuratively speaking, as a prisoner whose words were judged a violation of a law. Sharing her experience were a number of other Socialists, most notably Eugene V. Debs; anarchists, such as Alexander Berkman and Emma Goldman; Wobblies, such as Big Bill Haywood and Ralph Chaplin; Communists, such as Elizabeth Gurley Flynn, Julius and Ethel Rosenberg, and Eugene Dennis; black activists, such as George Jackson and Eldridge Cleaver, and less overtly political activists, such as birth control advocate Margaret Sanger. H. Bruce Franklin has observed that many were incarcerated for statements later generations would commend.

O'Hare's initiation into prison life was reminiscent of Jack London's twenty-five years earlier. Reflecting on his own jailing, he reported it to have had more impact than any other event of his life. London described his experience of being "dressed in" as follows: "carted down country . . . registered at the . . . Penitentiary, had my head clipped and my budding mustache shaved, was dressed in convict stripes, compulsorily vaccinated by a medical student who practiced on such as we, made to march the lock-step, and put to work under the eyes of guards armed with Winchester rifles." While the details were not exactly the same for O'Hare, the thrust of the experience was parallel. She later told her family that she felt stunned during her first day of prison. O'Hare, like London, abruptly became an individual who could show no independence, experience no freedom of choice, and who lived locked indoors with—in her case finally—a permanent address.

In the years since Jack London's prison experience a virtual revolution had occurred in the world of penology. Prisons ceased being bastions of punishment, and they were no longer expected to be financially self-sufficient. Through pressures from an increasingly effective American labor movement, prison labor contracts by independent entrepreneurs became outmoded. Reformatory impulses began to be the American standard, particularly in the northern states. Indeterminate sentences were introduced, parole and probation became commonplace procedures. Programs for first-time and youthful offenders were initiated; corporal punishment was minimized, and capital punishment less frequently utilized. Prison fare became more palatable and balanced, so that the earlier prevalence of scurvy in inmates disappeared. The traditional diet of mush, breads and other carbohydrates, and limited portions of meat was somewhat expanded to include fruit and other nutritional necessities. Dining halls were built, so that meals were less frequently eaten by inmates in their cells. In newly constructed buildings, advances in the standard of living were offered, such as electricity, running water, and showers and toilets in individual cells. In what was clearly a transitional era, the new penology epitomized an effort to rehabilitate so-called deviants, so that they could fit into society, rather than simply to punish them for their offenses. Advances in prison administration also occurred: potentially lucrative patronage appointment were discontinued and central prison boards to manage penal institutions became the norm.

Unfortunately, O'Hare was imprisoned in the Missouri State Penitentiary, the largest and one of the oldest prisons in the country, which had lagged behind professional developments. It clung to archaic practices, perhaps more so than any other penal institution in the United States. The Jefferson City institution still imposed on its inmates the nineteenth-century silence system, convict labor, and hideous striped uniforms. Moreover, it did not segregate prisoners by either seriousness of crime or by hygienic standards, and the women were in a section of a male institution, an outmoded practice. It did not offer prisoners many of the minimum educational or recreational amenities that were becoming customary. It was Kate O'Hare's ill fortune to be incarcerated in a prison that reflected discarded and discredited practices of an earlier generation of penology.

Thus, Missouri was one of the states that ignored many of the progressive developments practiced by other prisons. In fact, as a leading historian of American prisons, Blake McKelvey, has observed, "Missouri was the state that maintained the most wretched and congested prison in the country." McKelvery was referring to the Missouri State Penitentiary, which housed both state and federal prisoners. Missouri had witnessed few protests against contract labor for prisoners; rather, it had been praised for the profits the system earned. Toward the end of the nineteenth century, in fact, operations were expanded, and inmates were assigned work in coal mines. Political control, and patronage appointments, continued until after World War I, and no state board of control over the prison system was instituted. Reforms were attempted, notably by Charles A. Ellwood, who investigated county jails, and by three consecutive reform-minded governors, Joseph Folk, Herbert S. Hadley, and Elliot W. Major. Between 1904 and the war, they all tried to overhaul the system, but none were able "to carry out the Herculean reforms they recognized as necessary in Missouri." Although a State Board of Charities and Corrections and a juvenile court system had been established at the end of the 1890s, their impact was nearly nil. Governor Folk labeled the convict leasing system "a form of slavery," and Governor Hadley sought to humanize the treatment of prisoners. In 1911 the state legislature attempted to end convict leasing, but the implementation of this measure was stalled. In 1915 Governor Major forbade the signing of such contracts and authorized an extension of state-owned industries within the prison system, a modest victory by the State Federation of Labor. However, to inmates of the Jefferson City prison, those various legislative impulses held no meaning whatsoever.

In the country at large, female inmates had traditionally been overlooked by prison reformers. Because women were a small segment of the nation's prison population, it was viewed as inefficient to incur expenditures specifically on their behalf. Accordingly, women were a neglected prison population, whose particular needs were not recognized within a male-oriented system. Women were typically housed in the worst quarters, with any modern facilities or programming used for the larger (male) component of the inmate population. "Mixed institutions" typically denied women classes, exercise opportunities, or any other privileges available to the men, and women inmates were subject to sexual and other abuses. Furthermore, as Estelle B. Freedman, a historian of nineteenth century women's prison experience, has argued, not only did women tend to be marginalized in such institutions, but prison guards and officials were apt to treat them as "fallen women," who were considered to be more debased than the male inmates and less likely to be rehabilitated. The type of work and discipline that were normative in men's prisons were built on military models. A few states, notably New York, Massachusetts, and Indiana, pioneered a different approach with women prisoners: cottage accommodations in place of cells, training for domesticity rather than industry, women custodians instead of men, civilian clothing rather than uniforms, and there were nurseries for the inmates' infants and toddlers, meeting rooms, and gardening opportunities. By O'Hare's prison term, several other states had established such women's facilities and programs for women, but Kate O'Hare was not to enjoy such progressive programming.

Kate O'Hare was accompanied to the Jefferson City penitentiary by Grace Brewer. The O'Hares and the Brewers had shared almost two decades of socialist activities, dating back to Kate O'Hare's days with the Brewers on the *Appeal to Reason* in Girard. Kate no doubt would have preferred that Frank accompany her on the gloomy train ride from St. Louis, but Frank's parenting responsibilities required that he remain home with the children. The O'Hares had already said their goodbyes and made their plans. Frank would visit Kate weekly, if possible, sometimes accompanied by one or another of the children. O'Hare had forbidden her mother, Lucy, now ailing, to make the trip to Jefferson City so that she would not see her daughter in a prison. But at least O'Hare had the support of one of her few close women friends as she entered the fortress-like, eighty-year-old prison on the banks of the Missouri River.

O'Hare signed the prison registry and identified herself as a professional writer, 42 years of age, 5 feet, 8 inches, 143 pounds, with grey hair and hazel eyes. Kate became "number 21669." The "dressing in" was completed as she was given a few changes of clothing made of harsh fabric. She later wrote that the grade of muslin used for undergarments was more typically used for awnings and tents; it was unbearably hot in summer and provided no protection from the cold in winter. She described her basic work dress as coarse and hideous, and the occasional laundering never allowed for what she considered a decent standard of cleanliness. The most difficult aspect of her initiation occurred shortly thereafter, when her gross body measurements were taken. This practice, known as the *Bertillon,* had been adopted from the French penal

system. It was used for purposes of identification until 1929, when fin-
gerprinting was introduced. In describing her ordeal to her husband,
O'Hare noted that she had never been particularly prudish or squeamish
but found that this procedure, which she admitted was courteously administered, took all her poise and every shred of self-control she could
muster.

Aside from this humiliation, O'Hare's initial experiences were not
difficult for her. She had a cell to herself; it was small, seven feet wide,
eight feet across, and seven feet high, and had a steel bunk fastened to
the wall, a chair, a table, cold running water, and a toilet. Her cell had a
concrete floor with steel walls on three sides and bars in front. One of
the twins, Victor, installed chicken wire between the bars to keep out
the rats which plagued the inmates. O'Hare was provided with two bags
of straw to use as a mattress and a pillow, muslin sheets and pillow
cases, and coarse towels and blankets. She was allowed to decorate her
cell and proceeded quickly to put book shelves on one wall to hold her
reading material, knitting needles, knickknacks, photographs, and whatever else Frank brought her. Gradually, she covered the grimy walls
with snapshots of her children, her friends and their children, and other
photos supporters sent to her, learning from the other inmates to affix
them all with chewing gum. All in all, she brought a semblance of hom-
eyness to that most unlikely setting.

There were about eighty prisoners in the women's section out of a
prison population of over twenty-six hundred men. O'Hare was one of
only about twenty "federals." Had she been incarcerated a few years later, she would have served her time in the first federal prison for women,
which was opened in 1927 in Alderson, West Virginia. The inmates
lived in a stifling environment; it could be bitterly cold in winter and
swelteringly hot in summer. They spent five and a half days a week,
nine hours a weekday, working in one of the prison's industrial shops,
performing contract labor for a private manufacturer. Using archaic
sewing machines, they hemmed the fronts and bottoms of blue denim
jumpers and made and attached the collars. A beginner was expected to

finish fifty-five jumpers each day. Those not making their quota were verbally assaulted, denied the most minimal privileges, and required to complete their work at night in their cells (although O'Hare was not required to do so). The abuse that dogged the inmates' every move led O'Hare to characterize prison employees as cases of arrested development, degeneracy, and sexual perversion.

O'Hare, who immediately denounced the work as the worst kind of scab labor, later commented on how this system cheated the people of Missouri: "As nearly as I can determine the State received less than fifty cents a day for my labor, with which it threw in for good measure my maintenance; and I actually produced, at sweatshop wages, about six dollars a day in garments. I was paid fifty cents a month, the State was paid fifty cents a day, and the contractor had a clear profit of $5.48½ per day on my labor." She likened her situation to slavery. She declared, "The moment I entered the prison shop I had ceased to be a white woman belonging to a civilized race and a citizen of a civilized nation . . . and was an . . . exploited slave . . . [like] a white slave in Rome at the beginning of the Christian era."

The onerous task was made even more difficult by the working conditions. One of the political prisoners at Jefferson City likened the shop to Dante's *Inferno*. The building was one of the oldest in the prison complex. Ventilation was totally inadequate; the windows not only too small for the size of the facility, but they were nailed down and painted over to prevent inmates from gazing out. Because no sunlight came in, lights were kept on at all times, but they were too dim, and inmates commonly complained of eyestrain. The few fans in the shop were clustered in one corner, surrounding the shop matron's desk. O'Hare reported that no woman was able to keep up the pace for more than two years; long-term prisoners were transferred to lighter industrial jobs.

Mealtimes were hardly more relaxing than work, as the inmates were not allowed to socialize but forced to eat in silence. Meals were always served cold because they were delivered to the women's department hours before mealtime from the kitchen on the men's side of the prison.

Thus, the stew, oatmeal, and hash were inedible by mealtime, if they had not been initially. Food was unpalatable, nutritionally inadequate, and often spoiled with maggots and mealworms present. If possible, women either purchased food and had it delivered or depended on care packages. The result of this appalling situation was that the real meal-time for most of the inmates occurred in the evening when they swapped foodstuffs. Those who had outside sources of food shared their sup-plies. O'Hare received an enormous and eclectic variety of packages, including peanut butter, pickles, jellies, jams, cakes, candy, guava paste, butter, and gefilte fish and matzos from various supporters. Food was passed from cell to cell along the line. Morsels from cells in an up-per tier would be tied on strings and lowered to cells below. Everyone, O'Hare included, would take bits off the strings, laughing and whisper-ing all the while. The inmates joked about "feeding the monkeys" to one another. They also passed notes from one cell to another, called sending "kites" down the line, and in so doing, experienced unreal in-teractions with each other without seeing one another.

O'Hare found prison fare intolerable, and she registered formal com-plaints with the prison administration, but the situation that most ap-palled her was the constant danger of infectious disease. Women with influenza, tuberculosis, or venereal diseases lived among and shared bathing facilities with those in good health. O'Hare, normally a coop-erative prisoner, refused to bathe when she realized that the Native-American woman, Alice Cox, who had preceded her in the bathtub had open syphilitic sores. Justifiably terming the situation "really revolt-ing," she faced down a prison matron who insisted that she take the weekly bath. She again registered formal complaints. Her influence, even from prison, resulted in some positive changes in the facilities and the routine. In St. Louis, she had known the warden, William R. Painter, a political appointee and a former lieutenant governor. She had worked with Painter during the hearings on the minimum wage, and she knew his wife, too. Shortly after her incarceration, and clearly in re-sponse to some of her complaints, a federal inspection upheld a number of her criticisms. Efforts were made to segregate at least the syphilitic from the other inmates; showers were installed; for a while, the food was delivered warm; women were allowed access to the prison library; and the walls of the dining facility and the cellblock were whitewashed.

When they were not working, the inmates' regimented routine at least featured occasional leeway. On Monday and Tuesday evenings and Sunday mornings following chapel services, they socialized for an hour or so in a courtyard. On Wednesday evenings, lessons in chorale singing were provided. On Saturday afternoons during the summer, they had outings in a nearby park, and in winter during weekend afternoons, they were shown silent movies.

During O'Hare's first few months at Jefferson City, one of the other "federals" was Emma Goldman. Goldman spent eighteen months in Jefferson City, and for a short while, she, O'Hare, and the two other federal prisoners were housed in clustered cells. Although they represented radical movements that were hostile to each other—anarchism and socialism—the women became fast friends. They had met a few times before in St. Louis and also when O'Hare visited the prison shortly before her incarceration. O'Hare genuinely missed Goldman's company after the latter completed her sentence in September, and the two later corresponded with each other. To comrades who anticipated fireworks between them, each reported on the other's humane qualities and efforts on behalf of the inmates. Goldman wrote that they did not "compete in 'isms.' We compete in feeding hungry sparrows." Each stressed the mutual respect that they developed for one another. Their conflicting philosophies were irrelevant during their shared imprisonment. Kate O'Hare described Goldman as a wise and understanding woman who was a kind of "cosmic mother" to those around her, and Emma Goldman admired O'Hare's ability to make some changes in the prison, and she wrote that O'Hare's imprisonment damned the whole system.

Emma Goldman was notorious well before World War I for having conspired with her anarchist comrade Alexander Berkman in 1892 to assassinate a leading American entrepreneur, Henry Clay Frick. They had hoped to inspire an anticapitalist uprising of steelworkers. When President William McKinley was assassinated in 1901 by a self-described anarchist, Goldman, who had come to denounce violence as inappropriate, and who knew nothing about the event, was persecuted by the police. She had also been vilified and arrested for remarks publicizing her anarchistic philosophy and her views on sexuality and birth control, and at times she had to flee from mobs. During the war, Goldman and Berkman, her lifelong close colleague, had organized the No-Conscription League. They were convicted for conspiring against the draft and would eventually be first imprisoned under the Espionage Act and then deported to the Soviet Union. They left Russia after a short time there, following the Kronstadt Rebellion, as early critics of Bolshevik totalitarianism and wandered for years—legendary revolutionists without a country.

The two other political prisoners in the Missouri State Penitentiary were both young immigrant anarchists, Gabriella Antolini and Mollie Steimer. O'Hare developed great affection for twenty-year-old Ella, and she tried in every way she could to help her. Ella Antolini's family had emigrated to the United States in 1907; she was still a child when they were recruited as migrant laborers to work in the South. Influenced by a brother's radicalism, while still in her teens Ella became enmeshed in an Italian-American anarchist circle in Connecticut. A factory worker, she was arrested in 1917 for transporting a suitcase containing sticks of dynamite and was sentenced to eighteen months by the famous Judge Kenesaw Mountain Landis, who delighted in passing maximum sentences on the parade of radicals—Socialists, Wobblies, and anarchists—who appeared before him. To Kate O'Hare, Ella was "a dear little Italian girl." O'Hare supervised her education, encouraging Ella to read the American history books in the prison library and working with her to improve her English. O'Hare dubbed the two of them and Goldman "the American Revolutionary Soviet." They celebrated May Day as best they could, and also Ella's birthday. O'Hare wrote Frank that the three of them held "nightly conclaves to direct the affairs of the universe. Just imagine what interesting stories the historian of the future can write of this strange trio and our doings." When Ella completed her sentence and was released in January 1920, Frank O'Hare, at his wife's bidding, hired an attorney to handle Ella's legal struggle against deportation. The government could not prove that Ella was an anarchist, and she was not then deported to Italy.

The three political prisoners shared a perspective and experiences. They rejoiced, for example, when they received roses sent to them from Russian comrades. O'Hare described them as "great red roses, and the wonderful thing is that they came all the way from Moscow, straight from the bleeding, quivering heart of Russia. . . . Can you imagine anything more thrilling, more inspiring than that?"

The other young immigrant anarchist, Mollie Steimer, began her sentence the month of O'Hare's departure, so the two could not become close. Steimer was a twenty-three-year-old Jewish shirtwaist factory worker and well under five feet. O'Hare described Steimer as an "eighty-pound maiden," the epitome of youth suffering for its ideals. Frank O'Hare thought she was about the same size as thirteen-year-old Kathleen O'Hare. The radical journalist Agnes Smedley, who had encountered Steimer when they were both in the Tombs Jail in New York described Steimer as imbued with the spirit which had made the Russian Revolution possible. Smedley was held but never tried under the Espionage Act. Steimer had been arrested for leafletting against Allied intervention in Russia. She was one of the defendants in the landmark Abrams case in which Justice Oliver Wendell Holmes, with the concurrence of Justice Louis Brandeis, offered his famous dissenting opinion spelling out the doctrine of "a clear and present danger" as a means to define and uphold freedom of speech through the First Amendment. Steimer was so idealistic that even her anarchist comrades joked about her lack of realism. At one of her trials, she testified about the world order of the future, and predicted, "It will be a new social order of which no group of people shall be in the power of any other group. Every person shall have an equal opportunity to develop himself. None shall live by the product of another. Every one shall produce what he can and enjoy what he needs. He shall have time to gain knowledge and culture. . . . We workers of the world will unite in one human brotherhood."

Her views took her from the Tombs to Blackwell Island Jail and then to Jefferson City. There O'Hare, in response to a request from Steiner's lawyer, Harry Weinberger, tried to ease the young woman's adjustment to the penitentiary's routine. Steimer worked on the task in the industrial shop until her eyesight began to weaken and her right arm pain her. At the end of 1921 she was among a contingent of anarchists who were deported to the Soviet Union. Her beliefs did not find a receptive environment there, and she spent much of her long life in Mexico, a symbol of nineteenth-century anarchist philosophy in the twentieth century.

Kate O'Hare, however grateful she was for the company of the three other politicals, suffered in her unfamiliar isolation. She was locked away from family and friends. Her marriage to Frank had remained basically stable despite the constant separations imposed by her travels, but the stresses of her imprisonment and having to live apart for fifteen straight months were taking their toll. Moreover, it is feasible to assume that the fact of the onset of menopause added an additional complication for Kate O'Hare. Frank traveled from St. Louis to Jefferson City regularly to visit Kate, and his letters, more than hers, reveal the enormous strain the couple was under. He gradually had all their belongings moved to St. Louis from Florida. He took an apartment and hired someone to cook and clean.

Kate was also concerned about her children. The twins were only eleven when she was incarcerated. She sent word to the St. Louis branch of the Young People's Socialist League to include the twins in some of their outings and other activities. She encouraged the boys to write her notes, which they did only sporadically, and she had no sense that they paid much attention to her letters to the family. Kathleen was old enough to understand the need to write to her mother regularly, nevertheless, her letters were too infrequent to satisfy Kate. Kate O'Hare felt keenly the unraveling of her cord to her daughter just as Kathleen was entering adolescence. Dick, the eldest, was sixteen the year his mother was imprisoned. He sometimes visited Kate on his own at Jefferson City, in addition to his trips there with his father. In one of the most poignant moments of O'Hare's imprisonment, the prison warden refused Dick O'Hare permission to play his cornet for his mother in the facility, so he crossed the street and played in the gathering dusk, as the hushed inmates listened to the notes.

New inmates were permitted to write one letter per week. After three months, model prisoners were allowed two letters per week, after another three months of satisfactory behavior, three letters per week. These arbitrary standards limited O'Hare's contacts with her outside world. As Frank O'Hare informed friends and colleagues, Kate's letters would be written only to the immediate family. While she welcomed as many letters and packages as people cared to send, she would not write to others in place of her family. Of the over one hundred twenty letters that she wrote while at Jefferson City, only two or three were to people outside her immediate family. However, Frank published a booklet of the first sixteen of her weekly letters, and circulated it widely to help others understand her life in prison and to encourage sympathy and support for her.

The prison letter, it has been argued, is among the most cultivated literary genres of modern times. It demonstrates a writer's finesse in dealing with restrictions, and is perhaps more challenging than the principles of the Shakespearean sonnet or the limitations of Japanese *haiku*. Stanislaw Baranczak suggests that "the prison letter . . . is governed by a detailed set of strict prohibitions and injunctions regulating its size, structure, style, tone, and content. The author's mastery lies precisely in how he handles these rules, complying with them yet managing to slip his message through, remaining within the limits of a standardized model of utterance yet imbuing it with the urgency of his individual voice." For Kate O'Hare, the prison letter was the medium through which to send a message. She knew that all of her words would be screened by the authorities and that some of them would never reach their intended audience. In fact, a number of O'Hare's letters were confiscated, and others were mailed out minus offending paragraphs. Some of her comments on the state of the prison system and of society were permitted to reach the outside world; others were not. There seemed no clear standard of acceptability.

The letters, diaries, essays, and other compositions of political prisoners have often assumed a revolutionary perspective relating the oppression of workers to that of prisoners. Unlike literate nonpolitical prisoners, who tend to see themselves as isolated individuals, politicals impose a class perspective on what they experience; O'Hare's writings certainly did. Moreover, politically conscious women in prison tend to write broadly from the perspective of victimized social groups, and they may express a communal nature or a collective aesthetic. They are, after all, writing from what one author has called a "concrete womb" which they share with each other, and they represent, further, a doubly marginalized group as individuals in prison who happen to be women and therefore are greater outcasts than men prisoners. In the course of the twentieth century women in prison have increasingly developed a sense of solidarity with each other. Some note, as O'Hare came to in her own way, that life for women has been markedly unfree compared to men, and that prison is simply an elaboration of that condition.

The act of writing itself gives such individuals a sense of control over their environment and over their reality. They also, unlike men in the same situation, write letters that can be characterized as basically relational. Even though they know that their letters by their nature are public documents, their writings are typically family letters. And even while children are usually part of their intended audience, as they were of O'Hare's letters and also, for example, the letters of Ethel Rosenberg, nevertheless political concerns are also inherent so that a tension between the personal and political is present that is not so typical of men's writings. Such women display a clear need to instruct their children. The relational aspect appears in another guise, too, as women political prisoners often correspond afterward with one another, as O'Hare and Goldman did, as Agnes Smedley and Margaret Sanger did.

In addition to O'Hare's letter-writing while incarcerated in Jefferson City, she was also a voracious reader. First of all, she read everything that she could concerning the radical milieu. She read those socialist newspapers that war censorship had not destroyed, for example, the *New York Call,* the *Milwaukee Leader,* and *St. Louis Labor,* and she complained when issues did not reach her. She also read the nonsocialist St. Louis newspapers, such as the *St. Louis Post-Dispatch* and the St. Louis-based *Reedy's Mirror,* more of a cultural periodical than a news magazine. She read the progressive weeklies, the *Nation* and the *New Republic.* She also received and plowed through the cultural icon of the time, the *Dial,* and other current events periodicals, such as the radical *Liberator, Pearson's,* and the *Public.*

Unlike a number of other well-known radicals, O'Hare did not use the hours available to her to deepen or broaden her general education. In contrast, for example, Rosa Luxemburg (whose hours for reading were endless since she had no work assignment while imprisoned in Germany for most of World War I) delved heavily into serious literature, while building on her once strong foundation in biological sciences and also pursuing her own theoretical writings. Kate O'Hare's serious readings were devoted to the field of psychology which she hoped to put to a practical use while she was in prison. She read works by Sigmund Freud, Havelock Ellis, and Richard Krafft-Ebing. She had long been a student of Freud's, having developed an early interest in psychology based on her concern over the impact on the human psyche of desperate social conditions. She thought Ellis's works especially helpful in understanding the psyche of the inmates. His work, *The Criminal,* interested her as a psychological investigation of the causes and treatment of crime, and his multi-volume *Studies of the Psychology of Sex* a useful interpretation from a biological point of view to balance those from a clinical perspective. Krafft-Ebing's writings in the area of what was then known as sexual psychopathology attracted O'Hare, especially his work on sexual deviance and syphilis.

She also studied the writings of some of the New Penologists. She was especially fascinated by the work of Thomas Mott Osborne, who had been a reform-minded warden at Sing Sing Prison in New York a few years earlier. He wrote *Within Prison Walls* and *Society and Prisons,* both of which O'Hare devoured and in which he detailed his experience while posing for one week as an inmate in Auburn Prison. Later, after her prison term, she made certain that she got a chance to talk with Osborne about her experience compared with his artificial one. However enthralling some of these books were to her, given her circumstances, she believed that useful literature to help understand the psychology of prisoners had yet to be written. In fact, she doubted that anyone who had not lived the life of a convict could produce such work. As she explained to her family,

> How can anyone write intelligently about this life who has not lived it? What can anyone know of the effects of the constant galling of prison discipline enforced by those absolutely innocent of even the most rudimentary knowledge of human psychology until one's nerves have been worn to the raw by its stupidities? What can the professor in his college classroom, the physician in his study, the scientist in his laboratory know of the things that go on behind prison walls and their effect on human life?

She continued by writing, "There is a chasm that cannot be bridged, a gulf that cannot be crossed between the convict and the other men[sic] and only those who have lived behind stone walls, slept inside steel bars and eaten under the eye of official[s] . . . can sense what it means." She noted with sympathy the well-meaning efforts of the warden to help the inmates but said an unscalable wall existed between him and the prisoners. Her major life's work, she had come to think, was to study and write of prison life to enlighten the public.

O'Hare's original plan even before her incarceration was to conduct a series of investigative studies of the other inmates, and on the basis of those notes she could later write full-length case studies in criminology. She developed a detailed prospectus during the year prior to her imprisonment. Her concentrated work on the project might in fact have been her own way of shielding herself from the possibility of actual imprisonment. O'Hare discussed her proposed study with the governors of both Missouri and North Dakota, Frederick D. Gardner and Lynn D. Frazier, the only two possible states in which her incarceration was likely to occur. Each governor indicated support for her proposal to interview the inmates for the project, and Governor Gardner went on to say, according to O'Hare's version of their interview, that the eventual study would be of great social value. He promised that the officials at the Missouri State Penitentiary, should she be incarcerated within its walls, would cooperate with her project. O'Hare also conferred with officials of both the Department of Psychology and the Medical School of the University of Missouri at Columbia, and in both instances won support for her proposal as very worthwhile. Additionally, she talked to officials at the North Dakota State Penitentiary, and they promised that they would support her work, were she to be incarcerated there.

Once in the Jefferson City facility, O'Hare's assignment to the industrial shop precluded her committing much energy or time to the case studies. For that reason, she officially requested of Joseph F. Fishman, the U.S. Inspector of Federal Prisons, during his visit to her in August 1919, that she be transferred to the state prison at Bismarck, North Dakota. She described Fishman as well informed on scientific criminology for a prison official, and he invited her to write to him, discussing further her views on penology. But the Department of Justice refused her transfer to Bismarck where, given the political power of the Nonpartisan League, O'Hare would have found a more congenial and supportive environment.

Despite the lack of support in Jefferson City, O'Hare persevered with her project. She used some of her evenings to circulate her questionnaires among the female and male inmates, and in this manner she accumulated almost two hundred detailed case histories. The inmates provided information on their family history, occupational and educational background, and social factors in their lives, including childhood experiences, household composition, marital details, recreational interests, political and community affiliations, and the history of their encounters with the legal system. Hers was clearly an environmental approach to the subject, in tune with the current direction of the field of penology. It no longer emphasized heredity, and O'Hare as a socialist was comfortable with stressing societal culpability in criminality. She intended to analyze this wealth of information, and to invite specialists, a psychologist and a medical doctor, to write specific chapters of her proposed book based on data relevant to their expertise. However, when O'Hare was about to be released from Jefferson City, her field notes disappeared. She was permitted to pack her library of several hundred books and other personal effects, but her case studies had been confiscated by the matron. When she complained, she was informed that the data had been destroyed.

O'Hare's eventual comprehensive penal recommendations were based on her conviction that American prisons were the most hideous part of the existing social system, that they were institutional failures which inspired anti-social traits in both the prison staffs and the prisoners. All existing prisons should be abandoned as soon as possible, she argued. Prisons, she wrote, "violated every normal urge of human life and intensified every abnormal tendency." She recommended that the corrective institutions of Missouri, including especially the State Penitentiary, be immediately investigated by a blue-ribbon commission empowered to make sweeping proposals to the state legislature. While she believed that prison reforms could only have minimum significance, given that the prison system was a reflection of existing economic and social conditions, nevertheless she felt that transitionary efforts must be made prior to a systematic transformation. Her key recommendation was the establishment of a model federal female reformatory. Even though state female reformatories had been less than successful in the previous decades, she believed that society had to protect itself by incarcerating indi-viduals in what must be a decent environment. O'Hare favored the es-tablishment of an agrarian-based facility for women. The residents of her model reformatory would be assigned to useful labor under health-ful conditions, for which they would be paid a current wage, less room and board. They would be permitted conjugal visits with their husbands, a somewhat unique recommendation for reformers of that era, but re-flective of O'Hare's having served a prison term. She was anxious to minimize homosexual acts among inmates, about which she had be-come seriously concerned. Full segregation of the physically and men-tally diseased would be the norm, and scientific study of the inmates would be undertaken by appropriate experts. In these various sugges-tions, O'Hare proved herself still to be an offspring of turn-of-the cen-tury American social science which held to a bedrock position that data-gathering, analysis, and institutional responses would solve society's problems.

Like other educated political offenders in jail, such as journalist Ag-nes Smedley, O'Hare devoted herself to observing the other inmates. She tried to fulfill their glaring needs as she could. She offered to teach classes for them but was denied the opportunity by the administration, but she later concluded that the project would not have been feasible due to the prisoner's exhausting industrial labor. She requested permission to stage a Christmas play with the inmates, and that was denied. She tried to win approval to administer what she termed "a series of very simple popular lectures on modern psychology" but that request was also rejected. However, O'Hare persevered in other ways in what she clearly thought of as her efforts to uplift her fellows. Seeing the inmates as objects to study and help, rather than as colleagues whose situation she shared, despite changed circumstances O'Hare apparently clung to a perspective not unlike that of a Florence Crittenton worker trying to help the downtrodden. She always held the other inmates at arm's length while she tried to use whatever influence she had to humanize the condi-tions which they faced. After she won them access to the library books housed in the men's section, she read aloud to those who were illiterate. She lent her own magazines and books to those capable of reading them. She directed her own children and some of her correspondents to write to specific inmates, those without outside contacts of their own, and she had individual women showered with such attention. She shared with the others the myriad of gifts and trinkets that she constantly received in the mail from family, friends, unknown rank-and-file socialists, and other supporters. She used her special access to Warden Painter to discuss with him specific problems of individual prisoners, and arranged for her husband and others to handle legal aspects of some of the women's cases and even to employ them when they were discharged.

Kate O'Hare, set apart from the inmates by her perspective, and theirs, too, was a "lady" who happened to be in prison, while the others were society's unfortunates victimized by the system. In contrast to Emma Goldman, who related to the other inmates in a down-to-earth, direct, human fashion, O'Hare remained apart. While she became fond of many of the women, and evidence suggests that numbers of them had great regard and even affection for her, O'Hare stood her distance, catalogued them, and took notes.

O'Hare's prison letters were filled with generalized comments about the women inmates. She wrote,

> Between eighty and ninety percent . . . had committed minor offenses against property, and the others were about evenly divided between crimes against the person and homicide. They were almost without exception poorly educated, but very few having reached the sixth grade in school and many were entirely illiterate. A large percentage were feeble-minded, a smaller percentage were borderline cases between normality and subnormality, and practically all who were not dements were psychopaths . . . they were all very poor; all from the most poverty-pinched sections of the working class.

She emphasized how clearly the women loved adornment, and wrote that a piece of jewelry invariably "perked" them up, She diagnosed them as trained to hide their intelligence, and suggested that these women, unlike men, guessed at what they needed to know, while men (and perhaps she herself) undertook studies of issues which interested them. She saw these women as often child-like individuals who not only had been unfortunate enough to be exploited by society but who basically could not manage their lives. She wrote, "[T]he white women were usually 'sent up' for shoplifting, and almost without an exception they were charged with stealing clothing for their own use. The colored women were in the 'stir' generally for the classic crime of 'rolling.' Technically this means highway robbery, but in reality it is simply that many white men have the habit of consorting with negro prostitutes and then refusing to pay them."

She found that the most typical occupational background of the inmates was domestic service, a fact which seemed to refute a view which O'Hare had always challenged that domestic work was the safest vocation for young women on their own in big cities. She reported that every inmate there convicted of infanticide had been employed as a domestic, and almost all of them claimed that their employers had fathered their children. She found that a portion of the inmates were convicted of murdering their husbands. These women tended to be the most intelligent inmates, middle-aged and quiet, who had been worn out by poverty and abuse. She also discovered that at least one-third of the women were in prison because they had assumed guilt for men they loved. It seemed to O'Hare that women were much more apt to shoulder such guilt, and that, moreover, they were more likely to remain loyal to spouses who were "sent up" than were men in such circumstances, a view supported by Warden Painter. The exception to this rule was the "cadet" who supported his stable of women while they were in prison and worked for their release.

She wrote of individual women and of their fates at Jefferson City, for example, Minnie Eddy from Kansas City who simply could not "make the task" no matter how hard she tried. She was thrown into solitary several times, and after her longest stay of three weeks on a diet of only bread and water, she died, probably of a perforated intestine. Another inmate, a black woman whom O'Hare identified as demented, experienced brutal treatment after attacking an inmate whom she thought was bedeviling her. She was handcuffed to her cell bars with "a kind of bridle" in her mouth to prevent any screaming. She was also subject to beatings, a not unusual occurrence. O'Hare reported hearing not infrequently "the blows and cries and pleadings of inmates while they were being beaten by guards and matrons."

Through all this, O'Hare reminded herself, "The women here are real human beings, stupid and intelligent, educated and ignorant, normal and abnormal, just like any group of women of the same number anywhere. Unnatural, abnormal and brutalizing as life is here, like weeds by the roadside they manage to survive and maintain their individuality." In comments a few years later in a published article, O'Hare wrote even more emphatically about the humanity of the inmates. She noted that however "sinister and revolting" such "wrecked lives" appeared, nevertheless those individuals must be recognized as "flesh of our flesh, soul of our soul."

The only times she chided any of her fellow inmates was when they risked punishment by seeking to contact husbands or lovers in the men's section. Her blood ran cold, she commented, when she witnessed the risks some took to send what she termed "their tragically pathetic little love notes over the walls." But when reminded by an inmate that O'Hare did not have to wait months and years for word from a husband, she realized that without her personal support system she might be as foolhardy as some of the others.

Toward the two-thirds of the inmates who were black, O'Hare maintained at best a keen skepticism concerning their abilities. She, of course, had always been a firm believer in black inequality. She viewed blacks as incapable of competing with whites and unable to profit from higher education. Whatever evidence she may have encountered to the contrary, her views were not modified during her months living among black women. But, nevertheless, her humane instincts permitted her to interact with the black inmates as on agreeable a basis as with the Caucasians. She shared the innumerable gifts she received in the mail with all of them, and she distributed her candy and other sweets to the black inmates, too, wrote letters for some of them and sympathetically listened to their problems. O'Hare wrote about the black inmates to Frank, explaining to him that "It really is amusing to see how much joy . . . fifty colored girls can extract from a supply of gum." They were clearly childlike. Further, O'Hare believed, as did many other educated Americans of that time, that blacks could better tolerate heat than whites, she thought that they suffered less in the abominable shop conditions than did she and the other white inmates. But she did recognize that these black women were victims of society, victimized because they were black, because they were working class, and because they were women. She saw them representative of a social problem, in need "most of all [of] . . . justice, decent living conditions outside and sane, scientific handling here."

O'Hare's experience of incarceration almost imperceptibly began to modify her views on women and society. While before prison she had always seen women's issues as subsumed within the larger Social Question, as discussed earlier, and she believed that inequities which women endured would be undermined with the coming of the socialist system, her confidence in those ideas faltered. Despite herself, she developed a sense of sisterhood as she saw her own experiences as suggestive of the timelessness that characterized the plight of all women. In this way, she ceased being the observer. She now shared the status of all women. Within one month of entering prison, O'Hare's letters began to refer recurrently to the neglect of women in prison by society, by the media, and even by the Socialist party. She said that the press did not have "one spark of interest in the women," when it ran stories on the treatment of federal prisoners. It managed to focus on the Wobblies in Leavenworth while it ignored O'Hare and Goldman in Jefferson City. It did not have any concerns about the conditions of women prisoners, she commented angrily, after having been interviewed by a journalist who in his subsequent series for the *Survey* failed to include material on women prisoners. O'Hare noted that her own party focused its amnesty campaigns only on the men who had been caught up by the legal system under the Espionage Act—Debs and Berger but not Rose Pastor Stokes or herself. She interpreted such neglect not as purposeful but related, in fact, to what she called "the psychology of the male." Only men spoke at the rallies for amnesty for political prisoners and ran the campaigns, and so they saw only the plight of their imprisoned male comrades. There was a logic to it, she concluded bitterly. Accordingly, O'Hare began to comment on the marginal and inadequate treatment women received, and included herself. By the end of her prison term, she had transcended far beyond her earlier more restricted views on discrimination against women. In a letter that self-consciously referred to her pre-prison views, she wrote to Frank that: "You know that I have never been a particularly rampant feminist; . . . but my . . . months here have changed my views materially, and I know now, as never before, that 'women bear the heaviest burdens and walk the roughest road' and that this is true in all walks of life."

As a result of these views, O'Hare appealed to women on behalf of women prisoners. In a gender-based approach that was atypical for her, she asked Frank to encourage the establishment of several committees of women to promote amnesty for women political prisoners. She appealed to women, especially those in states where they were enfranchised, to write to their representatives and senators to demand a congressional investigation of her case. O'Hare had finally made common cause with other women as she could never have anticipated. She knew that her case was receiving less attention because she was a woman, and it was plausible that women could appreciate the dimensions of her situation and come to her aid. Women by their shared framework, whatever their walks of life, would understand and emphasize. In this instance, gender had become the most significant variable rather than class.

Another topic on which O'Hare focused her attention while in prison was organized religion. Her earlier views were strengthened by her

prison experience. She found that the Jefferson City clergy totally neglected the spiritual needs of the inmates. Visiting clergy, almost without exception, offered platitudes and were "professionally cheerful"
and therefore irrelevant to and contemptuous of the women inmates,
who in turn were contemptuous of them. The inmates did not need to
be told that they were fallen women whom God loved anyway, O'Hare
wrote, but they needed to be seen as individuals whom society had
knocked down. An occasional visit by a famous religious leader, for
example, Maud Billington Booth, daughter of the founders of the Salvation Army and founder herself of the Volunteers of America, served no
purpose. Sanctimonious uplifters violated the religious principles they
said they represented, O'Hare charged. The chaplain on the staff at
Jefferson City merited O'Hare's most biting comments. Only a second-
rate minister would accept such a poorly paid appointment, she said,
and the services he led could only make people loathe religion. O'Hare
came to believe even more strongly than before that clergy as a group
were "without moral courage . . . were so supine and spineless as a
class; "that they violated their charge. She wrote that: "The Protestant
Church professes to believe that the Bible is the way of salvation; and
there are no bibles here. Communion is supposed to be an essential of
church observance, and in the three months I have been here there has
been no communion . . . organized religion fails [the inmates] in the
hour of their need. What wonder then that they turn to Spiritualism for
help and comfort." Not uncommonly, some of the women tried to com-
municate at night with the spirits of dead loved ones so that "the cell
house is peopled by many ghosts."

O'Hare attended chapel essentially because that won her access to the
free hour thereafter in the fresh air of the prison courtyard. She skipped
it occasionally because of what she termed the "spiritual nausea" it inspired in her. She wrote that she had too much respect for the message
of Jesus to witness its violation. Many correspondents, both known and
unknown to her, sent her religious and theological writings. She received materials from "Christian Scientists, Russellites, New Thought

and Gospel Trumpets adherents." as well as others, which she read out of curiosity. But she, interested in religion as she always had been, followed her own path. She remarked in a letter to her family that "There is one thing certain, and that is I shall come out of prison understanding Jesus better and on terms of closer comradeship with him. Prison may increase my contempt for churchianity, but it will deepen my love and respect for Jesus."

She described her conception of God as essentially amorphous, but as something that embraced all that was good and which recognized love as the creative force of the universe. The God of orthodoxy was not her God, she wrote in a family letter that more self-consciously than others seemed geared for publication.

> As I look back over my life it seems that I have always vainly sought to "find Jesus." I sought him in church work and the rescue mission. I sought him in the labor movement and the Socialist party, but he always eluded me. In the Church I found an empty creed, in the rescue mission smug hypocrisy, in the labor movement a selfish policy of "save yourself" and in the Socialist party the soul of men bound and hampered by crass materialism. . . . One day I found myself in prison on Easter Day and there for the first time I felt that I knew Jesus; I could sit down and talk sanely and intelligently with Him and He could tell me out of His wide experience how to unstop deaf ears, open blind eyes, heal sick souls and bind up broken hearts! And from that day to this, Jesus and I have been good friends; we have had a common experience and we know and respect each other. . . . I know now why he . . . chose his friends among the outcasts and his apostles among the lowliest of the lowly.

Thus, O'Hare continued on the spiritual quest she had begun in the long-ago Kansas days when she groped for a direction in life. Nothing she observed in the months in prison convinced her that the representatives of orthodox religion held any answers nor that it had the least interest in those who were most in need in American society.

Kate O'Hare's most consuming interest during her months in the Jefferson City facility was in the socialist movement from which she was shut away. Fascination, anxiety, and bitterness in turn marked her observations about the future of the party to which she had given her life and which, during her imprisonment, virtually went through its death throes. The Socialist Party of America from spring 1917, when the United States intervened in the world war, through 1920, when O'Hare languished in prison, reeled from the impact of one event and then another. The wartime denial of the right of dissent cost the party many of its leaders including Debs who received a ten-year prison term for an antiwar speech in Canton, Ohio. The Russian Revolution, while at first an energizing force for the American left, traumatized and fragmented the party. A great spurt in membership and voters occurred in 1918. Association with the party was for some a means of demonstrating solidarity with the triumphant revolutionists in Russia. The largest growth took place in the party's foreign-language federations as Eastern European immigrants rushed to sign red cards here in lieu of being able to participate in events in their homeland. As a result the party took on a pronounced foreign flavor. The foreign-language federations swelled from 30 percent of the membership—before the war—to 51 percent—in 1919. While O'Hare concentrated on her legal battles, the federations demanded that the Socialist party ally itself firmly to the Bolsheviks then trying to solidify their control of Russia. The old party leaders such as Victor Berger and Adolph Germer, displayed some reservations about evolving events in Russia, and they were guarded about the new militancy all about them. They did not believe that the Bolshevik seizure of power could serve as a role model for the American movement, and they still hoped that any transition to socialist control in the United States would occur without violence and bloodshed.

An organized left-wing bloc emerged and demanded, in addition to tighter links to the Russian regime, an emphasis by the socialist movement on the class struggle rather than on electoral activity, and an end to cooperation with nonsocialists over issues such as amnesty for political prisoners. The increasingly bitter rivalry between the two factions led to disputed elections and the existence of two separate National Executive Committees by May, each claiming legitimacy. Individuals were expelled and entire state organizations ousted. The ideological infighting reached its peak at a national convention in August 1919, called to determine party policy and direction. At that convention in Chicago, the party split apart. Some walked out of the convention and established the Communist Labor Party while simultaneously a segment of the left-wing ignored the proceedings and formed the Communist Party. The Socialist party, at the end of two decades of growth, abruptly became a shadow of itself, shrinking from a pre-schism membership of 104,822 to 26,766. Moreover, it was shaken and uncertain about its future.

Kate O'Hare must have felt claustrophobic in her tucked-away cell. Her letters demonstrate great interest in every facet of party activities and developments in the world of labor. On the one hand, she maintained that she had more perspective on events than did the participants, writing that "Often those too near a great . . . event are too close . . . , and may see things in a distorted way." She was not discouraged by the factional disputes during the summer of 1919, and wrote sanguinely that "after the smoke has drifted away and the heated air cooled a bigger and better Socialist movement will come forth. The dross will have been burned out, and only the pure metal remain." But on the other hand, she felt frustrated. Impulsively, she wanted to dash off a telegram to the fateful convention that was gathering as she wrote to her family on August 28 but she shrunk back from doing so. Realizing that she might be out of touch with events, she regretted her absence "at this, the most important meeting the party has ever held, I can only be present in spirit. . . . I feel the whole thing very deeply."

O'Hare was heartened by the volatile activities of American workers during those months. She cheered on the Seattle general strike which took place the very month which she entered Jefferson City. While that strike was not successful, the great wave of strikes that rocked the country that year among clothing workers, steel-workers, and even police personnel seemed to her to be a harbinger of social revolution. The mindless violence that also marked those months, however, was disturbing.

She consoled herself that the turmoil had to be "the birth pangs of the coming of the new order."

Viewing the tears in the fabric of the party, she called it depressing "for me to realize that I have given the best years of my life to a movement that seems to be disintegrating." But again and again she maintained that: "life comes only through death and that all things decay and pass away when they have served their period of usefulness. All the work we have done in the past is not lost. It has been increased a thousandfold. The machine we have used to do the work may break down, but if so we will get a newer and better." She even decided that the fragmentation of the party was inevitable and would lead to some new "alignments, that will be bigger, broader and more serviceable to humanity."

She totally disagreed with those who abandoned the party that summer, and thought it was "criminal" to disrupt it. Four months after the fateful convention, she still dwelled on the events and the possibilities that might open to the remaining party fateful. While noting that she well knew the party's shortcomings, or particularly those of some of its officials, O'Hare hoped that all radicals— pink, cerise, and red—would yet come together in a movement of labor, Nonpartisan Leaguers, socialists and communists.

O'Hare referred to Socialist party officials to her husband that December, writing that "I doubt if any other person in the United States has suffered . . . from them more than I have." She had long felt unappreciated by the party leadership. Debs aside, and he, after all, never participated in the routine management of the party or established its policies, O'Hare felt that the leadership thought of her as a country bumpkin and only a woman. Her service in many party positions was due to the support of the rank and file rather than her popularity with party apparatchiks. Victor Berger and Morris Hillquit made little effort to disguise how slightly they regarded her. During O'Hare's legal struggle to avoid imprisonment, she and Frank felt that the party chose not to put energy and funds into her case in favor of concentrating on the legal struggles of other leaders. Once in prison, O'Hare caustically noted that she was ignored by her comrades. She commented after a large party rally that "none of the . . . speakers, . . . remembered that I existed." She told the National Secretary of the party, Otto Branstetter, that party rank and filers believed that she had "been most shamefully treated by the National Office." O'Hare asked him to hire an attorney to supplement the efforts of her lawyer, then seeking to push perjury charges against those who had testified against her. She maintained that she was not simply trying to help herself but that such an effort would aid party harmony if her followers saw that she finally had some support from the party's National Office. No assistance was forthcoming, however, as Branstetter angrily told her that the National Office was bankrupt. To O'Hare, his refusal was further proof of party neglect of its major female prisoner, for the National Office had not bothered contacting her regularly and had even neglected to send her the routine mailings that all party members received. A few months later, she was promoted for the party's vice-presidential nomination by some of the convention delegates, an effort that probably solidified her sense that the rank-and-file, if not the leadership, supported her. The nomination, in fact, may have represented the factionalism then rampant, with O'Hare's name put forward to stymie the chances of a Berger ally for the nomination. She was not nominated, however, because with Gene Debs, the presidential candidate, in Atlanta Penitentiary, the delegates reasoned that the party needed at least one of its nominees free to campaign.

The most prominent group raising money for O'Hare's legal struggle and working for amnesty for her was the Kate O'Hare Committee of New York, in which major radicals, such as Theresa Malkiel, Elizabeth Gurley Flynn, and Emma Goldman, were active. The other major effort to draw attention to O'Hare's case was the small publication that Frank put out for the duration of his wife's imprisonment, *Frank O'Hare's Bulletin*. This newsletter and the booklet containing some of her prison letters kept the public alerted to O'Hare's situation. In addition, ad hoc civil libertarian groups sprang up and promoted amnesty for O'Hare and other less-famous individuals convicted under the wartime measures. Probably the most well known such national group was the National Liberty Defense Union, whose leading figure was Roger Baldwin, himself having served a brief prison term for failure to report to his selective service board.

As these efforts proceeded, the seasons went by for O'Hare locked inside the central Missouri fortress. She was ill at least twice and also suffered one industrial accident in the shop when the needle with which she was sewing pierced her finger. She suffered heat stroke at one time because of the high summer temperature and humidity and unventilated condition in the shop. She was denied medical attention despite her fever and sent back to the shop after two days, where she collapsed. At that point, Frank O'Hare protested to the warden and won her permission to remain off work until she recovered. During the Spanish influenza, she and almost one-half of the other women were stricken. This time, she was allowed to remain in her cell, but no medical care was provided.

Visitors provided welcome breaks in O'Hare's routine. In addition to Frank O'Hare's weekly visits, sometimes with one of the children along, she occasionally received other visitors, although surely with less frequency than she would have had she been incarcerated in a more centrally located facility. In fact, the limited number of visitors stands in stark contrast to the enormous number of correspondents she had. Her dear friend and old comrade Caroline Lowe came to see her once, as did a couple of party officials late in her imprisonment. Government dignitaries, such as the federal prison official, Joseph Fishman, and an occasional journalist also called, and while these visits were not as meaningful as those from friends, still they broke the monotony. Roger Baldwin visited Goldman and talked with O'Hare, too. Mike Kinney, a Democratic machine politician from St. Louis whom O'Hare had dealt with in city politics, visited her, which seemed to touch her. Upon occasion, the prison administration turned back would-be visitors. In one instance, William Garvey, an organizer for the Missouri Socialist party and often a candidate for public office, was denied permission to see her when he arrived at the prison. He protested this inexplicable policy to the Department of Justice, which responded that such decisions were entirely the responsibility of local authorities.

On April 3, 1920, O'Hare wrote a long letter to her family in which she marked a year since her imprisonment. It was Easter, and that provided a certain framework to her thoughts:

> This is Easter eve and at last the long, weary, heart-hungry days have dragged their lonely hours through, and one year of our Gethsemene is passed. One year—how swiftly it passes when love and joy and useful labor gilds the hours with life's gold, but how slowly it creeps away when prison bars shut out life and love and joyful labor and shackles each weary moment with loneliness and longing, with degradation and the leaden ball and chain of chattel slavery. . . . Tomorrow in every church, . . . will clergy and choir sing and chant and preach, . . . deaf and dumb and blind to the fact that here—today— . . . is being re-enacted again, increased a thousandfold, the passion, the sufferings, the Gethsemene and the Calvery.

She went on to declare that she had few regrets after a year of time for introspection. She wrote, "I have tried to find some rational, logical explanation for the actions and reactions of mankind. Of course the eternal questions that have been always with me are WHY do semi-sane people submit to war and permit prisons to exist?" The first question she had raised well before she entered prison, and the second one would frame the rest of her life. Little did she know as she pondered these issues that the sought-after release from prison was only a few weeks away.

O'Hare, of course, had never wanted a pardon, the acceptance of which would imply guilt. A few years after her release, she would receive a full pardon and the restoration of her civil and political rights from President Calvin Coolidge, but while she was at Jefferson City, she pursued a commutation of her sentence. An orchestrated effort on O'Hare's behalf resulted in the Department of Justice receiving a steady flow of demands for her release, sometimes couched in the same words, as well as letters of concern about her condition and her health. Letters and telegrams came from unknown and famous individuals, some of whom indicated that they were not among her political supporters. An example of the latter was a letter from George S. Johns, the editor of the *St. Louis Post-Dispatch,* to Assistant Attorney-General John T. Creighton, whom he had once met. Johns enclosed an editorial demanding O'Hare's release on the grounds that she was unfairly convicted. Unions, including locals of the International Association of Machinists, the International Chain Workers' Union, various garment and bakers unions, as well as socialist locals, for example the YPSLs of the state of Wisconsin, wrote to the Department of Justice on O'Hare's behalf. Governor Frazier of North Dakota submitted a petition for her release (for which he was roundly condemned by some of his constituents) to the Department of Justice. A few members of the U.S. House of Representatives, such as H. M. Jacoway of Arkansas and John F. Miller of Washington State, sent inquiries about her case to the Justice Department in response to several letters from their own constituents. In contrast, Judge Wade, branches of the American Legion and of the American War Mothers, particularly North Dakota chapters, and many individuals wrote to the Department of Justice demanding that O'Hare remain in prison where, many said, she belonged.

A fateful meeting occurred on the O'Hare case at the Department of Justice on May 14, 1920. A. Mitchell Palmer, the Attorney General, an Assistant Attorney General, and the Pardon Attorney met with a Socialist party delegation, which included Seymour Stedman, a Chicago attorney who was the vice-presidential nominee on the socialist ticket, Freda Hogan of Oklahoma City, an old friend of O'Hare's, and Dr. Madge Stephens of Terre Haute, a correspondent of O'Hare's and a friend of Debs and his physician. This delegation from the recently concluded party convention presented a resolution asking for a general amnesty for political offenders. In the discussion, they emphasized the O'Hare case, arguing that she had not had a fair trial and that she was a victim of a political feud, which placed her case in a class apart from the others. Palmer, one of the most controversial attorneys general whose department's arrests and deportations without due process the previous winter had begun to haunt him, argued back and forth with Stedman about the validity of the espionage and sedition legislation. To the committee's demands, he explained that the United States lacked a statutory category of political offenders so that he could not support the concept of a general amnesty but that each case had to be considered individually. However, Palmer indicated that he personally believed that the time had come for O'Hare's release. She had been sufficiently punished, he said, not so much for the crime which he believed that she had committed but because she was a woman and a mother.

Two weeks later, on May 29, 1920, Kate Richards O'Hare walked out of the Missouri State Penitentiary. After fourteen months of imprisonment, her sentence had been commuted by President Wilson, and she was a free woman once again. She was also a changed woman. The O'Hare who had entered jail in April 1919, had been a committed militant whose entire attention was focused on the Socialist party and the impact of the recently ended war. The O'Hare who left prison was affected by her experience perhaps more than she at first realized. Her incarceration at Jefferson City, as well as the fragmentation of the socialist movement, had led her to begin to shift directions. The harshness and deprivations of her ordeal, her exposure to those she came to consider the most wretched of the earth, and her feelings of neglect had a deep impact on her. O'Hare experienced her first sense of sisterhood in prison, she became more intensely critical of organized religion for its neglect of the needy, and she also became alienated in new ways from the leadership of the Socialist party. While she still certainly identified with the party, nevertheless its changed fortunes and her new perspectives led her to devote her energy increasingly to the possibility of penal reform rather than to socialist revolution. Finally her experiences placed unbearable strain on her marriage to Frank O'Hare.

♈ 8
POLITICAL ORPHAN

W hen Kate Richards O'Hare was released from the Missouri State Penitentiary in 1920, it was as if a lifetime, rather that just fourteen months, had passed. The Socialist party to which she had devoted her adult life was no more than a skeleton of what it had been at the last convention which she had attended. That emergency meeting held in St. Louis in April 1917 was hosted by a vigorous local party built on a strong network of neighborhood locals, and O'Hare, the star of the local movement, was a dominating figure at the convention. In contrast, by 1920, the St. Louis Socialists had divided among themselves, some remaining loyal to the party and others immersed in the nascent communist movement. While much of the former leadership was intact, notably the working-class activists, G. A. Hoehn and William Brandt, and while the party still published its weekly, *St. Louis Labor,* it was no longer a dynamic and growing movement with locals in workers' and immigrant neighborhoods holding weekly meetings and sponsoring a plethora of social events. Members continued to enjoy the same types of events as in the past—lectures, bazaars, picnics, and dances—but political activities were much scaled down. The St. Louis microcosm was an accurate reflection of the party nationally, as branches everywhere were broken remnants of what they had been only a few years before.

Accordingly, O'Hare was somewhat rudderless, but the outline of the diminished environment was not yet clear to her. She focused on political issues that held personal significance for her. Devoted to the cause of amnesty for political prisoners languishing in penal institutions across the country, especially Debs, who was still in Atlanta, and also determined to undermine the loathsome practice of contract labor, O'Hare was able to plow forward, hardly affected by the shrinking of the socialist movement. Despite the fact that fewer party locals existed across the country to book her speaking dates, and that many prewar movement newspapers and periodicals to which she had contributed had disappeared, O'Hare, through her fame and contacts, her personal standing with the labor movement, and her grassroots following, was able to resume her life of constant touring and writing.

O'Hare barely touched bases at home when she was released. She arrived in St. Louis at Union Station on Sunday evening, May 30, 1920, from Jefferson City. Ten days later, on June 10, a huge welcome-home reception was staged for her by the local Socialists at the Odeon Theater. Two thousand people turned up and gave her a tumultuous reception replete with standing ovations. When she rose to speak, the cheering was deafening. She described her prison experience, which would be the hallmark of her talks over the next decade. The high point for the crowd was O'Hare's statement that she had entered prison "a nice ladylike pink, but I came out a genuine red."

At last she could revel in the nearness of her family. But home in St. Louis was not familiar to her. It was a rental which Frank had arranged during her absence. Indeed, St. Louis was now home to Frank but not to Kate O'Hare. Immediately demands on her time overwhelmed her; interviews, telegrams, and letters inundated her. Thousands of supporters wanted to see her and hear her, and while she herself noted that, "It seemed a crime against the children for me to leave home," they announced—or so she described their discussions—that she should meet those who had cheered for her during her incarceration. She took to the road to tour the country within two weeks of her return. Frank accompanied her for the first weeks, remarking that it seemed like their honeymoon all over again, together touring for the movement. Perhaps it helped erase some memories of the strains their forced separation had meant. He also noted that his wife always felt better on the road and removed from the demands of household chores.

Kate O'Hare toured from June to November, doing ninety dates on what was billed as her welcome-home tour. Crowds surrounded her, applauded and cheered her. They seemed to cling to her every word. Socialist locals and central labor councils as well as other groups hosted her in all parts of the country. Everywhere she talked of her prison ordeal, of the remaining political prisoners, and of the changes that she believed were necessary so that American penal institutions could become less barbaric. She appeared before audiences sometimes with other major figures, such as Big Bill Haywood of the IWW, just prior to his jumping bail and fleeing to the Soviet Union. Audiences contributed money in order that O'Hare could continue to travel and generate publicity. Friends and comrades thought of ingenious ways to underwrite her work financially. For example, socialist Mayor Dan Hoan of Milwaukee appointed her as his city's representative to the All-American Conference on Venereal Disease Control which allowed her to share her views on the topic with physicians, psychologists, and prison officials and, not incidentally, to enjoy a free lecture trip to Washington D.C. (although through an clerical error, she never received the promised funds from the city). Her tour over that five-month period raised the then not insignificant sum of twenty thousand dollars for the Socialist party's treasury, from which, however, she did not receive her salary and expense money for two years.

She and Frank traveled to the East Coast, speaking in cities such as Providence, Rhode Island, Hartford, Connecticut, Baltimore, Maryland, and Washington, D.C., and then south to Atlanta to visit Gene Debs. The next months she traveled alone, continuing to draw crowds eager to hear about her prison experience. O'Hare faced hostile mobs, too, and locked lecture halls which forced her sometimes to hold forth in makeshift settings. Posts of the American Legion and service organizations, such as the Kiwanis and the Rotary clubs, in various places opposed her appearances. At all of her post-prison speaking engagements, agents of the Justice Department were present, well-dressed figures quietly taking notes just as those had who followed her around the country during the war. Indeed, they would accompany her for most of the rest of her public life, with her Justice Department files growing ever thicker and with new O'Hare files initiated in various police departments and local offices of the Federal Bureau of Investigation. She was often identified by agents in those files as a communist agitator.

In 1921 Frank O'Hare scheduled another national tour for Kate that, on paper at least, was exactly in the pattern of her prewar touring. She accepted clustered dates by regions, the South, the Plains States and the Pacific Northwest, the southwest, and the east. Most of them took place without any major problems, and she reported that the size of the crowds was "far beyond the wildest hopes" of the sponsoring groups. On May Day she spoke to a capacity crowd in Cleveland under the auspices of a local Congregationalist Church. In Miami, Florida, she drew an audience of one thousand, after which local public school officials were attacked for allowing her to use their facilities. Sometimes washouts interfered with her train travel and caused her to miss her dates, for example, in Montana, but such transportation hazards were nothing new to this woman who was in her third decade of riding the rails. In Weston, West Virginia, the day of her talk an ordinance was passed at the behest of the local American Legion prohibiting public speeches that day. A local Socialist challenged the ordinance and was arrested. In Oakland, California, the police chief banned O'Hare's talk before she arrived but in Arizona she gave successful talks managed by an organization called World War Veterans. In Portland, Oregon, she held meetings sponsored by the local IWW Defense Committee. In North Dakota, most of her engagements went off very well, even though some antagonism to O'Hare could have been anticipated. She spoke in a half-dozen cities in that state, including Bowman. There she was enthusiastically welcomed back by an overflow audience of one thousand North Dakotans clamoring to get into the theater to hear her. A dance in her honor was held that evening. Her appearance scheduled for Minot, however, had to be relocated out of town, because of threats that local Socialists believed to be serious, and in Williston she first spoke outside of town for the same reason but the imposing turnout emboldened her to speak in town that evening.

The major event of the 1921 tour occurred in Twin Falls, Idaho, on July 1 where she was kidnapped by disgruntled war veterans. Prior to her arrival, the local American Legion and G.A.R. posts had petitioned the city council to prevent O'Hare from speaking in town, and other groups, such as the Elks and Knights of Pythias, had supported them. Accordingly, the city council passed an ordinance forbidding even street-corner talks. Whereas she had spoken in the summer of 1917 in the region without incident, since then Idaho had experienced its own Red Scare against the IWW and the Nonpartisan League, and her fame as well as the "flaming red attire" in which she appeared at some of her talks apparently enraged some Idahoans. A local socialist official telephoned her in Vale, Oregon, suggesting that she skip Twin Falls. O'Hare dismissed the idea with the remark that "barking dogs don't bite." Shortly after she arrived, three carloads of men arrived at her boarding house, asked to see her, and then drove off with her. Twelve hours later she turned up, shaken but unharmed, in Montello, Nevada, having escaped across the high desert in circumstances that have never been clarified. She tried unsuccessfully to get the authorities to press charges against her abductors, while the Socialist party telegraphed complaints to United States Attorney General Harry Daugherty. Incredibly undaunted, O'Hare resumed her schedule, and rejoined her fourteen-year-old daughter, Kathleen, who had been on this leg of the tour with her. O'Hare proceeded to speak on July 3 in Pocatello despite her nervous sponsors. She was locked out of the lecture hall by the panicky management so she spoke in front of a small crowd at a machine shop. But after that, the memories of what O'Hare termed the "rough handling" overwhelmed her, and she canceled the remaining dates of her tour. One month later she headed west to restart her work.

In addition to touring as soon as she was free, O'Hare plunged immediately into writing features for the remaining socialist press. She at once started a weekly column for a new Socialist party paper called the *New Day* and wrote booklets, usually on social conditions, crime or prisons, which Frank published. By November 1920, she and Frank transformed *Frank O'Hare's Bulletin* into a revived *National Rip-Saw.* They styled it "the voice of the voiceless" which would educate working people to the postwar world and develop opportunities for change. They specifically ignored any political label for the moment. The O'Hares moved back to Girard where they arranged to have the reborn *Rip-Saw* printed at the plant of the old *Appeal to Reason,* which in 1920 published as the *New Appeal.* The previous years had been hard on the *Appeal* as it had flipflopped over support or opposition to the war. Once it endorsed the war effort, it managed to continue publishing unlike so many socialist periodicals but it lost the bulk of its subscribers. The *New Appeal* was managed in 1920 by two journalists who had both been on the staff of the socialist daily, the *New York Call,* Louis Kopelin and Emanuel Haldeman-Julius. But their collaboration with the O'Hares turned out to be an unworkable and brief interlude.

A little over a year after establishing themselves once again in Girard, Frank and Kate O'Hare had to move the paper back to St. Louis. The *Rip-Saw* had been assigned working space of only an inadequate corner of the *Appeal* building, and had no access to staff time whatsoever. In fact, the O'Hare children had to be drafted to do the binding and other jobs. Under the circumstances, it was impossible to publish the *Rip-Saw,* and the ensuing arguments culminated in Haldeman-Julius firing the O'Hares, whom he chose to view as employees. By subterfuge, the O'Hares were able to smuggle their own mailing lists out of the building, and they stored them at old Mrs. Tubbs's, Kate's landlady in her single days in Girard. O'Hare then tracked down rumors that the *Appeal* was about to be purchased by Upton Sinclair, which might have allowed their association with the *Appeal* to continue. When it was clear that Sinclair was not going to take over the *Appeal,* the O'Hares floundered about for a workable arrangement for their newspaper.

Throughout these upheavals, Kate O'Hare continued to comment on and involve herself in militant political activities. She was moved by the hard times that working people, especially farmers, experienced in those postwar years. She reported to her readers that she had found everywhere "the same disillusionment, bitterness and despair. Never have I seen the soul of mankind so harried and distressed." Because of the marked disparity between the havenots and the haves, O'Hare sensed what she called the "smoldering fires of unrest." She was not certain in what form such unrest would eventually culminate but it seemed clear to her that the dispossessed would find some means to express their needs and hopes. She discounted the Socialist party. She argued that while the party had done significant work in educating the American public, some other vehicle would emerge as an expression of workers' hopes. She believed that rather than a political party, an economic organization, probably industrial unionization of some sort, would best represent American workers. She applauded the efforts of William Z. Foster, whom later she would oppose as a sectarian communist, for challenging the narrow and tepid craft unionism of the American Federation of Labor in favor of a more inclusive and aggressive industrial unionism.

O'Hare attended and reported on the meetings of the Conference for Progressive Political Action. Starting in 1922, she welcomed this series of coalition-building conferences of farmers, labor, Socialists, Progressives and others. She thought that these activities might result in the United States achieving a strong and nonideological movement for progressive change. Unconcerned about the possibility of party disciplinary action for incorrect positions, she applauded the collaboration of Socialists with non-Socialists and of workers with farmers, and wrote favorably about any farmer-labor joint actions. When activities culminated in the nomination of progressive Republican Senator Robert M. LaFollette, Sr. for the presidency on a third-party ticket in 1924 O'Hare did not think that this campaign was as important as the mere fact of the emerging progressive coalition.

The core of O'Hare's concerns in these years, as already has been noted, was two-fold. First, she was committed to obtaining political amnesty for those convicted under the federal Espionage and Sedition Acts and under comparable state legislation, and second, she was determined to stamp out contract labor in the prison system. In speech after speech, as she crisscrossed the country, she blasted the government for continuing to hold individuals convicted under unconstitutional measures during wartime hysteria. She raised funds during her tours to help with the legal costs of various political prisoners, whether they were Socialists, anarchists, or Wobblies, and she publicized their cases. Simultaneously, she argued that the plight of all prisoners had to be confronted. In her talks on behalf of amnesty, she emphasized that individual cases were not the important issue. While she would allude to Mollie Steimer, still locked up in Jefferson City, Gene Debs, confined to the Atlanta Penitentiary, Tom Mooney in San Quentin, and the over one hundred members of the IWW either in prisons or out on bail, she maintained that constitutional issues had to be posed. She asked audiences rhetorically: "[In] all the prosecution and persecution of people for political and economic beliefs in the United States during the last three or four years, has that been contrary to the Constitution, or has it been carried on in a Constitutional way?" Even more pointedly, she asked whether it was a punishable crime to maintain publicly that a violation of the constitution had occurred, as seemed to her the experience of many of those then in prison. If people could no longer enjoy freedom of speech and of the press, then the United States was no longer the republic with what she called the limited democracy of the past but in fact a despotic nation.

O'Hare came up with the idea of a testimonial fund on behalf of Katherine Debs, Gene's wife, in order to use her to dramatize his imprisonment as symbolic of all the political prisoners. The November 1921 issue of the *Rip-Saw* announced a fundraiser for Mrs. Debs. The latter, a withdrawn, taciturn, private, apolitical woman, who may have detested the world in which her husband spent his life, was appalled by the campaign, and as money arrived at her home in Terre Haute, submitted by various rank-and-file Socialists, she returned the contributions. The O'Hares, after meeting with Kate Debs, canceled the campaign and returned any funds sent to their office. That Christmas Gene Debs was freed from prison, his sentence having been commuted by President Warren G. Harding, and the O'Hares organized his welcome-home celebration at Terre Haute. O'Hare then devoted her time to winning the freedom of the less famous political prisoners.

To focus national attention on the prisoners, Kate O'Hare borrowed an idea which militants had used occasionally in the past. She decided to spotlight the families whose husbands and fathers were imprisoned, as she had tried to do through Katherine Debs. She organized and led a procession of women and children to Washington, D.C. to petition the president to grant amnesty for the remaining political prisoners. Such a bold and even melodramatic gesture had its antecedents in a number of earlier strike situations, such as at Lawrence, Massachusetts, a decade earlier in 1912, when the children of the strikers in a well-publicized effort were evacuated from the city for their own safety and sheltered in workers' homes elsewhere. The ploy earned public and even Congressional sympathy, and a committee of the House of Representatives, spurred on by Victor Berger, held hearings which helped end the strike. The following year in a strike in Paterson, New Jersey, strikers' children were also removed from their homes and sent to live in nearby cities, thus generating publicity, although no tangible benefits resulted for the strikers.

A special edition of the *Rip-Saw* announced that a "Children's Crusade" would travel to the nation's capitol to try to win freedom for the children's fathers. The O'Hares also published a booklet to generate publicity and to raise funds for the project. An initial group of at least twenty-two women and children assembled in St. Louis at Union Station— their departure filmed by a camera crew—and took on additional women and children on stops en route to Washington in over a dozen cities. The families of over thirty prisoners participated on behalf of one hundred thirteen men. Some of the prisoners were members of the Wobblies, such as Ralph Chaplin who had edited the IWW periodical, *Solidarity*. Others were unknown pacifists, and some were farmers charged with having taken up arms against the government in Oklahoma's so-called Green Corn Rebellion in which the Sooner State's Socialist party was destroyed. At each stop, rallies and demonstrations were held at churches and labor halls, and donations collected so that the group could proceed to the next stop on its itinerary. The national media covered the story, just as O'Hare had hoped. Not only the metropolitan daily newspapers, such as the *St. Louis Post-Dispatch,* the *Cleveland Plaindealer,* the *Cincinnati Enquirer,* and the *Washington Evening Star,* among others, but magazines and newsreels also featured the human-interest story. O'Hare tried unsuccessfully to minimize her own role to help the effort appear to be a grassroots crusade. She drummed up middle-class, progressive, and civil libertarian support so that the episode could not be dismissed as a radical scheme of Socialists and Wobblies, as she confided to Caroline Lowe. She was pleased, for example, when her dentist, no militant, offered funds to help underwrite the trip. O'Hare committed so much energy and time to the crusade that she seemed to be on the verge of collapse. Frank pleaded with her to take some time off so that she would not "go to pieces." but, true to her lifelong pattern, she persisted.

Kate O'Hare, using the departure scene for all it was worth, described the crusaders in the *Rip-Saw* in these words: "The very heavens wept at the spectacle and the children plodded wearily through rain, too inured to hardship and too intent on their mission to be disturbed by physical discomfort." Some children held aloft placards announcing that it had been "Four Years Since I Have Seen My Daddy."

At Terre Haute, Debs met them, despite an illness. A festive dinner was spread for them at the Central Trades and Labor Hall. In contrast, in Indianapolis, the national headquarters of the American Legion, no demonstrations or leafleting were permitted, so the crusaders just picked up the contingent waiting for them and moved on. From Chicago, a group met up with them that had enjoyed a send-off by Jane Addams, herself having faced criticism during the war for her pacifism, and also by Robert M. Lovell, the noted civil liberties advocate.

In Cincinnati, fifteen different civic and women's groups welcomed them. In Detroit, a comrade of Emma Goldman's, Agnes Inglis, headed a reception committee which fed them. In New York, where the Socialist party was noticeably unsupportive (perhaps, as Frank O'Hare suggested, fearful that its own efforts on behalf of amnesty would be undercut by this autonomous movement), Elizabeth Gurley Flynn was in charge of their stopover. The children dined sumptuously, were taken to the circus and were welcomed to the home of Dorothy Whitney Straight, who, a few years earlier, had used her fortune to bankroll the founding of the *New Republic*. In Philadelphia, the children were given tours of Independence Hall and other historic buildings. In Baltimore, the group was received by the daughter of the founder of The Johns Hopkins University, Elizabeth Gilman.

Once in Washington, D.C., as O'Hare anticipated, the group of thirty-seven women and children was not allowed to see President Harding, a fact which she was able to use effectively in her next column. She wrote that "The great man of whom [the children] had dreamed, turned them away from the White House door with the message that they were free to play on the White House lawn." A contingent of the crusaders was ushered in to see Attorney General Daugherty. During the conversation, he and O'Hare argued about the issue of a blanket amnesty but he did agree that the various cases would be reviewed on an individual basis.

The Children's Crusade marked the apex of O'Hare's achievements in winning national attention for a cause. The crusade had indeed gained the support or at least attention of the various groups which she felt it required to have any chance for success—progressives, pacifists, women's and religious organizations, and the media. While the actual impact of the publicity cannot be definitively assessed, in the following year and a half the sentences of the political prisoners were commuted. As late as the 1940s, Thomas L. Stokes, a nationally syndicated columnist, remembered O'Hare and her crusade, and he noted with irony that the crusaders seated in the outer office of the Attorney General's office heard the telephone receptionist answering the phone with one word, "Justice."

Kate O'Hare's post-prison lecture tours from 1920 throughout that decade dealt with conditions in American prisons as reflected in her own experience in the Missouri State Penitentiary. No matter what the topic or issue at hand, she always focused her audience's attention at some point on the inhumanity of the prison system. Sometimes attired in a hideous dress of green, purple and black stripes given to her by prison officials on the day that she was freed, she was a riveting figure. She strode the stage sketching the abysmal conditions under which people were incarcerated, quarters infected with rats and roaches, food infested with worms and maggots, and facilities shared with diseased inmates. She argued that some of the horrific foods and supplies which prisoners received stemmed from prison officials siphoning off funds for their own purposes. She described the lack of adequate recreational facilities and the cruel punishments, both daily and occasionally, such as bread-and-water diets or confinement in cold, barren punishment dungeons.

Her fundamental position on prisons and prisoners was expressed as follows in a talk in a dialogue format in Cleveland in 1921:

"What are prisons for?" You say, "For the punishment and reform of criminals." "What are criminals?" You say, "Criminals are people who violate the law." "What are criminal laws?" You say, "Criminal laws are statutes enacted for the protection of human life, human liberty and property. Then, if anyone violated a law made for the protection of life, liberty or property, he is a criminal. Here is a very interesting thing. We have volumes and volumes of criminal laws. Human life is after all the greatest thing, and yet, of all the volumes of criminal laws, 90% are for the protection of property and 10% for the protection of life and liberty."

While it was not possible, according to O'Hare, to develop an ideal reformatory system under capitalism any more than there could be an ideal educational system, nevertheless, ameliorative efforts had to be attempted. In her talks and her writings, she recommended that prisons be redesigned so that they were more hospital-like, devoted to healing by physicians, psychologists, and teachers of the unfortunate, the social delinquent and those she referred to as the "subnormal" in society. If penal institutions could be so reshaped, no longer simply holding tanks and punishment cells, then even though society had not yet transitioned to a system more caring than capitalism, a more sane and rational approach could exist. Ample state and federal funding, trained personnel, separate quarters for different types of inmates, and scientific methods might be first steps toward not simply the reformation of prisons but a true reconstruction of the system of dealing with the pathological segment of society.

As she toured and as the years passed, O'Hare integrated new topics and points into her lectures on crime and criminals. She described studies in which she had participated, for example, with the Housing Commission of New York City, the data of which suggested that criminal behavior increased in direct ratio to the number of people per room of housing units. She also reported that prisons by the mid-twenties were filling up with a hefty population of war veterans, men trained for war but without guidelines for civilian life. She also noted that more government funds, however poorly funneled, were being devoted to correctional institutions than to public schools. She termed this imbalance a very serious matter which was certain to affect the "very foundation and stability" of American society. Obviously, she still believed that environmental factors were crucial shaping variables. Society needed to rethink its priorities in order to develop a healthier public.

Appearing more and more routinely under the auspices of Central Labor Councils rather than locals of the Socialist party, O'Hare took special pains to attack the convict labor system that had so outraged her at Jefferson City. Industrial tasks assigned to prisoners through the penal institution but under the control of private contractors had offended her as akin to a system of slavery, as job competition, and as undermining union. O'Hare was a sufficiently well-known public figure so that her remarks on this topic drew attention. Moreover, by the mid-twenties, her lecture tours began to be jointly funded by an unusual partnership of the Garment Manufacturers' Association and the United Garment Workers' Union, and the subject of prison-made products competing with free labor became the theme of her talks. To further publicize the issue, she along with Frank highlighted the topic in their renamed *Rip-Saw,* which in November 1922, became the *American Vanguard.* In addition, Kate O'Hare was able to publish her articles on the subject in periodicals with greater circulation such as the *Nation.*

Kate O'Hare saw this cause as not only one which grew naturally out of her prison experience but also as another, and final, task which she had undertaken on behalf of the labor movement. She felt that she was moving on to other areas. The object of her current campaign was not to undermine prison labor itself for, as she had written much earlier, inmates needed the discipline of work and needed, more basically than that, something to do with their endless days. But their work should be at fair wages and with an appropriate return to the institutions which bore their overhead, and their labor should not compete with work outside the prison walls. In 1923, 6,083 convicts (6% of the U.S. prison population) worked under the contract system. The value of prison-made products sold on the open market was forty-three million dollars. O'Hare's object was to destroy the system of prison contractors, operational in forty-two states, she maintained with some exaggeration. Every state had to have comprehensive and effective legislation prohibiting contract labor, unlike laws such as in Missouri which had not weakened the system of contract labor at all. The jobbers involved must be put out of business. O'Hare wanted to educate the public to an awareness of prison-manufactured goods which, she argued, were foisted on unsuspecting customers. In addition to enlightening consumers, she wanted wholesalers, retailers, and unions to be more cognizant of the unfair labor practices which they faced. She also sought to rouse the public over the possibility of contracting whatever communicable diseases prison-made goods might carry. In the long-run, she hoped that only union-label garments would be bought or at least, those bearing the label of a reputable manufacture.

O'Hare worked with organized labor to establish a network of convict labor committees across the country. In Missouri, Illinois, New York and a number of other states, committees were set up, and Frank O'Hare printed circulars for them to distribute. They especially concentrated their efforts on areas where jobbers had managed to obtain exclusive contracts with prisons. The O'Hares tried to get the American Federation of Labor to allow them to work through its headquarters but that collaboration was contingent upon funding from the garment manufacturers which never was secured. Also, because organized labor in the decade of the twenties was on the defensive, besieged by employer anti-union campaigns, anti-labor court decisions, and a declining membership, the A.F.L. never played the kind of role in the campaign which the O'Hares wanted. But the A.F.L. cooperated as it could, and permitted O'Hare's articles to circulate through its news bureau. Through the efforts especially of the United Garment Workers' Union, O'Hare was programmed to appear at as many conventions of state federations of labor as possible as well as annual conventions of social service and religious groups and others whose interest in the issue might easily be awakened. She made use of her own contacts and experience in every way that she could to further the campaign. For example, she met with the Governor and the legislature of Missouri, and she was the star attraction at a conference on prison labor in Jefferson City, Missouri, her very presence in the city of her incarceration dramatizing the subject of contract labor. President Reuben Wood of the Missouri State Federation of Labor, with whom O'Hare's ties went back at least fifteen years, used his office to arrange additional speaking dates for her. She also made an effort to follow the trail of clothing produced at the Missouri State Penitentiary from jobbers to retailers. Results were slow but encouraging, and when prison contractors tried to coopt her to write prison research features for them, she knew the tide was turning. Federal legislation, the Hawes-Cooper Bill, was passed in 1929, allowing states the power to prevent the transportation of prison-made goods across state lines. Thereafter, prison-made products were increasingly made for the use of government agencies and departments and the contractors were put out of business. Thus, by the 1930s O'Hare's goals were generally achieved.

In the midst of the campaign, O'Hare wrote to her old prison comrade, Emma Goldman, in London, England, that she was about ready to "to stop saving the world." She told her that she felt as if she were doing the work for them both since Goldman, a woman without a country, was not in the United States. She had her applications repeatedly turned down by the State Department even to visit the country which had arbitrarily denaturalized her. O'Hare, confiding to Goldman as she would to few others, remarked that she felt herself to be "sort of a political orphan now with no place to lay my head." The bond between these two political activists who would once not have considered that they could have a common perspective, was reflected by O'Hare agreeing with Goldman "that the Communists" in their own way were "as reactionary as the Coolidge gang," and more ruthless, she added. Prison had indeed made for strange bedfellows. Both women by 1925 were without causes in which they could feel the confidence of their earlier years. They each lived a nomadic existence, Goldman, subject to the whims and mysteries of government authorities and regulations, and O'Hare, touring for one cause and then another, with her focus dependent on which group sponsored her lectures. While touring seemed to be in her blood, comparable to traveling hucksters and entertainers, and it always had perked her up, she was approaching the age of fifty and increasingly the old routine had diminishing returns for her.

During the prison contract labor campaign, Kate O'Hare embarked on what would be the last deep, all-engrossing commitment she would make, and it was also the last adventure shared with Frank O'Hare. Throughout her adult life, she was interested in the subject of worker's education. Ever since she and Frank O'Hare had met at the International School of Social Economy at the beginning of the century, both of them had been drawn to various experiments in labor education. She cared deeply about the quality of the education offered to working people; she also wanted to see them educated in accord with their own class interests. She had been influenced by J. A. Wayland who wrote that "To remain ignorant is to remain a slave." This perspective has been elaborated on by a contemporary educational historian, William J. Reese, when he discussed American public schools as "contested terrain." He wrote of education as inherently political in its training of its students in value-laden directions and its shaping them into becoming adjuncts of the market economy.

Kate O'Hare several times visited the People's College in Fort Scott, Kansas, which emerged from the remnant of the International School. The college was partially supported by funds from the *Appeal to Reason,* and nationally known Socialists worked on its staff, such as Arthur Le Sueur, an attorney who became the socialist mayor of Minot, North Dakota, and who ran for the socialist nomination for the presidency in 1916. O'Hare's interest in education was a factor in the family taking up residence in the Ruskin Colony in Florida during World War I. Although it was Frank O'Hare who was especially identified with Ruskin since Kate was on the road constantly at the time and then caught up in her legal struggles, Kate and socialist educator, William Zeuch, analyzed the failure of Ruskin to see if they could design a more successful experimental school for workers.

Programs of workers education originated in Europe. Accordingly, American labor colleges were influenced by European examples as they set out to educate working people, especially in the skills that could help them serve the labor movement. The Socialist party, too, endorsed the idea of education that upheld workers' culture and was fitted to their needs. The party sponsored its own Sunday Schools, summer classes, and weekend schools for adults. The most well known party-related educational institution was the Rand School for Social Science founded in

New York in 1906, and the most famous southern-based training school for a new social order was the Highlander Folk School in Tennessee which opened in 1932. So O'Hare was very much in tune with socialist thinking when she enmeshed herself in educational and curricular development.

Zeuch, O'Hare's collaborator and publicist during her incarceration, had been a research assistant to John R. Commons, one of the founders of the field of labor studies at the famous Wisconsin School at Madison, where the young man had earned his doctorate in 1922. Zeuch remembered that he and Kate O'Hare had "talked over [our] own educational ideas, and decided to work together to establish a school for workers [after the war] we took up our plans again. For a period of six years, all told, we searched for an opportunity to launch our experiment."

An appropriate opportunity caught their attention in 1922. Fortuitously, it occurred at the same time that the O'Hares were casting about for a home for their newspaper. In the village called Newllano, Louisiana (formerly known as Stables), a cooperative colony had been established a few years earlier by Job Harriman, a Socialist who had run for the vice-presidency as Debs's running mate in 1900 and for mayor of Los Angeles in 1911. The Llano Cooperative Colony was established in Antelope Valley in the Mojave Desert in 1914 and seemed to thrive. But because of water scarcity, hostile neighbors, and other problems, Harriman had relocated the colony to southwestern Louisiana in Vernon Parish near the town of Leesville in 1918. While the trauma of the move resulted in a membership decline from perhaps over 200 to 65, by 1922 the colony seemed to be prospering once more, and it eventually expanded to a population of 400.

Kate O'Hare visited Newllano in 1922 to look it over, and as Frank later described it, she was "swept overboard," convinced that they should join the colonists. Kate and Frank O'Hare agreed that the colony would be the perfect base for them, and they quickly worked out arrangements with the colony's administrators. Their newspaper, the *American Vanguard,* was to be printed in the colony's printshop at no cost for one year, after which time its ownership would be transferred to the colony. The O'Hares would be assigned membership in the colony, the one thousand dollar fee waived. She and Zeuch would establish their long-dreamed of workers' college at Newllano on forty acres donated by the colony, in return for which colonists were eligible for free tuition. Perhaps most important to the O'Hares was that they would live and work among like-minded people in a cooperative setting and be able to integrate many of their interests.

The O'Hare family moved to Newllano in March 1923. By then, several cottage industries had been established, such as a saw mill, a grist mill, a sash factory, a brickyard, a bakery, and a dairy, as well as assorted farming ventures such as raising cattle, and rice and other crops. Kate O'Hare immediately began to prepare the plans for the residential labor college so that it could open in the fall, and within a month she set off on a lecture tour to raise funds. So, as always, she was on the road while Frank and the children remained at Newllano. Frank rejoiced in the routine which permitted him to concentrate on the editing and production of the newspaper, freed of all responsibilities for meals, lodging, and monthly bills.

Kate O'Hare's first fundraising expedition from Newllano was successful. Backed by the *Vanguard's* publicity about the forthcoming opening of Commonwealth College, she was able to generate funds and numerous letters of inquiry from prospective students. Once back in Newllano, she became dangerously ill that July with typhoid fever, running a temperature of 103 degrees. Owing to the colony's primitive plumbing and sewerage facilities—not so different from the summer encampments—typhoid was not an unexpected visitor. O'Hare lost more than twenty pounds, which did not in itself displease her, but the illness threatened the opening of the college in October. However, true to form, she was soon traveling again. She devoted considerable energy toward convincing the United Mine Workers of Illinois to invest in the college following the union's initial expression of interest. However, she was disappointed when she went to confer in person and, in fact, had to wire for funds to permit her to return home from Illinois where she was stranded. Thereafter, she travelled under the auspices of the contract labor campaign, and she was able to use those talks also to publicize Commonwealth College.

Commonwealth College opened in October 1923, for the first of what would be seventeen academic years. Kate O'Hare, the key figure in Commonwealth's early history, served in a variety of capacities including trustee, instructor, curriculum coordinator, and field director. She was the keynote speaker at the opening ceremonies for the college, and in her talk provided the audience with both a history of education and the goals of the college. She explained,

> The history of education in the United States has been very largely the story of the efforts of the ruling classes to impose their ideals of culture upon the growing generation. Historians now admit that our free school system, and our state-supported institutions of higher learning are monuments to the tenacity, genius, and struggles of unknown and unhonored trade unionists who waged the battle for free schools for more than half a century. But . . . the free schools are too powerful a force in shaping the ideals of the coming generation to be overlooked by the ruling class, and . . . our public school system has been seized upon by the owning class and made a most effective machine to shape the development of the coming generation in accordance with its ideals of life.

She declared that workers needed access to the new social sciences in programs which harmonized with their lives and culture. Accordingly, Commonwealth College was opening as a needed institution. It would be a college by the workers and for the workers. It signified the development of "institutions . . . , suited to the needs of the common people." In conclusion, O'Hare stated, "Commonwealth comes into being to build a culture in overalls and workmarked hands; a culture whose ideal is a working class fit to inherit and hold the earth and the fullness thereof . . . [It] means to the workers the opening of the long-locked doors of learning . . . , a laboratory for working out the technique of co-operative life, and a crucible for refining the ore of common humanity into pure and precious metal."

The students were to work for the colony four hours per day after attending classes in the mornings in a three-year program. But facilities were wholly inadequate for the ambitious plans of the college, and in no time factions emerged fighting over limited resources. Both the colony through its dictatorial administrator, George Pickett, and the college, through the O'Hares and Zeuch, the director, applied for assistance from the American Fund for Public Service. Known also as the Garland Fund, it provided grants to a great variety of progressive and radical causes between the two world wars. Roger Baldwin was one of the key figures at the Fund, but this did not help the O'Hares because the two Newllano applications canceled each other out. The colony administration moved against the O'Hares, and sought to absorb the college's programs. Kate O'Hare and Zeuch presented an eleven-point rebuttal to charges against them, arguing that the college needed to be structurally independent so as to insure its academic freedom. Following that imbroglio, the *Vanguard* was attacked on the grounds that the O'Hares had not cleared it of debt as they had promised. After some colonists petitioned the administration to expel the O'Hares in May 1924, the Newllano Board of Directors instead voted to terminate the publication of the newspaper.

The end of the brief partnership was clearly in sight. While the college had had a successful first year by most standards, the newspaper had not. Beyond that, the factionalism, always so endemic in the history of cooperative colonies, had erased the initial goodwill. The Newllano experience was simply a reenactment of earlier episodes, whether New Harmony, Indiana, or Brook Farm.

The O'Hares and Zeuch, and a Newllano secessionist faction loyal to the colony founder, Harriman, spent frantic months trying to relocate. Unable themselves to collaborate amicably, they ended up settling separately less than ten miles from each other in Polk County in western Arkansas. Dick O'Hare rented buildings for the college in Mena, Arkansas, and a tired contingent of staff and students arrived there at the end of 1924. Commonwealth College was established as a cooperative community in its permanent home the following spring in Mill Creek Valley nestled under Rich Mountain, a few miles from the Oklahoma border and looking toward the Southern Ozarks. A new Commonwealth College Association was formed, with Kate O'Hare, Zeuch, and W. C. Benton, an attorney who had been in the O'Hares' class in 1901 (and who would soon serve as Frank O'Hare's attorney in proceedings against Kate), as the trustees. Zeuch went to New York and obtained some operating monies from the Garland Fund, and O'Hare traveled there also to win support for the college.

The acreage the College acquired contained an old farmhouse and two barns, and timber and pasture land. Tents were at once raised, and construction began on classrooms, a library, and housing units, while simultaneously crops and a garden were planted hurriedly. Soon unpainted buildings of rough-sawed lumber with red roll asbestos roofing were completed and a dairy and chicken coops were set up. When O'Hare arrived that spring, she was apparently nonplused by the primitive living situation, and immediately she subsidized the completion of her own cottage. When Frank O'Hare came through later, he finished building a chimney for her cottage. She then lived comfortably during her periods of residence at Commonwealth, with the two youngest female students residing in her cottage so that she could chaperon them.

O'Hare served as field director and Professor of Sociology. She seemed to be everywhere. She pitched in and taught the students how to launder and cook, and in so doing, broke through whatever barriers they felt about her as a strong and famous personality (she wrote, apparently jokingly, that they initially viewed her as "an arrogant, tyrannical, narrow-minded Victorian"). A student recalled that the ultimate tribute to Kate O'Hare was that the students were proud of her rather than in awe. While she often wanted to be catered to, nevertheless, she inspired positive responses. She sometimes spontaneously baked biscuits for whoever showed up in the kitchen, and she was generally viewed as the Grand

Hostess of Commonwealth College. She gave talks to the community meetings to which the college invited farm neighbors and Mena residents. Her formal teaching consisted of a class on women and the home. Its lectures were drawn from her prewar writings entitled "The Tale of A Rib." It was a popular offering, and auditors crowded in with the enrolled students.

A survey of the student body was conducted in 1926. Limited by space considerations to fifty students, Commonwealth enrolled forty-two: twenty-eight men and fourteen women. The median age of the students was twenty-two, with the oldest fifty. While no educational prerequisites had been established, half the students had at least attended high school. They hailed from throughout the United States. Not surprisingly, many came from labor backgrounds: fifteen were union members and twelve belonged to one or another radical political party.

The curriculum included history and government, economics and literature, law, mathematics, sociology and psychology, stenography, languages, and music. As at the College's previous site in Louisiana, the students attended classes in the mornings and worked on behalf of the school in the afternoon. In the evenings, general discussions were held, poetry readings and plays given, with dances scheduled on some Saturday evenings. Visitors sometimes addressed the students. They included representatives of other labor schools, officials of labor federations and unions, Charles H. Kerr of the socialist publishing company of that name, and Roger Baldwin who had agreed to serve on Commonwealth's advisory board.

Despite financial and physical problems, Commonwealth College was off to a good start in Arkansas. But O'Hare's days with the school were numbered. In fact, she was seldom in residence for long. More and more, she resided in New York City. She remarked that she needed to be near publishers in order to "vamp" them into acceptance of her manuscripts on behalf of Commonwealth and the convict labor campaign. But in actuality, she was beginning to feel that the most major chapter of her life had ended. Ironically, during the time of the relocation to

Arkansas, she had written that she could well imagine abandoning the political battles and campaign trails in order to spend her "declining days" at Commonwealth.

During the colonists' strife-torn year of 1924, the correspondence between the O'Hares became quite strained. At best, it was simply businesslike as they discussed funding, contracts, and touring schedules. But they also carped at each other in ways that had not marked their previous correspondence. Kate sharply rebuked Frank for finding it necessary "to make critical remarks concerning me" in a letter he wrote to an associate. Frank, in a letter to relatives written during a stressful moment when he felt he needed her to be with him, compared Kate in a disparaging way to Woodrow Wilson, who had to go to Paris and be in the limelight. That year, Kate and Frank O'Hare separated. Not many observers recognized it since the O'Hares acted as if nothing unusual had occurred. Kate O'Hare was on the road, operating out of what was increasingly her New York base, but her relocation was explained away as only a slight variation of the normal work-driven routine. But from December 1924, when Frank wrote that they should announce their separation and make it official, no longer having to rationalize their living arrangements, until 1926, they refrained from any public notification. Kate began to push for a divorce, even suggesting that Frank sue her on grounds of desertion, and that if he refused, she would go to Mexico to file there. Frank, however, was by then holding back and delaying. He had fallen into a deep depression, and at least one colleague, Covington Hall, recalled that he was suicidal. To hurt his wife, he destroyed her files and correspondence. In a sorrowful Christmas letter to his son, Dick, Frank regretted that he did not have even "diplomatic relations" with his estranged wife, or with daughter, Kathleen, either, who had temporarily broken with Frank.

In March 1926, Kate O'Hare wrote to Frank from San Francisco that she was observing another birthday, and she felt the need to have their affairs settled. She said that she "simply cannot conceive going back to the stress and strain, conflicts and brain storms, wretchedness and misery of other days. I am far more healthy, happy and content than for many years. And I am sure you are also . . . we make life hell for each other. Economic conditions never permitted me to leave my work, maybe I could not have done it if they had, and you are not so constituted that you can be my husband."

Rather than celebrating a twenty-fifth anniversary, Kate O'Hare chastised Frank with not having been a good husband but she also assumed some responsibility for the breakdown of the marriage. She was able to say that she sometimes drove him "to do insane things." At other times, however, her alienation from Frank was more pronounced. Ten days later, she wrote to him from Portland, Oregon: "I feel almost sure now that all the love I once had for you is quite dead. It died very hard—took many years of endless suffering and misery to kill it—but I fear that it is as dead as my youth. . . ." But then again, she wrote that: "I did the best I could, the best I knew, but it was not sufficient. You wanted more than I was, wanted me to give more than I could—and—well it was just hell."

She acknowledged loneliness at times but did not know if she would every wish to marry again. She reflected that the last year apart, despite working as hard as ever, was "a Heaven of peace," which was marked by appreciation from those she worked with and freedom from nervous strain, in contrast to the usual conditions she experienced around Frank. She continued to rebuff his suggestions that they try a reconciliation. Kate declared that she would need a guarantee from a crowd of psychologists and psychiatrists that Frank had mastered what she called his "complexes and conflicts" before she would be able to consider a reconciliation. Eventually, she told Kathleen that the only place she would even see Frank was "in the office of a psychiatrist." She would no longer allow herself to be drawn into his "whirlpool of . . . emotional instability." After twenty years of trying to get him to consult specialists for his "neuroses" whether or not he did so now, she said, was up to him. She was finished with what she seemed to feel was perhaps a manic-depressive personality. She also felt finished with an aspect of their life which she had never referred to before in her extant letters, what she saw as his tendency to plan their ventures on imaginary foundations. Somewhat later, in an acrimonious moment of stress over the emotional wreck of daughter Kathleen's life after her marriage, Kate rebuked Frank emphatically as she asked if he could "come across just once in a whole lifetime."

Despite what she termed her long-held antipathy toward the idea of divorce, she was resolved that they be free of each other. In 1928, the O'Hares were divorced. Each of them remarried later that year and on the same day, thus suggesting that ties remained to each other. Later, when Frank pleaded for a written statement from Kate to allow him to get an annulment of their marriage for the sake of his new wife's Catholicism, Kate tried to be cooperative. She agreed to acknowledge that she had never held a Catholic-like view that marriages could not be dissolved but she would not state, and thereby make a sham of what they once shared, that they had entered into a trial marriage in accord with then-current free love theories.

Kate O'Hare married Charles C. Cunningham, an engineer and businessman from the South who was known as "the Colonel." They were married in San Jose, California, with Walter Thomas Mills presiding at the ceremony. She settled down for the first time in her life to what she described as perfect companionship, peace, and economic security, with "a yard full of flowers, and . . . days full of sunshine and leisure." She occasionally saw comrades from the old days, such as Grace and George Brewer who lived in San Francisco, but she did not feel the need to seek out those connections.

Three years later, she wrote to Theodore Debs, the brother of the then-deceased Gene Debs, in what was a kind of eulogy to her past life.

> Sometimes I get rather restless feeling that there is energy and training going to waste that should be used in some socially useful manner. But when I look around I can see no organization or movement that seems to offer a satisfactory field for my services. The organized labor movement seems to be slowly dying of dry rot, and the poor, pitiful . . . Socialist Party is to me a heart-breaking tragedy. So I cook my husband's meals and darn his socks

and pamper him shamefully. I putter about my flowers and read and write as the spirit moves me and wonder if fate has decided that its [sic] time for me to call it a day's work and sit down to rest. And perhaps, thank God that I have so nearly an ideal haven after a storm-tossed life.

She was then in her mid-fifties and thought her public life was behind her. The previous decade had been perhaps too volatile a time for her. O'Hare began that decade as a prisoner in Missouri State Penitentiary. When she was released in May 1920, she immediately jumped back into the fray. But society and her own priorities had changed. O'Hare's speaking tours were no longer focused on the message of socialism. She campaigned for the release of American political prisoners and the end of prison contract labor. Her successes in those areas saw her turn to an old interest, labor education, and she became a founder of Commonwealth College. While she was energetically committed to labor education, her attention increasingly was drawn to her personal life. The strains in her marriage, exacerbated by the impact of World War I and the tensions of her imprisonment, resulted in the O'Hares separating during the Commonwealth College years. When they divorced, Kate O'Hare remarried almost at once, and while she wanted to devote herself to a placid and secure life with her second husband, she had a few more episodes in the public arena ahead of her.

9

ENDINGS

In her mid-fifties, Kate Richards O'Hare Cunningham confided to a correspondent, with apparent relief, that the "storm-tossed" era of her life was behind her. Settled in California, with a financially established second husband, she had given up the grueling pace of public life: she was done with incessant train travel, lengthy speeches, and deadlines for newspaper columns. She was finished with the stresses and strains of ideological infighting and with the endless struggles on behalf of campaigns confronting discouraging odds. She could now relax; nothing required her to reenter the fray. However, Kate O'Hare remained a political creature. She still cared about public issues, and she still wanted to promote meaningful change. O'Hare saw enormous suffering during the Great Depression, and she could not stand aloof. New political movements, left of the New Deal, emerged. In the 1930s, Kate Cunningham—still known as Kate O'Hare publicly— reentered the public arena and stood at the rostrum before audiences as in the old days.

Details of her life after 1930 are not well documented. In the early years of the depression, she seems to have clung to her private routine. Then, O'Hare witnessed a new left emerge in California as well as in some other states. One historian, James N. Gregory, has referred tellingly to an "unconventional left" appearing in those desperate years. The old left of the Socialist party and the Communist party was not able to attract masses of Americans in the electoral campaigns of the 1930s, but new groups did so. While some were merely vehicles for the ambitions of demagogues, most notably the Share-the-Wealth movement of Huey P. Long, others were genuine efforts to redistribute the abundance that existed in the country even in the midst of the depression.

In California, Upton Sinclair founded and led the End Poverty in California (EPIC) movement, which emerged as a grassroots campaign complete with volunteers, pageants, newspaper brigades, and tinges of evangelic revivalism somewhat reminiscent of the southwestern encampments. Sinclair, who had previously run for the United States Congress and the governorship of California on the socialist ticket, in 1934 ran for governor on the Democratic ballot. At first he was not taken seriously by mainstream politicians and the mass media. The Sinclair campaign was managed by the End Poverty League, independent of the Democratic party. One thousand EPIC clubs organized throughout the state. Sinclair managed to attract voters with his platform of production for use rather than for profit. He proposed the creation of an autonomous economic system within the existing capitalist structure: self-sufficient cooperative colonies of unemployed workers would be established on idle land, which the state would condemn and purchase; other jobless people would be put to work in state-purchased factories. Additionally, public pensions and taxation policies would be used to redistribute the wealth. The program was very attractive to many Californians and, not for the first time, a major reform movement swept the state. In a field of ten candidates, Upton Sinclair won the Democratic primary with 52 percent of the ballots cast.

Collectivist schemes were not new to California. Dozens of Bellamy Clubs, named for Edward Bellamy, who wrote a futuristic novel, *Looking Backward,* about the socialization of the American economy, had once organized in the state. California had also been offered some support for Marxist socialism. The quixotic socialist publisher and entrepreneur, Gaylord Wilshire, for whom Wilshire Boulevard is named, published his magazines and ran for office in Los Angeles in the late nineteenth century. In the years before World War I, six socialist weeklies were published in California: four in English, one in German, and one in Armenian. Socialists were elected as mayors and state legislators, and a network of Socialist locals crisscrossed the state.

In 1934 Kate O'Hare ventured out of her San Francisco home and signed on with the EPIC campaign. She welcomed the movement's effort to bring together diverse groups in a grassroots campaign. O'Hare had known Upton Sinclair for thirty years, through the Socialist party and also through other common causes, and they had occasionally corresponded. O'Hare joined the EPIC staff for the fall gubernatorial campaign. She wrote and toured, propagandizing for the movement as she traveled up and down the state. She worked with old colleagues; many of those highly placed in the campaign staff had also come out of the old Socialist party. O'Hare tried to win over various interest groups, and she used her old ties with labor to build support for EPIC. As always, she drew large audiences. She found it exhilarating to be joined in battle once again, and it obviously suited her to be back on the hustings. "We are living in a madhouse," she reported, "but with all the terrific strain things are going splendidly."

The election was the most bitter in California history, in the appraisal of historian Robert E. Burke. Virtually the entire mass media of the state supported the Republican candidate, James Rolph, Jr., attacked Sinclair as an atheist and a Communist, who would "Russianize" California. Meanwhile, the old left lambasted Sinclair as a social fascist and a traitor to the workers. Despite the battering he took, Sinclair doubled his vote in the general election, but it amounted to only 37.8 percent in a field of three. EPIC candidates won other offices—twenty-seven were sent to the state legislature.

Kate O'Hare stayed with EPIC following Sinclair's defeat, unlike the founder himself. O'Hare wanted to continue to build on the existing support for fundamental changes in the economic system. The critical mass for change must not be abandoned, O'Hare believed. She was thrilled that the EPIC campaign had accomplished what earlier progressive forces had not: the domination of old party political machinery. The campaign also developed, she believed, "the most militant economic-political organization that ever existed in this country," with the exception, she suggested, of the Nonpartisan League.

For six months, O'Hare served as the chair of the Executive Committee of the league and headed its educational department, working in the field and at headquarters. After decades of experience in political hierarchies, she was able to demonstrate a seasoned approach to her colleagues. Operating out of the league offices in Los Angeles, she tried to restore the financial health of the organization. She insisted that, above all, the *EPIC News,* the mouthpiece of the movement, continue to publish. It was of fundamental importance, she argued, that EPIC maintain a propaganda outlet for its loyal workers to distribute to potential supporters. Campaign debts simply had to be settled without sacrificing the newspaper. Another emphasis of O'Hare's was the expansion of EPIC's youth group. A youth movement was an insurance policy for any organization, she reasoned. However, she remained vigilant concerning possible communist influences in the Young EPICs. Certain that Communists would destroy EPIC to suit their own purposes, she insisted that infiltrators had to be ousted. Ironically, at that very time she was being investigated secretly by the Los Angles Police Department (which referred to O'Hare as "this ex-convict,") for "communistic activities."

Her key concern, which she continually raised with the board of directors, was of the dangerous vacuum left by Sinclair's departure. O'Hare knew that such a vacuum would somehow be filled. She watched her old colleague, J. Stitt Wilson, once the socialist mayor of Berkeley, siphon off some members for a spin-off organization, and worse, she saw "a plague of communists and shysters" circling like vultures over the movement. She deplored the board's inability to take decisive action to solve existing problems. O'Hare also had serious concerns about the effort to integrate the league and the Democratic party. She viewed it as a disastrous muddle. But the board of directors either would not or could not offer leadership for the league's activists, and that, she felt, placed her in an untenable position. Under the circumstances, all she could be was a "thumb twiddler." Writing that she was no good at that, she sorrowfully tendered her resignation from the executive committee in December 1935. Over the next three years, the End Poverty League collapsed and was swallowed up by the Democratic party.

O'Hare left public life again, but only for a year or so. In 1937, she joined the staff of a Wisconsin member of the House of Representatives, Thomas R. Amlie, and served in his Washington, D.C. office for over a year. Amlie represented the First Congressional District of southeastern Wisconsin, and he was a key member of an upper Midwest liberal coalition in Congress. This was another example of the unconventional left of the 1930s, which criticized New Deal efforts and wanted to push American progressivism and liberalism to the left.

O'Hare and Amlie were natural allies, having emerged from the same background and sharing the same beliefs. Amlie, a generation younger than O'Hare, was born in 1897 on a farm in North Dakota. While still a student, he had served as an organizer for the Nonpartisan League, and thereafter he had earned a law degree at the University of Wisconsin. He entered Congress as a Progressive Republican in 1931, and in his two other terms from 1935 to 1939, he served as a representative of the Progressive Party of Wisconsin. In the meantime, he led ultimately unsuccessful efforts to form a nationwide third party of various dissident movements, except Communists. To that end, he organized both the Farmer-Labor Political Federation and the American Commonwealth Political Federation. Kate O'Hare's presence on his staff was potentially very useful. She viewed the liberal groupings as "less left than we might wish" but worth working with and thought she might go on the road again to encourage a great coalition. She offered to represent Amlie in congressional staff meetings, believing that she could serve as a bridge between liberal Democrats and the left. Amlie was a Socialist in all but name, having denigrated the Socialist party for its dependence on unnecessarily foreign formulas. He believed that capitalism had run its course and that the government eventually would be forced to move beyond regulation to some form of collectivization. O'Hare, of course, had always held such views and was very comfortable working in such an ideological milieu.

While in Congress, Amlie supported many New Deal measures, although contemptuous of Franklin Roosevelt's efforts as mere palliatives ("charity capitalism," he termed them), a position with which O'Hare was in total agreement. She wrote about the administration's efforts to combat the depression in the same vein:

> All the powers of government were turned to salvaging the wreck and attempting to get it started under its own power. The Federal Government, poured billions into wrecked corporations, bankrupt railroads and wobbly banks. Congress worked frantically at "priming the pump" of private industry by hectic financing, subsidies and purchases of vast quantities of commodities, often at fantastic prices. The government hoped that if it poured enough money into the pump that had lost its priming, private industry might right itself and reabsorb the millions of unemployed. This did not happen, then the government started the most colossal job of charity dispensing ever conceived by the mind of men. . . . It was a spending debauch such as the world has never seen, but all directed towards turning civilization back to a system of scarcity which modern mass production methods had destroyed. . . . Washington has drawn its inspirations from graveyards, worn its eyes in the back of its collective head, and progressed like a crab, traveling backwards.

O'Hare heartily endorsed Amlie's efforts to move the United States toward a planned economy, reminiscent of Sinclair's ideas. The issue was posed as abundance versus scarcity. Amlie and his colleagues in the liberal congressional bloc, which included Gerald J. Boileau of Wisconsin, Jerry Voorhis of California (a colleague of O'Hare's in the End Poverty League), and Maury Maverick of Texas, promoted a planned economy based on production for use in contrast to the first New Deal's promotion of artificial scarcity. The measure they introduced was called the Industrial Expansion Act. It was intended to reverse the thrust of

Franklin Roosevelt's National Industrial Recovery Administration and Agricultural Adjustment Administration, orchestrate coordinated production increases, and divide the ultimate income. Such planned production would create jobs and expand purchasing power, and in addition it would limit any individual profits to 10 percent. In sum, it would mean planned abundance for Americans. As O'Hare wrote in an article published to promote the legislation: "We might . . . move out of the wreckage and shadows of the past and forward into an economy of abundance that will permit each human being to 'eat his bread in the sweat of his brow' and toss doles and relief clean out of our civilization." O'Hare, who had always aimed for a society in which everyone enjoyed independence, held no brief for the make-shift job programs that often characterized the second New Deal. Circumstances required that she support some of those policies in the face of desperate human need. But a planned system in which all shared in what the American economy could produce would mean, if not the socialist cooperative commonwealth of her earlier dreams, an America without want. In the 1930s, she was satisfied to be working for that.

Amlie also designed a farm tenancy bill in which O'Hare had great interest. It unsuccessfully opposed the Bankhead-Jones Farm Tenancy Act, which created the Farm Security Administration. Amlie and O'Hare both agreed it would not meet the basic needs of tenant farmers and sharecroppers. They were interested not only in addressing problems more fully, but also in approaching legislation pragmatically, and so they opposed, too, an alternative bill by a member of Amlie's congressional bloc that they felt had no chance of passage and was simply grandstanding. O'Hare, compared it to communist-like propaganda efforts. In support of Amlie's legislation, she again wrote features, which appeared in about one hundred newspapers and which she circulated to members of Congress.

O'Hare's work on Amlie's staff put her in the corridors of power for the first time in her life. She was at last where policy was made on economic issues with which she had been concerned for forty years: the plight of the unemployed, the exploitation of the tenant farmers, the need to harness the productive capabilities of the American economy on behalf of the people as a whole, and, most fundamentally, the shaping of a planned economy. She was serving on a congressional staff when one of the few measures ever directed toward a planned economy was introduced into the House of Representatives. She was simultaneously drawing together many of the key socioeconomic interests of her life, and also touching on new issues which the 1930s had brought to the forefront. Moreover, in this engaging role, O'Hare was often thrown together with many colleagues from earlier days. As examples, Milwaukee Mayor and former Socialist Dan Hoan, Oscar Ameringer, then editing the *American Guardian* in Oklahoma, and the educator W. E. Zeuch, then at Black Mountain College (who advised O'Hare to run for Congress) were all in Amlie's circle. It had to be a heady time for O'Hare.

In September 1938 Tom Amlie was defeated when he ran in Wisconsin's Progressive primary for the United States Senate. By then the Roosevelt record, however flawed, had destroyed any possibility of a new national party dedicated to economic equality becoming a major factor in American society. At that point, Kate O'Hare, who had acknowledged that she was homesick, left Washington and political life. She must have thought that she had at last reached the end of her career.

Kate Richards O'Hare had been home in northern California for only a few months when, late in 1938, a new position was offered to her. Culbert Olson, her colleague from the EPIC campaign, had been elected governor of California in November 1938. He was the first Democrat to hold that office in forty-four years, and one of the major issues with which his liberal administration was concerned was the revitalization of the penal system. At the time, the prisons of California were ranked next to last in the nation, and the new governor was interested in reforming and modernizing them. Kate O'Hare, who lived in the vicinity of San Quentin, the maximum security prison believed that no prison reformer who had not lived within the system could fully understand the dimensions of the issues, and so she could not refuse an opportunity to work on improving the system.

Olson appointed John Gee Clark as director of penology to clean up the prisons. Clark was a state assemblyman who lacked experience in penal work. He wisely hired O'Hare as his assistant. Although she had no formal training as a penologist, she was certainly a respected figure in the field. An investigation of the prison administrators was opened at once. O'Hare was nervous about festering problems, particularly at volatile San Quentin. Its inmates had just staged a hunger strike, and it had the undoubtedly earned reputation as "the most primitive penitentiary in the world." She wrote to Governor Olson, arguing that it was mandatory to move quickly through the hearings. She feared, she stated, "the ever present danger" of more food riots and further unwarranted, harsh discipline for the inmates. Within months, all members of the board of prison directors were dismissed for incompetence and neglect of duty, and a more centralized system was designed. In conjunction with the arrival of San Quentin's new warden, who would become one of the most popular and fabled wardens of all time, Clinton T. Duffy, flogging, torture, and other cruel and unusual punishments (including headshaving) were banned, the infamous dungeons were closed, the use of gigantic numbers on uniforms was discontinued, and efforts were made to improve the food and hygienic conditions. Those guards and other officials implicated in abuses were fired, and the new team moved toward introducing civil service in place of the existing practice of political appointments.

Many of these measures had O'Hare's stamp on them. Since her own incarceration (1919–1920), she had deplored the unnecessarily inhumane conditions that prisoners faced. Even the uniforms, emblazoned with stripes or numbers, of outlandish styles, colors or fabrics, marking people off as separate from the human condition were an unnecessary affront to inmates, she pointed out. Overcrowding, poor food, and inadequate bathing facilities were also matters which she had long ago drawn to the attention of the authorities. These various reforms clearly brought her great satisfaction. As in service on a congressional staff, she had the pleasure finally of being able to see her ideas win serious consideration.

Probably the innovation which O'Hare would have rated as the most significant was the establishment of a minimum security prison at Chino, California. As a former inmate, she well knew how insidious the prison environment was for the young and unsophisticated forced to live among older and toughened criminals. The reformers, including Governor Olson, saw to the establishment of the country's first minimum security prison for men. O'Hare and the prewar penologists whose work had influenced her had argued for decades for the need to diversify penal institutions, and at last the program was implemented. Soon thereafter, the segregation of different groups within institutions was initiated, including homosexuals and those with a variety of illnesses. O'Hare had made such recommendations twenty years earlier at a time when no one had listened to her.

After one year, Kate O'Hare retired at age sixty-four. Her final public activity no doubt had brought her a sense of closure. When she left the Department of Penology, the state of California was on the path to designing the most progressive penal system in the United States. When the next governor, Earl Warren, assumed office in 1943, he recognized the value of her service to the state of California and invited her to sit in on sessions of the State Crime Commission. She regularly attended its meetings, and might well have reflected on the fact that the last half-dozen years had brought her the official legitimacy that had been denied her in the previous decades.

Kathleen Richards O'Hare Cunningham attended a last meeting of the State Crime Commission in the winter of 1947–1948. That winter she also, as was her habit, addressed local civic groups such as the PTA and the Kiwanis. On Saturday, January 10, 1948, Kate was stricken suddenly with a heart attack and died in Benicia, California, on San Pablo Bay across from San Francisco. She was nearly seventy-two years old. She had completed her work; this time there were no encores. Services were held for her at the local Congregational Church, and cremation followed. A large memorial service was held a few weeks later in Los Angeles. She was survived by her second husband, Charles Cunningham, who was nearly eighty years old. She also left behind her four children, Dick, Kathleen, Gene, and Victor, and grandchildren. None of the O'Hare children were political activists. Dick was a businessman; Kathleen was a dress designer and also worked as a reporter briefly. Gene had worked with the WPA and was a journalist and a businessman at various times, and Vic worked in city government for a while.

It might also be said that Mrs. Cunningham left behind another survivor, Frank O'Hare. He lived in St. Louis until his death in 1960. He worked as an efficiency expert for various businesses and as a tinkerer who invented various machines for which he never bothered to obtain patents. Increasingly described by some as a curmudgeon and even cantankerous and viewed as a sage by others, he kept up a voluminous correspondence with old comrades. He also produced runs of informally put together newsletters, *Dunkerdoings* and *Frank O'Hare's Weekly Commentary,* in which he criticized mainstream politicians, as he had done his whole life.

Kate O'Hare's death was not much noticed by the American public. True, the wire services reported her passing, and obituaries appeared in all the major newspapers from coast to coast. The *New York Times,* the *St. Louis Post-Dispatch,* the *San Francisco Chronicle,* and others carried the news, as did some of the liberal and labor press. But no period of national mourning was called. No monuments or statues were commissioned in her memory. Public schools were not named after her. Legislation can offer immortality—such as in the case of a Robert La Follette, Jr., a Robert Wagner, Sr., or a J. William Fulbright—but none carries the name of Kate Richards O'Hare. She was never elected to either a state legislature or the United States Congress, and she was not similarly immortalized because she was a radical whose activities were viewed as outside the mainstream and, thus, anathema.

O'Hare's career has been remembered most concretely in the research and publications of those scholars who study the issues in which she was involved: socialist politics, war dissent, or penal reform. But their articles and books, familiar to only a narrow spectrum of readers, often mislabel O'Hare and distort her work. She appears as a background figure whose role has never been placed in center stage and is usually not clearly elucidated. O'Hare, however, has remained alive in memories long after her death. The rank-and-file of the old socialist movement and even their children still remember her. They kept alive stories about the old days when the struggle for economic equality was being waged and of one of its leaders, Kate O'Hare. In 1992, almost a century after a young and eager O'Hare began her barnstorming across the country, an eighty-eight-year-old Californian recalled hearing O'Hare speak at a three-day socialist encampment in his native western Oklahoma in 1913. She was both "winning" and "instructive" and remained in his memory and his heart "with nostalgia and appreciation." It is the most fitting tribute to O'Hare's life that her immortality came through those to whom she dedicated her life.

Kate O'Hare was a New Woman of turn-of-the-century America. Those women coming of age at that time were emancipated from some of the limitations that the women of the nineteenth century had borne. They were the recipients of the gains made by the first generation of women's rights advocates. They enjoyed new opportunities for education and employment, and experienced social freedoms and what might be called early sexual liberation. While still facing gender discrimination and socioeconomic and political barriers, nevertheless they were able to function much more freely than the women who preceded them. Their generation of middle-class American women was able to plot its own course, freed of earlier religious and social restraints, at least in the few years between the conclusion of formal educations and settling into marriages. Accordingly, such women pursued various cultural, social, civic, and intellectual interests that brought a new burst of energy to American life.

Kate O'Hare embodied a specific version of the New Woman. She

enjoyed the benefits of a postsecondary education and the social freedom which allowed her to find her own way. The direction she chose to
follow was a function of the intersection of time and place with her
own psychological drive to pursue some version of the public good. The
agrarian radicalism and rural upheaval of the 1880s had uprooted her
from her family's homestead and placed her in an urban setting, while
simultaneously influencing her toward an interest in the downtrodden of
society. Cultural variables of the 1890s attracted her to the religious and
social purity activities so prevalent among young women of her background. Ultimately, at the very end of the century, she stumbled upon a
movement that had arisen in the name of the working people of America. She was responsive to her times, and so this particular New Woman
had found her work. Unlike the majority of such woman, hers was to be
a lifetime commitment rather than a few years of activism in the cause
which she had chosen.

Curiously, during the heyday of O'Hare's socialist career she was
sometimes referred to by the name, "Red Kate." The label implied that
she was a member of the leftist faction of the party as opposed to the
center or right (a division never very well defined) revisionist reformists
who were sometimes described as yellow Socialists. Not one policy
position with which O'Hare was aligned could justify tagging her as a
member of the revolutionary wing of the Socialist party. Over the years,
O'Hare's positions were consistently reformist. She never varied from
that ideological position.

O'Hare believed that the goal of the cooperative commonwealth had
to be pursued gradually, as has been discussed. She was a step-at-a-time
Socialist who was anxious to do everything possible to improve the lot
of the working people in the here and now. She never doubted that the
government could be controlled by the people and harnessed to serve
their interests, and she harbored no fears over possible dangers inherent
in expansive governmental power. She was not worried that reforms en
route to the socialist transformation of the economy would satiate the
workers so that they would lose interest in the ultimate changeover from

capitalism to socialism. Indeed, she was fiercely condemnatory of the irresponsibility of those Marxists who opposed reforms because of their perceived potential to satisfy the people's interest in change.

In the name of humanity and personal responsibility, she served on or participated in more than one party committee or government hearing focused on reforms of living or working conditions, and through her years of writing and editing socialist periodicals she continued to high-light the need for such reforms. In 1902 when she conducted her under-ground exposé of New York City working conditions, she did so in the hope of convincing legislators not to adopt a collectivist system but of the need to prohibit inhumane conditions. In that same year, when she and Frank O'Hare toured among miners in Pennsylvania, they were try-ing to support those strikers pressuring for better working conditions and wages. In neither case did Kate O'Hare advise workers to organize on behalf of an *attentat* that with a single well-planned blow would trans-form the system from one of worker exploitation to worker control. In 1913 when she investigated wages and living conditions of working women in St. Louis, she was trying to persuade municipal authorities to insist upon a realistic minimum wage for women in the local labor force. In 1914 when she accepted an appointment from Mayor Kiel to survey unemployment issues, she enthusiastically participated in wide-ranging recommendations on behalf of the needs of the jobless. In accord with her belief system, she served on that committee not seeking to persuade the city or its residents to neglect housing conditions until a municipal socialist administration would arise to construct worker owned and managed housing units. Rather, in this case and the others, she always tried to alleviate suffering and neglect through improving existing con-ditions, while in the meantime seeking to educate and convince workers to support socialism as the ultimate goal.

Others with whom she worked either were contemptuous of or disil-lusioned with step-at-a-time gradual efforts and looked for immediate means to change the system, while O'Hare always maintained faith in the people's ability to accept and believe in her socialist ideology. Unlike her comrade and sometimes nemesis, Victor Berger, she never flirted with the idea that a violent takeover of the existing system might be necessary. Berger, who regretted expressing such fleeting thoughts that haunted his career, had once published an editorial called "Bullets and Ballots." While he concluded that the facts of universal manhood suffrage in the United States and the availability of various avenues for pursuing changes legally made any resort to violence unconscionable, still he had given it some consideration, unlike O'Hare. Eugene Debs, whose presence was so marked in O'Hare's life, also allowed himself to be linked with violence, at least in the minds of some. In his case, it was through his association with the Wobblies and their linkage to the use of the tactic of industrial sabotage. Debs had joined the Industrial Workers of the World, as had a few other Socialists, in 1905 at its inception; in fact, he attended its founding convention. His membership in the Wobblies was rather brief, as he withdrew after a couple of years, repelled by divisiveness and factionalism, but he felt close to the rank and file Wobbly working stiffs whose spirit he admired. O'Hare also felt warm toward individual Wobblies but because she opposed any semblance of violence and also because she believed that the Socialist party must support the mainstream labor movement, she kept the I.W.W. as an institution at a distance and never joined it.

Finally, on this point, O'Hare certainly never related to the young Emma Goldman's vehement opposition to a gradualist approach and her commitment to violence as a strategy for meaningful change. But Goldman came to oppose individual acts of violence as inappropriate and counterproductive although she was loyal to those driven to violence against the system. Her reputation, however, as a dangerous woman dogged her steps for the rest of her life, leading to both mob action and police persecution against her.

O'Hare was a radical who consistently fought for change in the capitalist system from within through democratic means. It was the core of her political perspective. As she sought in speech after speech and column after column to persuade her audiences to the importance of that approach, she simultaneously worked with non-Socialists to achieve mutually valued goals. She collaborated with consumer advocates and civic reformers, with suffrage proponents and social settlement house activists, and with progressives and pacifists on a whole range of issues. Until the Socialist party schism and decline, she found it necessary to take pains to show that her collaboration across class lines in no way compromised party policy. She was sometimes put on the defensive over her willingness to take such chances, but she never wavered from her path. After the collapse of the party, her interest in working with like-minded non-Socialists faced no obstacles, and she was very comfortable in the 1920s working with the Committee for Progressive Political Action and in the 1930s, with liberals in the EPIC movement and the campaign to establish a planned economy.

O'Hare lacked the intellectual depth and breadth of a theoretician, such as marked the work of some of the leaders of the Second International. She certainly did not produce tracts of Marxist rigor as did, for example, Rosa Luxemburg. Indeed, the American party as a whole was not known for its contributions to the intellectual thought of the socialist movement. O'Hare's creativity did not lead in that direction. But she was imaginative, and she demonstrated it in the anecdotes and parables with which she captured the attention of the farmers and workers who listened to her speeches and avidly read her columns in the *Appeal to Reason,* the *National-Rip-Saw,* and the *Vanguard.*

Writing about the dangers of sexually transmitted diseases, for example, in her booklet, *What Happened to Dan,* she spun a tale which every reader could understand, and placed the subject in a socialist context. It became a best-seller on the socialist circuit. When she wrote of women's economic and sexual exploitation in "Wimmin' Ain't Got No Kick," her readers were held by the sarcasm and satire, admittedly heavy-handed, which brought her points home to her audience better than would a sociological treatise. Speaking in condemnation of the world war in 1915 and 1916, she offered an economic analysis of its causes, and her listeners seemed to agree, but when she wrote and produced an antiwar play which personified villains and heroes, her audience was captivated, and she had another socialist best-seller.

The consistency that marked her career is most readily seen in her failure to break with the Socialist party after it collapsed. She readily conceded its weaknesses and inadequacies, and her own bitterness over what she thought of as her unfair treatment by other party leaders. But she chose not to abandon the party for new movements of left or right. Instead, between the world wars, she worked with any Socialists in or out of the party and with any progressive group in order to obtain her goals. As she had shown, the only leftist movement with which she would not work was the Communist party. From its emergence, during her incarceration, until O'Hare's death, in the early years of the Cold War, she always believed that communist insistence on the ends justifying the means led it to wreak havoc, first on the Socialist party and then on whatever next crossed its path.

She pulled together some of her reflections on the political party which had been her life in a letter written in 1945. She believed that the European-born reformist leaders had helped derail the party. She described Victor Berger as a devotee of the German Social Democrats who never understood the United States, other than his Germanic home base, Milwaukee. She thought Morris Hillquit was also too European in his orientation to the detriment of the party's prospects. Both leaders were hostile to the socialist rank-and-file across the country, she wrote. They were also antagonistic, she believed, toward Debs, whom she called the soul of the party, and toward W. A. Wayland, whom she called its pioneer. The Berger-Hillquit nexus, she maintained, bore a good deal of responsibility for the demise of the party as a promising political force, as much, she said, as did the governmental campaign which destroyed her newspapers and imprisoned both her and Debs.

But O'Hare stayed in the fold, however disillusioned she was at times, and she never broke with the organization she had joined in 1901. The longevity of her commitment distinguished her from thousands of other Socialists. Many members switched allegiances, especially during World

War I and in the immediate postwar era of repression and of communist ascendancy. Caroline Lowe, for example, had become an attorney just before the war. She joined the legal team defending the Wobblies at their mass trials, and they became her prime concern. Another Socialist, much better known than Lowe, who also moved away from the party was Rose Pastor Stokes. Excluding O'Hare, she was the most prominent woman Socialist convicted under the Espionage Act, though she never had to serve time in prison. Stokes had lived a fabled life. She went from an immigrant adolescence in factories and sweatshops to marriage to a wealthy, socially prominent American, scion of a family whose forebearers had come to Massachusetts in the first generation of its settlement. Stokes left the party and became a founding member of the Communist Party of America, serving on its central committee. May Wood Simons, longtime associate of O'Hare's and the most prominent figure in the establishment of the Socialists' Women's National Committee, dropped out of the party in protest of its antiwar policies. Simons then devoted herself to Americanization programs aimed at immigrants, to voter education campaigns, and to the League of Women Voters, eventually becoming the state chair in Illinois. These miscellaneous, nonpartisan civic and women's club activities replaced the ideological politics which she and her husband, Algie, had formerly pursued together. Countless others made even greater shifts in direction, from the Socialist party even to right-wing republicanism. O'Hare did not wander.

Kate O'Hare left behind an impressive record. As an American radical, she challenged virtually all of society's institutions. She worked to focus attention on solutions to a variety of issues which the public faced in her time, and she anticipated many that the nation would deal with during the rest of the twentieth century. O'Hare identified and addressed conflicts that arose as the United States was transformed into an urbanized and industrial world power. She focused on the costs of that transformation of American life to working men and farmers and women in factories and rural areas. She took on the battles of every forgotten American, from working children to prison inmates, and placed their struggles in the context of the fight between capitalism and socialism. She explored and publicized aspects of social and cultural change, including educational and sexual topics, and never hesitated to attack secular or religious authorities if she believed they bore responsibility for injustices. Her interest in consumer and industrial environmental issues foreshadowed later movements. Her concerns about racial inequities demonstrated an awareness that many of her contemporaries lacked, but her own racism limited the value of her efforts there. In her forceful demands for an end to war, she was one of those who exposed the roots and costs of war that later generations would, if unknowingly, echo. Finally, O'Hare's awareness of the inequities that plagued women went further than that of most feminists of her time, even though she clung to a traditional framework on gender. Kate Richards O'Hare was a woman of vision whose concerns, however marred by blind spots, and whose struggles, however seemingly hopeless, spoke to generations to come.

❦ BIBLIOGRAPHIC ESSAY

K ate Richards O'Hare (or Kate Cunningham, as she was known when she died) did not leave behind a body of papers, nor has any repository established an O'Hare collection. While it is common knowledge among scholars that many famous women did not have their papers collected, in contrast to men of similar renown, O'Hare's public prominence would almost certainly have guaranteed her papers an institutional home. However, Frank P. O'Hare destroyed the overwhelming bulk of her papers when the couple was considering a divorce. Thus, a researcher has no central repository to which to refer students interested in O'Hare's papers and correspondence.

Kate Richards O'Hare did, however, leave a lengthy paper trail. As a writer, editor, and columnist for almost thirty years, from the beginning of the century until the eve of the Great Depression, she commented regularly on the issues of the times from her specific ideological perspective. Some of the publications for which O'Hare wrote disappeared quickly; but enough of O'Hare's work survives to enable a student to trace the evolution of her thought.

O'Hare wrote for J. A. Wayland's newspapers in the first decade of this century, submitting columns and occasional pieces for the *Appeal to Reason* and *Wayland's Monthly*. She was a columnist from 1902 through 1903 for the *Coming Nation* (Rich Hill, Mo.), and for the *Publicist* (Chandler, Okla.) from 1904 through 1905. In 1913 she wrote for the *Melting Pot*. In 1911 she became an editor and columnist of the widely read monthly *National Rip-Saw*. Her features appeared regularly, and her own newsworthy events were covered until the demise of the periodical in 1918 (under the name *Social-Revolution*). She and Frank O'Hare revived the *National Rip-Saw* in 1921, and she continued to write for it as the renamed *American Vanguard* until it expired in 1924. Newspapers to which O'Hare occasionally contributed in the years up to World War I included the *Socialist Woman* (which was renamed the *Progressive Woman,* and then later renamed the *Coming Nation*), which was published from 1907 to 1913, the *International Socialist Review, Wilshire's Magazine,* the *Chicago Daily Socialist,* the *New York Call,* and many other socialist sheets of the era. She also published columns upon occasion in the mass media, for example, the *Arena* and the *Nation.* O'Hare published a handful of short booklets or pamphlets, most of which were printed and circulated widely by the Socialist party. These include *The Sorrows of Cupid, What Happened to Dan,* "Law and the White Slaver," "Wimmin' Ain't Got No Kick," "Church and the Social Problem," and "Common Sense and the Liquor Traffic."

The most extensive body of O'Hare's writings consists of the letters that she wrote to her family from the Missouri State Penitentiary during the fourteen months of her incarceration at the Jefferson City facility in 1919 and 1920. Many of these 122 letters were circulated at the time by Frank O'Hare to draw attention to her case, and the first sixteen letters were printed in booklet form in 1919 under the title *Kate O'Hare's Prison Letters.* A complete set of the letters is housed at the Missouri Historical Society in St. Louis. A bound set of the mimeographed letters exists under the title *Dear Sweethearts: Letters from Kate Richards O'Hare to Her Family.*

No copies exist of O'Hare's birth certificate or educational records. At least one distant relative, a descendant of a paternal uncle, Mary Beth Figgins, who resides near Topeka, Kansas, has attempted to develop a genealogy for the Richards family, which she has traced to Virginia as far back the Revolutionary War era. A dozen or so letters from O'Hare to Frank, to her children, and to her sister-in-law, Gertrude Petzold, may be found in the Frank P. O'Hare Papers at the Missouri Historical Society in St. Louis. A few of her letters may be found among the papers of her colleagues, such as in the Eugene V. Debs Collection at the Tamiment Institute at New York University, the Victor L. Berger Collection at the Milwaukee County Historical Society, the Upton Sinclair Papers at Indiana University, the Emma Goldman Papers at the University of California, Berkeley, and the Emma Goldman Archives at the International Institute of Social History in Amsterdam. But for the most part, it must be emphasized that there is a paucity of O'Hare letters in any of these collections; O'Hare's letters have been virtually lost to history. For example, while she carried on a correspondence of over twenty years with her lifelong idol, Gene Debs, in J. Robert Constantine's excellent three-volume collection *Letters of Eugene V. Debs*

(Urbana: University of Illinois Press, 1990), O'Hare letters are not represented. Her absence is enough to make an O'Hare student grieve.

One collection of O'Hare's correspondence and other writings has been published. Philip S. Foner and I coedited it, and it is entitled, *Kate Richards O'Hare: Selected Writings and Speeches* (Baton Rouge: Louisiana State University Press, 1982).

Glimpses of O'Hare can be found in the Socialist Party of America collection, which is housed at Duke University's Perkins Library and is available on microfilm. Socialist party newspapers should be perused for O'Hare's party-related activities. These include the *Official Bulletin of the Socialist Party* (1910–1913), the *Party Builder* (1912–1914), and the *American Socialist* (1914–1917). The proceedings of the Socialist party's national conventions and congresses provide a view of O'Hare and her milieu. The relevant meetings occurred in 1904, 1908, 1910, 1912, and 1917, and the proceedings were published by the National Office of the Socialist Party in Chicago.

While O'Hare has not been the subject of a biography up to now, various scholarly articles have appeared on episodes of her career. These articles include Stanley Mallach, "Red Kate O'Hare Comes to Madison: The Politics of Free Speech," *Wisconsin Magazine of History* 53 (Spring 1970): 204–22; Bernard J. Brommel, "Kate Richards O'Hare: A Midwestern Pacifist's Fight for Free Speech," *North Dakota Quarterly* 44 (Winter 1976): 5–19; Hugh Lovin, "The Banishment of Kate Richards O'Hare," *Idaho Yesterdays* 22 (Spring 1978): 20–25; Neil K. Basen, "Kate Richards O'Hare: The 'First Lady' of American Socialism, 1901–1917," *Labor History* 21 (Spring 1980): 165–99; Sally M. Miller, "Kate Richards O'Hare: Progression Toward Feminism," *Kansas History* 7 (Winter 1984/1985): 263–79; David Roediger, "Americanism and Fordism—American Style: Kate Richards O'Hare's 'Has Henry Ford Made Good?'" *Labor History* 29 (Spring 1988): 241–52; and Erling N. Sannes, "'Queen of the Lecture Platform': Kate Richards O'Hare and North Dakota Politics, 1917–1921," *North Dakota History* 58 (Fall 1991): 2–19. For briefer treatments of O'Hare, see Sally M. Miller, "Other Socialists: Native-Born and Immigrant Women in the Socialist Party of America, 1901–1917" *Labor History* 24 (Winter 1983): 84–102; and Neil K. Basen, "The 'Jennie Higginses' of the 'New South of the West': A Regional Survey of Socialist Activists, Agitators, and Organizers, 1901–1917," in *Flawed Liberation: Socialism and Feminism,* edited by Sally M. Miller (Westport, Conn.: Greenwood Press, 1981).

A number of encyclopedia entries offer sketches of O'Hare's life. In her own lifetime, she was included in *American Labor Who's Who,* ed. Solon DeLeon

(New York: Hanford Press, 1925), 177–78. More contemporary entries include the following: David A. Shannon, "Kate Richards O'Hare Cunningham," in *Notable American Women: A Biographical Dictionary,* vol. 1, edited by Edward T. James, Janet Wilson James, and Paul S. Boyer (Cambridge: Belknap Press, Harvard Univ. Press, 1971), 417–20; Melvyn Dubofsky, "Kate Richards O'Hare Cunningham," *Dictionary of American Biography, Supplement 4* (New York: 1974), 635; Sally M. Miller, "Kate Richards O'Hare," in *Handbook of American Women's History,* edited by Angela Howard Zophy with Frances M. Kavenik (New York: Garland, 1990), 447–48; Peter Buckingham, "Kate Richards O'Hare," in *Encyclopedia of the American Left,* edited by Mari Jo Buhle, Paul Buhle, and Dan Georgakas (New York: Garland Press, 1991), 544–45; and Sally M. Miller, "Kate Richards O'Hare," *American National Biography* (New York: Oxford University Press, forthcoming).

A few of O'Hare's comrades in the socialist movement refer to her in their memoirs. These include Oscar Ameringer, *If You Don't Weaken: The Autobiography of Oscar Ameringer* (New York: Henry Holt and Co., 1940); Morris Hillquit, *Loose Leaves from a Busy Life* (New York: Macmillan Co., 1934); and Emma Goldman, *Living My Life,* 2 vols. (New York: Alfred A. Knopf, 1931).

O'Hare appears on film in the background of a home movie made at the celebration for Gene Debs upon his release from prison in 1921. A print exists at the Tamiment Institute.

In the secondary literature on the Socialist party of America, historians often distort O'Hare's work and minimize her contribution, seldom treating her as a central party figure. These works, which need to be consulted as party histories in and of themselves, include David A. Shannon, *The Socialist Party of America: A History* (New York: Macmillan Co., 1955); Ira Kipnis, *The American Socialist Movement: 1897–1912* (New York: Columbia University Press, 1952); James Weinstein, *The Decline of Socialism in America, 1912–1925* (New York: Monthly Review Press, 1967). Also see for treatments of O'Hare: Mari Jo Buhle, *Women and American Socialism, 1870–1920* (Urbana; University of Illinois Press, 1981); and James R. Green, *Grass-Roots Socialism: Radical Movements in the Southwest, 1895–1943* (Baton Rouge: Louisiana State University Press, 1978). Some of the biographies of Eugene V. Debs consider O'Hare; see, as examples, Ray Ginger, *Eugene V. Debs: A Biography* (New York: Collier, 1962) and Nick Salvatore, *Eugene V. Debs: Citizen and Socialist* (Urbana: University of Illinois Press, 1982). A recent journalistic treatment of the life of an equally famous socialist woman, Rose Pastor Stokes, contains a few references to O'Hare; it is by Arthur Zipser and Pearl Zipser, *Fire and Grace: The Life of Rose Pastor Stokes* (Athens: University of Georgia Press, 1989).

The pages that follow, which treat general historiography, are meant to be suggestive rather than comprehensive. Works that examine the basic history and geography of post-Reconstruction Kansas during O'Hare's childhood include Kenneth S. Davis, *Kansas: A Bicentennial History* (New York: W. W. Norton and Co., 1976); William Frank Zornow, *Kansas: A History of the Jayhawk State* (Norman: University of Oklahoma Press, 1957); John D. Bright, ed., *Kansas: The First Century* (New York: Lewis Historical Publishing Co., Inc., 1956); Robert W. Richmond, *Kansas: A Land of Contrasts,* 3rd ed. (1988); Homer E. Socolofsky and Huber Self, *Historical Atlas of Kansas* (Norman: University of Oklahoma Press, 1972); Scott G. McNall and Sally Allen McNall, *Plains Families: Exploring Sociology through Social History* (New York: St. Martin's Press, 1983); Homer Croy, *Corn Country* (New York: Duell, Sloan and Pearce, 1947); and William B. Bracke, *Wheat Country* (New York: Duell, Sloan and Pearce, 1950). The Kansas State Historical Society in Topeka has some useful local histories and records that relate to O'Hare's background in central Kansas, including Ottawa County, but only slightly to her as a person. See a nineteenth-century history, A. T. Andreas, *History of the State of Kansas* (1883); *Ottawa County Centennial, 1866–1966* (no publishing information, 1966); Ottawa County History Book Committee, *History of Ottawa County, Kansas, 1864–1984* (no place or publisher: 1984); and Muriel Greene, *Of Floods and Flowers: The Tescott Story* Ellsworth, Kan.: Ellsworth Printing Co., 1986).

For the social and political milieu during O'Hare's early years, one might start with the classic work by Everett Dick, *The Sod-House Frontier, 1854–1890: A Social History of the Northern Plains from the Creation of Kansas and Nebraska to the Admission of the Dakotas* (New York: D. Appleton-Century Co., 1937); see Howard Ruede, *Sod-House Days: Letters from a Kansas Homesteader, 1877–78,* ed. John Ise (Lawrence: University Press of Kansas, 1983), which offers an invaluable first-person peek into the life of homesteaders; Joanna L. Stratton, *Pioneer Women: Voices from the Kansas Frontier* (New York: Simon and Schuster, 1981); Julie Roy Jeffrey, *Frontier Women: The Trans-Mississippi West, 1840–1880* (New York: Hill and Wang, 1979); Glenda Riley, *The Female Frontier: A Comparative View of Women on the Prairie and the Plains* (Lawrence: University Press of Kansas, 1988); Scott G. McNall, *The Road to Rebellion: Class Formation and Kansas Populism, 1865–1900*

(Chicago: University of Chicago Press, 1988); Walter T. K. Nugent, *The Tolerant Populists: Kansas Populism and Nativism* (Chicago: University of Chicago Press, 1963); Peter H. Angersinger, *Populism and Politics: William Alfred Peffer and the People's Party* (Lexington: The University Press of Kentucky, 1974); O. Gene Clanton, *Kansas Populism: Ideas and Men* (Lawrence: University Press of Kansas, 1969); Stanley B. Parsons, Karen Toombs Parsons, Walter Killilae, and Beverly Borgers, "The Role of Cooperatives in the Development of the Movement Culture of Populism," *Journal of American History* 69 (March 1983): 866–85; Robert Smith Bader, *Prohibition in Kansas: A History* (Lawrence: University Press of Kansas, 1986); and Hal D. Sears, *The Sex Radicals: Free Love in High Victorian America:* (Lawrence: The Regents Press of Kansas, 1977).

For the history of Kansas City, Missouri, see Theodore A. Brown and Lyle W. Dorsett, *K. C.: A History of Kansas City, Missouri* (Boulder, Colo.: Pruett Publishing Co., 1978), and Lyle W. Dorsett, *The Pendergast Machine* (New York: Oxford University Press, 1968); also see Henry C. Haskell, Jr., and Richard B. Fowler, *City of the Future: A Narrative History of Kansas City, 1850–1950* (Kansas City, Mo.: Frank Glenn Publishing Co., Inc., 1950). On "rescue" efforts in Kansas City and elsewhere, see Patricia Youmans Wagner, "Voluntary Associations in Kansas City, Missouri, 1870–1900," Ph.D. diss. (University of Kansas City, 1962); Katherine Gertrude Aiken, "The National Florence Crittenton Missions, 1883–1925: A Case Study in Progressive Reform," Ph.D. diss. (Washington State University, 1980); Peggy Pascoe, *Relations of Rescue: The Search for Female Moral Authority in the American West, 1874–1939* (New York: Oxford University Press, 1990); Regina G. Kunzel, "The Professionalization of Benevolence: Evangelicals and Social Workers in the Florence Crittenton Homes, 1915 to 1945," *Journal of Social History* 22 (Fall 1988): 21–43; and Beverly A. Smith, "Female Admissions and Paroles of the Western House of Refuge in the 1880s: An Historical Example of Community Corrections," *Journal of Research in Crime and Delinquency* 26 (February 1989): 36–66.

Studies on human development, the area in which the work of Erik H. Erikson has been seminal, have tended to focus on the lives of men only. While this essay will not attempt to review this burgeoning field, authors whose work has begun to introduce women into the study of human development include Carol Gilligan and her associates; see her first book, *In A Different Voice: Psychological Theory and Women's Development* (Cambridge: Harvard University Press, 1982). Another writer whose work has given me insight into Kate O'Hare's psychological evolution has been Carolyn G. Heilbrun; see her *Writing A Woman's Life* (New York: Ballantine Books, 1988) and *Reinventing Womanhood* (New York: W. W. Norton and Co., 1979).

The history of the unique town of Girard and of the career of W. A. Wayland and the *Appeal to Reason* has yet to be given the full attention that it merits. Gene DeGruson of Pittsburgh State University of Kansas and Sharon E. Neet of the University of Minnesota, Crookston, may soon remedy that omission in the historiography. For now, see Paul M. Buhle, *"The Appeal to Reason, New Appeal"* in *The American Radical Press, 1880–1960*, vol. 1, edited by Joseph R. Conlin (Westport, Conn.: Greenwood Press, 1974), 50–59; Elliott Shore, *Talkin' Socialism: J. A, Wayland and the Role of the Press in American Radicalism, 1890–1912* (Lawrence: University Press of Kansas, 1988); and also John Graham, ed., *"Yours for the Revolution": The Appeal to Reason, 1895–1922* (Lincoln: University of Nebraska Press, 1990), including its material on the International School of Social Economy. Additionally, see "The International School of Social Economy," *Comrade 1* (July 1902): 217–19, and the *Socialist Teacher,* which published at least three issues in 1903. Also see *The Little Balkans Review* 4 (Fall 1983): 42–75, which contains six articles on the socialist milieu of Girard.

The history of Oklahoma during its territorial days and its early statehood, when the O'Hare family lived there, can be traced in the following works, among others: Roy Gittinger, *The Formation of the State of Oklahoma (1803–1906)* (Berkeley, Calif.: University of California Press, 1917); Edward Everett Dale and Morris L. Wardell, *History of Oklahoma* (Englewood Cliffs, N. J.: Prentice-Hall, Inc., 1948); and H. Wayne Morgan and Anne Hodges Morgan, *Oklahoma: A Bicentennial History* (New York: W. W. Norton and Co., Inc. and the ASLH, 1972). Particularly useful on Oklahoma's political and social history is Anne Hodges Morgan and H. Wayne Morgan, eds., *Oklahoma: New Views of the Forty-Sixth State* (Norman: University of Oklahoma Press, 1982); see especially chapter 3, "Pioneers and Survivors: Economic and Social Change" by Sheila Manes. Worthwhile is Ellen L. Rosen, "Peasant Socialism in America? The Socialist Party in Oklahoma Before the First World War," Ph.D. diss. (City University of New York, 1976). In addition, see John Thompson, *Closing the Frontier: Radical Response in Oklahoma, 1889–1923* (Norman: University of Oklahoma Press, 1986), and the already cited above, James R. Green, *Grass-Roots Socialism;* also helpful is Garin Burbank, *When Farmers Voted Red: The Gospel of Socialism in the Oklahoma Countryside, 1910–1924* (Westport, Conn.: Greenwood Press, 1976), and his earlier published article, "Agrarian Radicals

and Their Opponents: Political Conflict in Southern Oklahoma, 1910–1924,"
Journal of American History 58 (June 1971): 5–23; also see H. L. Meridith,
"Oscar Ameringer and the Concept of Agrarian Socialism," *Chronicles of Okla-
homa* 15 (Spring 1967): 77–83, and his "Agrarian Socialism and the Negro in
Oklahoma," *Labor History* 11 (Summer 1970): 277–84; and Keith L. Bryant,
Jr., "Kate Barnard, Organized Labor, and Social Justice in Oklahoma During
the Progressive Era," *Journal of Southern History* 35 (May 1969): 45–64.
Finally on Oklahoma socialism, see two items by the O'Hares themselves:
Kate Richards O'Hare, "The Land of Graft," *International Socialist Review* 6
(April 1906): 598–604, and Frank P. O'Hare, "The Oklahoma Vote," *Interna-
tional Socialist Review* 9 (1908): 519–20.

On the history of St. Louis, an interested reader might start with Lawrence O.
Christensen, "A Survey of Historical Writing on Missouri from 1860," *Missouri Historical Review* 82 (April 1988): 299–311. The Western Historical
Manuscript Collection at the University of Missouri–St. Louis contains useful
material on the labor movement in St. Louis and also on the Socialist party,
including some sketchy biographical data on the major local leaders, G. A.
Hoehn and William Brandt. It also holds incomplete proceedings of some of
the conventions of the Missouri State Federation of Labor, as does the Missouri
Historical Society in St. Louis. The Western Historical Manuscript Collection
at the University of Missouri–Columbia has some related, if sparse, holdings.
As already mentioned above, the Frank P. O'Hare Papers are located at the
Missouri Historical Society. The weekly newspaper, *St. Louis Labor,* is an indispensable source of information on the local socialist movement; it was published from 1893 to 1930, and its German-language counterpart, the *Arberiter
Zeitung,* was founded in 1898. The State Historical Society of Missouri, Columbia has a rich collection of Missouri newspapers, most of which is available on microfilm.

Major secondary works for the O'Hare years in St. Louis include David
Thelen, *Paths of Resistance: Tradition and Dignity in Industrializing Missouri*
(New York: Oxford University Press, 1986); James Neal Primm, *Lion of the
Valley: St. Louis, Missouri* (Boulder, Colo.: Pruett Publishing Co., 1981);
Gary M. Fink, *Labor's Search for Political Order: The Political Behavior of
the Missouri Labor Movement, 1890–1940* (Columbia: University of Missouri
Press, 1973); Gary Ross Mormino, *Immigrants on the Hill: Italian Americans
in St. Louis, 1882–1982* (Urbana: University of Illinois Press, 1986); Chris-
topher C. Gibbs, *The Great Silent Majority: Missouri's Resistance to World
War One* (Columbia: University of Missouri Press, 1988); John Clark Crighton,

Missouri and the World War, 1914–1917: A Study in Public Opinion (Columbia: University of Missouri Studies, 1947); David D. March, *The History of
Missouri,* 4 vols. (New York: Lewis Historical Publishing Co., 1967). Also
see Lee Meriwether, "Labor and Industry in Missouri during the Last Century," *Missouri Historical Review* 15 (October 1920): 163–75; and Margaret
Lo Piccolo Sullivan, *Hyphenism in St. Louis, 1900–1921: The View from Outside* (New York: Garland Pubs., 1990). The *St. Louis Post-Dispatch* may also
be consulted.

A voluminous secondary literature exists on the Socialist party and World
War I. While the Socialist Party collection at Duke University's Perkins Library is extensive and can be reviewed in files organized by states, it has relatively little on the party before the 1920s. More than one collection of documents has been published detailing the evolving position of the Socialist party
on the war; for examples, see William English Walling, ed., *The Socialists and
the War: A Documentary Statement of the Position of the Socialists of All Countries; With Special Reference to their Peace Policy,* 1915, reprint (New York:
Garland Publishing, Inc., 1972); and Alexander Trachtenberg, ed., *The American Socialists and the War: A Documentary History of the Attitude of the Socialist Party Toward War and Militarism Since the Outbreak of the Great War*
(New York: Rand School of Social Science, 1917). For O'Hare's evolving
views, the *National Rip-Saw* is indispensable, because her monthly columns
reveal her reactions to ongoing events. Her play on the war, coauthored with
Frank O'Hare, was entitled *World Peace* (St. Louis: National Rip-Saw, 1915).
Her standard antiwar stump speech, which she gave throughout the spring and
summer of 1917, was published by Frank O'Hare in 1919 as a pamphlet called
"Socialism and the War." For O'Hare's activities and speeches after her arrest,
at the time of her trial, and up to her incarceration, the National Archives contains excellent records of files kept on her by both the Justice Department and
the Federal Bureau of Investigation (FBI). The University of North Dakota at
Grand Forks has detailed records (many of which duplicate the National Archives' files) pertaining to her trial and subsequent legal actions, including
files of participating attorneys and relevant reports of the Federal Bureau of
Investigation and of the United States attorney general. Contemporary pamphlets relevant to her case include "The Conviction of Mrs. Kate Richards
O'Hare and North Dakota Politics" (New York: National Civil Liberties Bureau,
1918); Kate Richards O'Hare, "Americanism and Bolshevism," *The Kate
O'Hare Booklets* (St. Louis: Frank P. O'Hare, 1919), which was O'Hare's so-
called farewell address before she entered prison; and W. E. Zeuch, "The Truth

About the O'Hare Case," (St. Louis: Frank P. O'Hare, n.d. but probably 1918), Also see John D. Lawson, ed., *American State Trials: A Collection of Important and Interesting Criminal Trials* which have taken place in the United State from the Beginning of our Government to the Present Day (St. Louis: F. H. Thomas Law Book Co., 1920), 1–51.

For the political climate in North Dakota during the time of O'Hare's arrest and trial, see Robert L. Morlan, *Political Prairie Fire: The Nonpartisan League 1915–1922* (St. Paul, Minn.: Minnesota Historical Society Press, 1985); Robert Wilkins, "The Nonpartisan League and Upper Midwest Isolationism," *Agricultural History* 39 (April 1965): 102–9; Jackson Putnam, "The Role of the NDSP in North Dakota History," *North Dakota Quarterly* 24 (Fall 1956): 115–22; and William C. Pratt, "Socialism on the Northern Plains, 1900–1924," *South Dakota Quarterly* 18 (Spring/Summer 1988): 1–35. General works on dissent, the "Red scare," and the issue of civil liberties are almost as voluminous as works on the war itself. Old standards include Zechariah Chafee, Jr., *Free Speech in the United States* (Cambridge: Harvard University Press, 1942); H. C. Peterson and Gilbert C. Fite, *Opponents of War, 1917–1918* (Madison: University of Wisconsin Press, 1957); and Robert K. Murray, *Red Scare: A Study in National Hysteria* (New York: McGraw-Hill Book Co., 1964). Recent useful works include Richard Polenberg, *Fighting Faiths: The Abrams Case, the Supreme Court, and Free Speech* (New York: Viking, 1987) and M. J. Heale, *American Anticommunism: Combating the Enemy Within, 1830–1970* (Baltimore, Md.: Johns Hopkins Press, 1990).

For O'Hare's prison experience, her already cited letters from prison are fundamental. While addressed to her family, they were also written for public consumption, and that fact must be kept in mind, as well as the fact that prison censors excised some passages and even a few letters. Her later publications on penology include her *In Prison* (St. Louis: Frank P. O'Hare, 1920), and her lengthier *In Prison* (New York: Alfred A. Knopf, 1923); also see Kate Richards O'Hare, *Crime and Criminals* (Girard, Kan.: Frank P. O'Hare, The Kate Richards O'Hare Booklets, n.d.).

The Missouri State Archives at Jefferson City, Missouri, houses only two reminders of O'Hare's incarceration: her signature in the register of inmates and the record of the Bertillon measurements taken of her on the day she entered the prison. For the context of O'Hare's prison experience, see Blake McKelvey, *American Prisons: A History of Good Intentions* (Montclair, N. J.: Patterson Smith, 1977); Estelle B. Freedman, *Their Sisters' Keepers: Women's Prison Reform in America, 1830–1930* (Ann Arbor: University of Michigan

Press, 1981), and her "Sentiment and Discipline: Women's Prison Experiences in Nineteenth Century America," *Prologue* (Winter 1984): 249–59; and Paul W. Keve, *Prisons and the American Conscience: A History of U.S. Federal Corrections* (Carbondale: Southern Illinois University Press, 1991). Two useful anthologies of women's prison experiences and writings are Kathryn Watterson Burkhart, *Women in Prison* (Garden City, N. Y.: Doubleday and Company, Inc., 1973); and Judith A. Scheffler, ed., *Wall Tappings: An Anthology of Writings by Women Prisoners* (Boston: Northeastern University Press, 1986). On prison writings as literature, see H. Bruce Franklin, *The Victim as Criminal and Artist: Literature from the American Prison* (New York: Oxford University Press, 1978); and also see Stanislaw Branczak, *Breathing Under Water and Other Eastern European Essays* (Cambridge: Harvard University Press, 1990).

The so-called New Penology of the pre–World War I era, which shaped O'Hare's thoughts on prison, is reflected in Thomas Mott Osborne, *Society and Prisons: Some Suggestions for a New Penology* (New Haven: Yale University Press, 1916). For overviews of the topic, see Gerhard O. W. Mueller, *Crime, Law and the Scholars: A History of Scholarship in American Criminal Law* (Seattle: University of Washington Press, 1969); and David J. Rothman, *Conscience and Convenience: The Asylum and Its Alternatives in Progressive America* (Boston: Little, Brown, 1980).

In regard to O'Hare's prison comrades, Emma Goldman's collected letters are now available on microfilm through the Emma Goldman Papers at the University of California, Berkeley. In addition to Goldman's autobiography mentioned above, of the many Goldman biographies available, recent ones include Candace Falk, *Love, Anarchy and Emma Goldman: A Biography* (New York: Holt, Rinehart and Winston, 1984); and Alice Wexler, *Emma Goldman in America* (Boston: Beacon Press, 1984) and *Emma Goldman in Exile: From the Russian Revolution to the Spanish Civil War* (Boston: Beacon Press, 1989). Glimpses of Molly Steimer can be caught in the works by or on Emma Goldman, in the Polenberg monograph cited above, and in Paul Avrich, *Anarchist Portraits* (Princeton: Princeton University Press, 1988). Gabriella (or Ella) Antolini has not figured in many of these works, but biographical material on her is found in Paul Avrich, *Sacco and Vanzetti: The Anarchist Background* (Princeton: Princeton University Press, 1991). See also, "Mother and Teacher as Missouri State Penitentiary Inmates: Goldman and O'Hare, 1917–1920," *Missouri Historical Review* 85 (July 1991): 402–21.

For O'Hare's post-prison activities, the National Archives files from the Justice Department and the FBI are quite helpful for their reports on her post-prison speaking tours. The revived *National Rip-Saw* also provided a running account of her interests and activities. On O'Hare's amnesty campaign for political prisoners, see Marla Martin Hanley, "The Children's Crusade of 1922: Kate O'Hare and the Campaign to Free Radical War Dissenters in the Era of America's First Red Scare," *Gateway Heritage* 10 (Summer 1989): 34–43; also see the daily press in the cities that the "children's crusade" visited. Her work on convict labor can be traced through correspondence in the Frank O'Hare collection as well as in the National Archives files cited above.

O'Hare's work in labor education can be seen best through documents on Commonwealth College at Wayne State University in its Archives of Labor and Urban Affairs at the Walter P. Reuther Library. The archives contain issues of the *Lodestar,* a fortnightly published in the early Mena, Arkansas, years of the college. See its copy of the O'Hare essay, "Kuzbasing in Dixie," which was originally published in the *American Vanguard* in 1923. For perhaps the fullest development of her educational views, see her article, based on her keynote address given at the opening of Commonwealth College, "What Common-wealth College Means to Me," *American Vanguard* (October 1923): 6–7. Also useful at the Reuther Library are materials in the Raymond and Charlotte M. Koch Collection and the Edward J. Falkowski Collections, among other items. Studies of Commonwealth College include Raymond and Charlotte Koch, *Educational Commune: The Story of Commonwealth College* (New York: Schocken Books, 1972), the authors having participated in the educational experiment. See also William H. Cobb, "Commonwealth College Comes to Arkansas, 1923–1925," *Arkansas Historical Quarterly* 23 (Summer 1964): 99–122, his "From Utopian Isolation to Radical Activism: Commonwealth College, 1925–1935," *Arkansas Historical Quarterly* 32 (Summer 1973): 132–47, and his "Commonwealth College and the Southern Labor Movement, 1931–1940" in Merl E. Reed, Leslie S. Hough, and Gary M. Fink, eds., *Southern Workers and Their Unions, 1880–1975* (Westport, Conn.: Greenwood Press, 1981). Of the several works on labor colleges, see Richard J. Alten-baugh, *Education for Struggle: The American Labor Colleges of the 1920s and 1930s* (Philadelphia: Temple University Press, 1990); and Marcus Hansome, *World Worker's Educational Movements: Their Social Significance* (New York: Columbia University Press, 1931). For the Llano and Newllano colonies, see Robert V. Hine, *California's Utopian Colonies* (Berkeley and Los Angeles: University of California Press, 1953); Paul K. Conkin, *Two Paths to Utopia: The Hutterites and the Llano Colony* (Lincoln: University of Nebraska Press,

1964); Delores Hayden, *Seven American Utopias: The Architecture of Communitarian Socialism, 1790–1975* (Cambridge: MIT Press, 1976); Mike Davis, *City of Quartz: Excavating the Future in Los Angeles* (London: Verso Books, 1990); and Bill Murrah, "Llano Cooperative Colony, Louisiana," *Southern Exposure* 1 (March-April 1973): 88–100.

On the O'Hares' divorce in 1928, both Kate's and Frank's views are represented in a richly suggestive handful of letters in the Frank O'Hare collection, including material on Frank's remarriage and his effort to obtain Kate O'Hare's cooperation as he sought an annulment. Letters from a priest and an attorney add a dimension to the correspondence.

For O'Hare's life, once she settled in California at the end of the 1920s, materials are virtually extremely scarce. For example, she is not listed on the *California Roster* of officials of the Department of Penology, where she worked in 1938 and 1939 on the staff of John Gee Clark, the director of penology. No reference seems to exist to O'Hare in the vast oral history collections at the Bancroft Library of the University of California, Berkeley. For O'Hare's work in the California prison system, no primary sources on her are available. But see Clinton T. Duffy (as told to Dean Jennings), *The San Quentin Story* (Garden City, N. Y.: Doubleday and Co., 1970); and Lloyd L. Voigt, *History of California State Correctional Administration from 1930 to 1948* (San Francisco: 1949). Other sources which might be consulted include Robert E. Burke, *Olson's New Deal for California* (Berkeley and Los Angeles: University of California Press, 1953); Kenneth LaMott, *Chronicles of San Quentin: The Biography of a Prison* (New York: David McKay Co., Inc., 1961); and Shelley Bookspan, *A Germ of Goodness: The California State Prison System, 1851–1944* (Lincoln: University of Nebraska Press, 1991).

Her involvement in the Upton Sinclair campaign in the 1930s is most clearly documented in her letters in Sinclair's collection at Indiana University's Lilly Library. For that campaign, see secondary sources, such as Greg Mitchell, "Summer of '34," *Working Papers Magazine* part 1, 9 (November/December 1982): 28–36, and part 2, 10 (January/February 1983): 18–27, and *The Campaign of the Century: Upton Sinclair's Race for Governor of California and the Birth of Media Politics* (New York: Random House, 1992); Royce D. Delmatier, Clarence F. McIntosh, and Earl G. Waters, *The Rumble of California Politics, 1848–1970* (New York: Wiley-Interscience, 1970; and Michael Paul Rogin and John L. Shover, *Political Change in California: Critical Elections and Social Movements, 1890–1966* (Westport, Conn.: Greenwood Press, 1970).

For O'Hare's work on the staff of U.S. Representative Thomas R. Amlie, his papers may be consulted at the State Historical Society of Wisconsin. They contain at least a few of O'Hare letters, and they demonstrate the nature and range of issues upon which she worked while on Amlie's staff. Articles of interest on Amlie include Theodore Rosenof, "The Political Education of an American Radical: Thomas R. Amlie in the 1930s," *Wisconsin Magazine of History* 58 (August 1974): 19–30; Stuart L. Weiss, "Thomas Amile and the New Deal," *Mid-America* 59 (January 1977): 19–38 and "Maury Maverick and the Liberal Bloc," *Journal of American History* 57 (March 1971): 880–95.

Obituaries of Kate O'Hare appeared in the *St. Louis Post-Dispatch*, January 12, 1948: 8A; in the *New York Times* on that same day, 19; and in the *Benecia Herald*, January 15, 1948: 1. A eulogistic tribute to O'Hare appeared in *Solidarity* 43 (March 1948): 44.

👉 INDEX